Ain't Got No CIGARETTES

Memories of Music
Legend Roger Miller

Lyle E Style

GREAT PLAINS
PUBLICATIONS

Great Plains Publications
420 – 70 Arthur Street
Winnipeg, MB R3B 1G7
www.greatplains.mb.ca

Great Plains Publications gratefully acknowledges the financial support
provided for its publishing program by the Government of Canada
through the Book Publishing Industry Development Program (BPIDP);
the Canada Council for the Arts; as well as the Manitoba Department
of Culture, Heritage and Tourism; and the Manitoba Arts Council.

Design & Typography by Relish Design Studio Ltd.

Printed in Canada by Friesens Printing

CANADIAN CATALOGUING IN PUBLICATION DATA

Main entry under title:

Style, Lyle E
   Ain't got no cigarettes : memories of music legend Roger Miller /
   Lyle E Style.

   ISBN 1-894283-60-0

1. Roger Miller, 1936-   2. Singers--United States--Biography.
3. Composers--United States--Biography. 4. Musicians--Interviews.

   I. Title. II. Title: Memories of music legend Roger Miller.

ML420.M649S93   2005   782.42164'092
C2005-903319-3

Table of Contents

It Happened Just That Way...

Front cover photo of Roger Miller courtesy of The Country Music Hall of Fame.

Opinions expressed by interviewees are not necessarily the opinions of the Publisher or Author and as such assume no liability for the accuracy of stories, dates, names and/or memories shared by the interviewees.

Edits and Enhancements by Jenna Young and Gregg Shilliday

"Roger was a great musician and a soulful man. His influence on music will never be forgotten."

–Tony Joe White

Foreword

Throughout our lifetime, we are influenced by things people say to us—our parents, teachers, family members, mentors and spiritual advisors. We are inspired by things in almost everything we do. I was tremendously influenced by Roger Miller, just like countless others. All of the writers that I look up to—Willie Nelson, Waylon Jennings, and others have said how important he was to their music world. No one said it quite like Roger, before or after. He was truly an American original. There were only a few people I felt the need to seek out and get to know at some point in my life. Roger was the only one I never got to meet. He passed on before I got to Nashville. However, I felt like I knew him inside-out through his music and clever sayings. Ask someone who knew him personally to tell you a Roger story, and they will smile and tell you something great he said, always something he said. That is what made him extra special. How many great songwriters are known among their peers as having just as much to say in person as in song? That is a short list, huh?

As far as songwriting goes, he never seemed to compromise his integrity for success. He made rhymes that shouldn't rhyme, he said things you shouldn't say, always clever and almost always with a smile. Hoboes, railroads, funerals, coffins, reincarnation, kiddie shows, moonshine, love, lost love, women; he backed off of no subject. He won Grammys and Tonys, he wrote everything from tender love songs to Broadway musicals. I hope in your lifetime you find that one person that inspires you and what you do more than anyone else. I can only hope some of Roger's influence shows up in my work. Again, after reading this book, ask someone who knew him to tell you a story. Enjoy. Then get a Roger Miller boxset. Enjoy. Was he a genius? The ones who know think so.

–Toby Keith

Introduction

By Lyle E Style

T he question I am asked most of all, next to "Is Lyle E Style your real name?", is "How did you start working on this Roger Miller book?" See, some people think it's a little strange that a guy born in 1971 in Winnipeg, Canada, wrote a book on an American music legend whose career had its zenith before the author was even born. In fact, I didn't even know who Roger Miller *was* until 1998, six years after he died, but once I discovered him, things were never the same.

Growing up I survived a strict all-boys high school/minor seminary in Roblin, Manitoba, called St. Vladimir's College. It was a scary experience for me—the kind of place where students are encouraged to become priests. As you probably guessed, since the cover of this book doesn't say "Written by Father Lyle E Style," I never did get the calling. After graduating from St. Vlad's I went to university and fell in love with a girl. Long story short, three years later it was over, and with all the new heartache and pain I finally "got" country music.

I guess finishing university just wasn't in the cards for me. I found it more therapeutic to write my own songs about lost love and misery than to study, so I quit just shy of getting my degree, got a day job working for the government, started singing in a band, eventually recorded a CD and attempted to "take it on the road." Fast forward to 1996 and I was on the way home from my first visit to Nashville, Tennessee. A scenic detour to check out Branson, Missouri led to a variety of very strange coincidences that landed me an introduction to legendary songwriter Bill Dees. Dees wrote over sixty songs with Roy Orbison, including "Oh, Pretty Woman" and "It's Over." He invited me to his house to listen to some of his new songs. I was blown away by how someone could make a great living off of writing songs, especially ones that were written over thirty years ago! I was equally impressed that he was still making great money, even though he was on wife number four at the time and was himself receiving only a small portion of the royalties earned on those songs.

While I was at his house I asked if he would consider co-writing with me, something I've never done but was told to do by a few people in Nashville. He kindly said, "No, the only artist I've ever written with is Roy Orbison and

I'm going to keep it that way." I totally understood, but nonetheless I said to his wife (now ex-wife), Leesa, as I was leaving, "If he ever feels like writing with a Canadian, let me know and I'll be here within forty-eight hours." She said to Bill in a beautiful southern persuasive tone, "He's willing to drive all the way from Canada to write with you. Why don't you give him a shot?" So Bill said to me, "Don't make a special trip, but if you're ever out here again you can give me a call and we can sit down and try to write something." Well, I "happened" to be out there two weeks later, and since then we've become very good friends. I really lucked out—my first co-writer had written "Oh, Pretty Woman," a song that almost everyone in the world knows the words to, and which is rated by *Rolling Stone Magazine* as one of the top twenty-five pop songs of all time.

After meeting and writing with Bill Dees, I really started to pay attention to the art of writing songs. I began taking seminars and reading books on it to learn all the "rules" of songwriting. Eventually, two years later, I discovered Roger Miller and his one rule of songwriting: *There are no rules.*

After my inspiring adventures down South (including meeting my hero Johnny Cash), I felt like I needed to move away from Winnipeg, to get away from the mosquitoes and the insanely cold winters and to go somewhere I thought had a happening music scene. I wanted to relocate to Nashville, but it's almost impossible for a Canadian without a university degree to move to the USA, so instead I moved to Vancouver to be a singer/songwriter/actor. In other words, I was waiting tables. I turned out to be a terrible waiter. I was even written up in the Vancouver *Sun* for being the "worst waiter" in the city.

One night in 1998, after a shift, I was flipping channels when I came across Dean Miller on TNN (when it was *The Nashville Network*) saying, "My dad wrote this song for me." He launched into "Old Toy Trains," one of the few country songs my parents played when I was a kid that I really loved. Watching the show, I recognized many of the songs that were played: "Husbands and Wives," "King of the Road" and "Dang Me." Then I heard "My Uncle Used to Love Me (But She Died)" and I was hooked! Hearing that song for the first time changed my life. The next morning I went to a record store and bought one of the Roger Miller *Greatest Hits* CDs. I loved it, every song. However, each song was only two minutes long and there were only ten tracks on the CD. Twenty minutes was not enough

Roger Miller for me, so I went back the next day and bought the Roger Miller Mercury boxset. I had never enjoyed anyone's music so much in my life! With just a few songs, Roger Miller became my favorite singer and songwriter of all time.

When I become a die-hard fan of any artist, I try to get my hands on every song that artist ever recorded. But most of Roger's material that has been released consists of the same twenty songs on different *Best Of* collections. I found a few rare albums, like *1970* and *Making a Name for Myself*, and I loved the lesser-known stuff even more than his hits. I've always been that way. The rare Johnny Cash, Bobby Bare, Elvis Presley, etc., are the ones that I enjoy the most. Totally hooked on Roger Miller, I tried to look up as much information on his life as I could, but there were no books written about him, only a little information in music encyclopedias and on the Internet. It seemed strange to me that so huge a talent wasn't well-documented for the public. Not many artists write and record their own songs, have their own television shows (*The Roger Miller Show*, which ran on NBC in 1966), cross over into so many genres of music, including Broadway, and get inducted into the Country Music Hall of Fame (posthumously, in 1995). And yet, I couldn't even find a full discography of Roger's work.

By 1998, things in my music career were going pretty well. The Lyle E Style Show was playing music festivals, theatres and casinos, and I was starting to meet people who were from Nashville and from that golden era of country music. Whenever I met someone whom I thought might have crossed Roger Miller's path, I'd ask if they knew him. No matter who it was, if they knew him their eyes would light up and they'd share a crazy Roger Miller story or one of his one-liners. A man's life can often be measured by the memories of those who knew him, and I soon discovered that everyone who worked in the entertainment industry had a tremendous amount of respect and admiration for Roger. It seemed that Roger Miller was the entertainment industry's best-kept secret. The more I heard about him, the more I wanted to know, and I decided that it was time to start documenting some of these stories before they were forgotten or no longer available.

It took me roughly four years of traveling back and forth across North America to conduct these interviews and document the legend of Roger Miller. The world of country music is flooded with colorful characters, and, as you can imagine, strange things often happened when I ran into these folks who lived, loved, drank, fought and played their way around Nashville and beyond, so I've included the odd behind the scenes story. I've tried to focus here on Roger Miller stories that haven't been told in public over and over again, and to ask questions that true fans of Roger would like to know the answers to. I've also included stories about some of the interviewees themselves that I haven't read anywhere that I think a music fan might be interested in hearing about. Interviews in the book appear more or less in chronological order.

Roger Miller died on October 25, 1992, from cancer, way too young at the age of fifty-six. He never got a chance to grow old with his friends, but he left many behind, and, like all great artists, he left us wanting more. If you don't already know then you will soon find out what I discovered: Roger Miller had one of the most brilliant minds in the history of entertainment.

Merle Haggard

Gordy Collins

Merle Haggard, the Outlaw's outlaw from Bakersfield, California, is one of the best singer/songwriters in country music, and one of the most successful—having more than forty number-one singles. Merle is the epitome of a music artist; his songs, voice and delivery technique are like that of a master painter. He was close friends with Roger and even recorded an incredible song with him called "I Won't Give Up My Train." I met up with Merle in Grand Forks, North Dakota. He was my first interview for this book. How's that for a start?

Merle: Roger and I were real close. Some of my favorite memories were in the mid-sixties when he was doing real good and I was working [in Las Vegas] at the Nugget and he worked at the Sahara. We spent a lot of time together during that period. We flew some Lear jets together! I admired him as much as you could admire anybody. Whenever he came in to where I was working, he always shook me up because I knew he knew what I was doing. I guess probably the worst memory I have of Roger is when he came in one night to Harrah's and I broke both my guitar and my fiddle because I didn't feel like I did a good show. The carpenter threw his hammer. It was all because Roger was there.

Lyle: Did he make you nervous?

Merle: I don't know what it was, but things just didn't go the way I wanted them to go, and when I got downstairs to my room I just threw the guitar and fiddle both right into a mirror. It was a '45 Martin and I still have it. They put it back together for me but the fiddle is a thing of the past. Roger came down and had seen what had happened and said, "Nobody knows but me and you."

Lyle: Under what circumstances did you first meet Roger?

Merle: I was working in a place called The Blackboard in Bakersfield, and he came in—must have been around 1963. He sat in, played piano and sang "In the Summertime."

Lyle: Did you guys ever write anything together?

Merle: You know it's strange that we didn't. He was always talking about wanting to cut "You Don't Have Very Far To Go," a song that I wrote. Every time he was around me, he'd compliment me on that song. "I'm gonna cut that one of these days," he'd say, but I don't guess he ever did.

Lyle: How was it that Roger was chosen to present your award to the Country Music Hall of Fame?

Merle: I don't know exactly but there is nobody else in the world that I would be as thrilled to have do it as him, and that includes everybody in the entertainment business. He was my favorite guy.

Lyle: Did you guys ever do any shows together?

Merle: Oh yeah, I did shows with Roger. I think I did his television show—that could be true or not true, I'm not sure. There have been a lot of television shows. Most of our association came from Las Vegas. We were in and out of Las Vegas through the years.

I remember the first time I ever seen a portable phone, Roger Miller had it. He called me one morning around six a.m. and said, "You and Bonnie still awake?" This must have been around 1965.

I said, "Well, yeah."

"Well, can I come over and play?"

"Sure." I expected him to be somewhere out around the Sahara. I was out on the other part of town and figured it would take him an hour to get there. Well, he hung up the phone and somebody started knocking on the door and I went to the door and he was sitting in the hallway leaning against my door with that damn big old portable phone in his hand!

I think the first thing that we'd always say to each other when we'd be away from each other for a long time was, "How long you been up?" I remember that time he came over with that phone, him and I went somewhere, stayed up and didn't go to sleep. We were downtown and he bought Bonnie [Owens, Merle's second wife and Buck Owens' first wife] a real pretty dress, just for no reason. We were just messing around gambling, and we walked by this pretty dress shop and Roger went in and bought her this dress.

I remember one time when we were at the King of the Road Hotel and Jerry Lee Lewis was in the little lounge there. There was a little stage. Jerry Lee called me up in my room and said, "Why don't you come down? I'm playing here—why don't you bring your fiddle?" And I went down there, and Jerry Lee ended up getting in a squabble and hit this guy with a shot glass in the face! I don't know why I'm telling you this story, but it happened at the King of the Road.

Lyle: Who was it that Jerry Lee threw the shot glass at?

Merle: It was a piano player that worked with my drummer Biff Adam. I think his name was Clyde Griffin. He played just like Jerry Lee and asked Jerry Lee to play a song, and Jerry Lee picked up a shot glass and rammed it in his face. Old Biff was going to kill him! They grabbed Jerry Lee—a bunch of his bodyguards—and got him out of there. Old Biff spent three days and nights looking for Jerry Lee. He didn't go to bed. He was going to kill him. What made me think of that was I went upstairs and spent the rest of the night laughing with Roger. He had sort of a suite on top of that thing where everybody used to go to and hang out.

Roger was always funny. He kept my sides hurting. If he came around you'd just have to laugh because he would make you laugh no matter what it took. He knew I thought he was funny so he had a heyday when he was around me. I remember him looking straight down at the floor and singing that song "My Window Faces the South." You know, Roger was always the same with me. He never got serious for more than thirty seconds at a time. If there was something that happened that we both knew about that hurt both of us, we would talk about it for a period of about thirty, forty-five seconds, and then it was on to something funny again. The funny thing about Roger was that you never could remember anything he said. He was so original and he was so quick that before you could analyze or remember something he said, he was off to something else. He was really something. I don't think I've ever been around a guy that had a mind quicker than Roger Miller's.

I heard a story one time that Roger's guitar player, Jerry Cole, asked him if he could ride his motorcycle and Roger told him, "No." A few minutes later Roger went out to get his motorcycle and it was gone. Jerry took it anyway. When Jerry got back Roger whopped him and knocked him out. When Jerry woke up, Roger said, "You're fired."

The last time I saw Roger was I think the time that he put me in the Hall of Fame and we all left in a limousine. He had us all in tears by the time we got to where we were going. Then after, when he had the cancer, he called me, and he called me on average of once every three months. It might be two o'clock in the morning, it varied. He called me one day and said, "I'm almost back to normal. I can't hit those high notes, but I got most of the low notes back." It just so happened that I was working on a couple of his songs and I told him that I just recorded "Leavin's Not the Only Way To Go." He was real excited about it. That was the last time that I ever talked to him.

Johnny Cash, Willie Nelson, Merle Haggard and Roger Miller were real close friends, all four of us. It's a funny thing that none of us ever bring up Roger when we're together. It's too tender. You know, I don't know of anybody that would say anything bad about Roger. I don't think there is any bad. He was loved by everybody who knew him. I really cared a lot for him and I miss him every day.

Biff Adam

Biff Adam has been Merle Haggard's drummer off and on for the last forty years.

Biff: One of my favorite memories of Roger is when Merle was just learning to play the fiddle. Merle had this fiddle that Bob Wills gave to him and he was real proud of it. So we were doing a show at the Hollywood Bowl and of course Roger came out to the show. Roger had this old fiddle that he picked up at a pawnshop, and when Merle introduced him, he came out and stumbled and fell and broke that fiddle all over the stage! Merle could have died because he thought it was his fiddle. Roger came out and said, "Hey Merle, I got your fiddle here. Can I come out and play fiddle with you guys?" Merle said, "Yeah," and Roger came out and stumbled and the fiddle broke in a hundred pieces. Merle didn't know what to do!

We were the house band at the Palomino and Roger used to come up and play every once in a while. After we'd get done working the Palomino, we'd go to his house and just sit around and jam and tell stories. Roger had this black lady that took care of his house and everything. I don't even know how to say it—they were like man and wife, only not sex-wise. They used to argue all the time. She dearly loved Roger and he dearly loved her as a respect type of thing, and I just thought that was the neatest thing in the world.

I remember that Roger used to rent a Lear jet. He used to send one back to Nashville to get them little bitty Krystal Burgers! He loved them. He'd send for about a hundred of them and fly them back to Hollywood and pass them out to everybody.

Lyle: Merle told me a little about you wanting to beat up Jerry Lee Lewis at the King of the Road Hotel. What happened?

Biff: Clyde Griffin was the biggest Jerry Lee Lewis fan in the world. Clyde asked Jerry Lee to play his favorite song and Jerry Lee said, "I isn't gonna play that song," and threw a shot glass at him. I was feeling pretty good at the time and went after him, but Jerry Lee's bodyguard got him out the door. The drunker I got, the madder I got. I walked all over that hotel trying to find him because I was going to kill him—or whip his ass anyway.

Mickey Newbury

Gordy Collins

Mickey Newbury was a tremendous singer/songwriter with a distinct voice and guitar playing style. In most of his songs he left a lot of room for interpretation, which to me is the mark of a genius. I think the only reason he isn't as well known as Johnny Cash, Waylon or Willie is because he valued his privacy more than anything else. Some of the many unbelievable songs he wrote and recorded are "Swiss Cottage Place," "Why You Been Gone So Long?," "The Dragon and the Mouse," "Going to Alabama," and "American Trilogy" (made famous by Elvis Presley). Many of the people I interviewed for this project were hit hard when they found out about Mickey's passing in September 2002 from emphysema. I was fortunate to do this interview with him, as he was very ill at the time. Even though he was bedridden for quite a while, Mickey was cutting records right there in his bedroom!

Lyle: I have always been fascinated by the song you wrote that Roger recorded called "Swiss Cottage Place." What's the story behind the song, and how did Roger end up recording it?

Mickey: Well, the song title is about Swiss Cottage Place, which is an area I used to live in in London. Like all songs, the names had nothing to do with the song—you know what I mean? You write a song that took place in California and it could end up taking place in New York. I mean, it's just the way it is.

Roger just called me and asked me if I had a song for him, and I told him, "Yeah, I've always got a song, and especially for you." I'm going to tell you right up front that Roger Miller, aside from being one of my best friends, was probably my favorite. He was the most talented singer, the most talented and gifted person of the century. He was exactly what he appears to be. He was sensitive, he was funny, he was highly intelligent, and I don't go a week that I don't think about him. I wished I had known he was so ill. I didn't know.

Lyle: I've gotten the impression that he was the kind of person that didn't want anybody to worry about him.

17

Mickey: Well, that's the natural thing for somebody like Roger. Roger was a very private person. The only time he and I ever got crossed rays was when I was doing *The Tonight Show. The Tonight Show* was an awful show. The only reason I did it was because I liked Johnny Carson. I mean, he and I got along together. I really did like him personally. We had many things in common. Both of us had a bad back. We'd sit there like a couple of old men talking about our problems. We both had very similar personalities. Both of us kept to ourselves and were private and didn't like talking about our personal lives too much.

Anyway, Johnny asked me to do his show and it was the first time, I understand, that he ever asked anybody to do the show. I started doing the show but the show could do me no good. I didn't want to be a performer, and the only time doing the Johnny Carson show could do anybody any good is if they wanted to do Las Vegas. It would help you get there. My wife Suzie and I had long since decided that that was one place I did not want to work. We went over there and watched John Denver do a show in Tahoe, and after seeing one show I looked at her and she looked at me and we both said, "No way."

I've never really had a venue, I've never really been a hillbilly singer, and I've never really had a band. The only time I'd ever worked was for eight months during the late sixties, early seventies when I was on Electra Records. I did a bunch of college concerts in little coffeehouses and I enjoyed that. That folk singing went by the way real fast, though.

When you do *The Tonight Show* they always say, "Be up! Be alive! Be real happy!" I'm not an "up" kind of a guy. That's just not my personality unless I'm with somebody and we are kidding around. But I just can't turn it on. That's why I was never a performer—I mean I am not a performer. I don't dance.

So I went out there, and Carson does it so well that you don't even realize it's being done. Carson says, "So what have you been doing?" I was gonna say, "I just spent a week one night with Roger Miller," but when it came out I said, "I just spent a week with Roger Miller." But I just spent one *night* with him.

Carson said, "Roger is kind of strange, isn't he?"

And I said, "Yeah, well, Roger's squirrelly."

So Roger came on the next night and said, "Here I'm trying to get my reputation squared away and an example of what happens to me is Newbury comes on here and said we spent a week roarin' away in Nashville and we were only together one night."

I never really did get into ever telling him what that was all about because that doesn't matter now. It blew over. It didn't make me mad, but to be called a liar on national television is not something that you want. I never did the Carson show again after that. I just figured television isn't worth it. It wasn't fun for me.

Lyle: Was Roger guest-hosting *The Tonight Show* at one time?

Mickey: Roger would have been a great host. They really missed a bit. Everybody really missed a bit with Roger. Roger would have been great on film as an actor. He was just a funny guy, naturally funny. He was also a very sensitive guy. I mean if you want to hear some sad songs... All his songs weren't just "Dang Me." Roger called me one time and said, "How do you keep writing all of those songs? What drives you to just keep writing?"

And I said, "What drives you not to write? Why aren't you writing?"

"I just don't have anything to write about."

"Well, have you ever just thought about writing about it?"

And he started writing again. Whether that triggered it, I don't know. Shortly after that he put an album out called *Dear Folks, Sorry I Haven't Written Lately*.

I was probably the first person to hear the songs from *Big River*. I didn't even know at the time that they were in a play. He just played me the songs. We were in Australia at the time. That was the last time that I spent any length of time with Roger and [his wife] Mary, any really good quality time. He played me those songs and they were great. I said, "Man, you are right on the wire again. They're great. That's Roger Miller." They stood without the play, just as songs. They didn't need the play as an excuse to exist.

We were all out at Johnny Cash's house one night. Cash has got really elaborate carved furniture like you see in museums—huge kind of gothic carvings. He had a huge piece that was carved and Roger was standing there looking at it. He had a way about him when he was getting ready to say something that was really good. He said, "That guy really liked to whittle, didn't he?"

Lyle: How did you first meet Roger?

Mickey: I really don't recall how I met him. It seems like I've known him forever. It must have been around '64 or '65. He had already had a hit with "Dang Me." I met him right after that, when he wrote "The Last Word in Lonesome Is Me." That song just killed me. Poor dumb me, for years I didn't realize that the last word in "lonesome" is "me". The song stood up to me without that cute little extra bit. I mean, that is how wonderful his mind was. There are probably a ton of people who love that song to this day that are probably not aware that "lonesome" ends with "me." It takes a really brilliant mind to be able to spot something like that, to be just able to look around and be thinking or seeing something in words. What makes a mind think like that? It's just really wonderful. A creative mind like that is a thing of beauty to me. You know, half of the stories that you hear about him being a drunk are from people that didn't know him. Like a lot of us, we all had our times, but people like to name drop, and one of the most famous name droppings would be Roger's. People would say, "Roger and I snorted a house full of cocaine last week," when I would know for a fact what they were saying was a lie because I had just been with him. Yeah, a lot of that went on.

Lyle: In the country music books you can't find much about Roger even though he is so respected in the industry. Why do you think that is?

Mickey: My name probably isn't there either. When you don't talk to them, your name isn't there. I mean, I was in the Hall of Fame with my name misspelled. When you walked into the Hall of Fame they had sheet music for "Sweet Memories" written by Mickey N-E-W-B-E-R-R-Y. For twenty years! My wife Suzie said, "When are you going to tell them about that?" "Never!" I said. I think it's the funniest thing in the world—I'm so famous that they don't even know how to spell my name!

Roger treated everybody the same. He was never condescending to anyone. I don't give a damn if you were one of the guys who swept up the floor or if you were the president of the company. I remember one time he was talking to the head of Warner Brothers or one of these big companies about a movie contract, and he put his head down and went to sleep on their desk! They were so upset about it because of course their egos are so big. That just crushed any chance he had of doing anything in Hollywood after that.

Lyle: Did you hang out at the King of the Road Hotel at all?

Mickey: Yeah. When Roger first got involved with that it was a neat deal. The top floor of that thing was a nice place to go and listen to music. It was only good for about six months, then that part of the town started turning slummy. I don't know what happened. You don't know what causes these things to happen. You ask, "What in hell could cause this?" There was not a decent kind of hotel like that on the freeway at the time. You would think that it would have just kept booming, but it didn't. We used to all hang out there in the lobby. There was always music going. It was a great place.

Lyle: Could you tell me anything about Roger that most people wouldn't know?

Mickey: Well, I think the thing I could say that people didn't know about was how intelligent Roger was. They thought of him as being a comical kind of tutti-frutti, nutsy guy. I don't think they realized how brilliant he really was. We never really talked about anything that serious, though. We both talked about how bad the music business was, which it was and still is. I don't think you could even call it a business right now. As far as I'm concerned it's right where it belongs.

Lyle: One more question: In the song "Swiss Cottage Place," why was she leaving? I must have listened to that song a hundred times and I can't figure it out, and it's been a mystery that I've always wondered about.

Mickey: Well, you know, I'm kind of private too. If anybody has a reason, they can apply it to their own life. It's like an abstract artist. It would be cheating if you told whoever is looking at the painting what it meant.

Jimmy Dean

Gordy Collins

Jimmy Dean is a legend. Many people recognize his name now only in connection with Jimmy Dean sausages and don't realize that he was a hit songwriting and recording artist ("Big Bad John," 1961). He was also a television personality with The Jimmy Dean Show, first on CBS-TV from 1957-1958 and then on ABC-TV from 1963-1966. The Jimmy Dean Show gave Roy Clark, Patsy Cline and Roger Miller their first big breaks and introduced the world to many country music artists.

Jimmy: First of all, I'd have to say that Roger Miller was the most spontaneously creative human being I've ever met. I mean just off the top of his head. There was a comedic side of him, but there was also a very serious side. I remember I interviewed him on a syndicated show that I had and I asked, "Who is Roger Miller?" And he said, "Well, he's a composite of an awful lot of different people." And he was. He was a multifaceted human being. Did you hear about the award he presented me?

Lyle: Yes, the Golden Doorknob. Could you share some details on that?

Jimmy: Well, we introduced "King of the Road" on our television show, and shortly thereafter he sent us the Golden Doorknob Award. It has a little plaque below the golden doorknob that says, "To Jimmy Dean, for a million doors you opened for me."

Lyle: How did you guys become friends? Was it after his appearance on your show?

Jimmy: Ah, gee whiz, boy, you are really digging back. No, I knew Roger a long time before that. Roger appeared several times on my ABC show and also when I sat in for Carson. I think one of the most effective things in the advancement of Roger's career was when Johnny Carson used to go off on a tangent and NBC would call me and ask me if I would fill in for him. I brought Roger Miller on one of those and he was *right*. I mean, he was just a *hit*. Of course Johnny had him back several times after that, but Roger was loose with me. He could turn loose. He was just hysterical.

Lyle: Do you remember any of Roger's one-liners?

Jimmy: I don't know why it hit me as funny, but one time he said, "Remember one thing, Dean: a bird in the hand will shit in your fist." There were oodles of wild things. We did a television show, *Reach For a Star*. It was a pilot-type thing and they only did one. Johnny Russell came on and he had on kind of a funky looking shirt and Roger said, "What'd you do John, shoot your mattress?" And it did look like a mattress!

Lyle: Did you ever record any of Roger's songs?

Jimmy: I recorded the first song he ever had recorded. You never heard it. It was called "The Good Lord's Happy Child." The first song he ever had recorded, that was before he had a recording contract.

You know it was kind of interesting: I had just done *The Statler Brothers' Show*, and [my wife] Donna and I had come back to the hotel and went down to the lounge. It was kinda late but they served us one drink and we were sitting there having a glass of wine, and she looked up and said, "By God, that's Roger Miller over there." And here comes his head bobbing around, and sure enough, it was. He was delighted to see us and naturally we him. He came over and sat down, and then a little later on Jimmy Fortune came in and we just sat around and talked about this, that and the other. I went over to the piano, and everybody wished we had a guitar but we didn't have one. I remember we were getting ready to leave and Roger said, "You know, Jimmy, that's what's the trouble with this business: We don't do this. We don't get together. We used to get together and sing each other songs and tell stories. A lot of wonderfully creative things came out of those meetings and get-togethers. We don't do that anymore. We have got to start doing that. We've got to just set aside time and say we're going to get together." And I really meant it when I said, "You're exactly right. We've got to start getting together." But we never did. It's sad.

The last time I saw him was at a tribute we did for Minnie Pearl. As a matter of fact, Roger used the same dressing room as Donna and me. Barbara Mandrell was one of the emcees on the show. Donna had a beautiful red dress and it was hanging there in the dressing room, and the wardrobe lady came in and said, "Who's wearing that red dress?"

Roger said, "Me."

She proceeded to say, "Well, Barbara is wearing a red dress and we don't want to have anybody else in a red dress on the show."

And Donna said, "Well, that's the only one I brought with me."

The wardrobe lady said, "Go home and get another one." And we lived in Richmond! So we used the red dress anyhow. At that time, Roger had the marks on his body where the doctors were going to zap him with the chemo. Now that he's gone, naturally I cherish every minute that I spent with him and wish that I had more. But you never know. You just never know.

Bubba Brown

Bubba Brown is a songwriter/musician who wrote the song "The Sunny Side of My Life," which Roger Miller recorded in 1972.

Bubba: Roger was playing in Dallas around the same time he cut my song, so I went up and met him at the hotel he was playing at. It was a fancy hotel. Hell, I had to go buy me a suit just so I could get into the place! He took me backstage, handed me his guitar and said, "Show me how you play the beginning of that song." It was really just a simple little lick on the very beginning of it, but he said, "I've been working on that and I can't figure it out." So I showed him and he just kind of laughed. I couldn't believe that here's Roger Miller asking me how to play something!

The best visit I had him with him was up at Willie Nelson's recording studio, when him and Willie and Ray Price were doing the *Old Friends* album. That was a very interesting session that night. A lot of people showed up. They cut all night long and we were visiting off and on. They did the whole album in a matter of two or three days. One funny thing that I remember is the next morning, just as the sun was starting to come up, me, Roger, Willie's bass player, Bee, and a couple of other guys were sitting around in the lobby of the studio out there. You could see out the lobby through this big picture window out over the hills and Roger looks out the window and says, "Oh boy, here he comes."

I said, "Who?"

"Here comes God with his brights on." The sun was coming up.

My wife Patsy also knew him. She's a singer also. She went on a tour with Willie and him back in the late sixties. She was opening shows for him. They went to L.A. and played the Troubadour out there and stayed at Roger's house that night. There's a pretty funny story about that. It was actually supposed to be Willie playing, but Willie rented a car and drove out to pick up Roger [at his house] and got lost. Roger waited until it was almost show time and wound up getting in his own car and driving down to the club. Willie still hadn't gotten there. They introduced Willie Nelson and opened the curtains and it was Roger sitting there! He just started doing Willie Nelson songs because nobody could find Willie.

Mel Tillis

Jim Lersch

Mel Tillis is an extremely talented singer, actor, businessman and entertainer. He has written over one thousand songs including such timeless classics as "Ruby (Don't Take Your Love to Town)" and "I Ain't Never." More than six hundred of his songs have been recorded by other major artists, including Patsy Cline, who recorded "It's Strange" and "So Wrong," which Mel co-wrote with Carl Perkins. He was a regular guest on the hit CBS television show Hee Haw, co-hosted by Roy Clark and Buck Owens, and in 1976 was named Entertainer of the Year by the Country Music Association.

Mel: Roger had genius. He didn't have all that much schooling—I think he quit school in the ninth or tenth grade—but he knew what he wanted to do. There's a certain amount of writers and a certain amount of good songs out there. I think they're blessings and I think he knew that and got every one of them. Every blessing that was supposed to come his way he got. You know, Roger could see something funny about anything he'd look at. He'd look and see it different than you would and he'd put it into his songs. For example, he said something like 'maple syrple.' Hell, who'd put that in a song? Maple syrple!

I met Roger, I believe, in '57. I first went to Nashville in '56 but I didn't move there until '57. I think he had been coming over there from Atlanta. He was in the army and he'd get weekend passes and come over there, but he didn't move there until '57. I met him about the same time he came to town.

I had written a few songs for Cedarwood Publishing Company and they were recorded by Webb Pierce. One of them was "I'm Tired." That was a big hit for Webb, and also "Honky Tonk Song." I had an in. Mr. Denney, one of the owners of Cedarwood Publishing Company, had put me on a $50 a week draw against my royalties and also got me a job with Minnie Pearl. Minnie Pearl was gonna do some fair dates in the Midwest and she was putting together a little band. She needed someone who could play the rhythm guitar and a singer that could sing a little bit, and she hired me and said, "I need a fiddle player." And I said, "I met one today. He just moved to town and hangs out at the Clarkson Hotel Coffee Shop."

In those days that's where everybody hung out. They'd be drinking coffee and discussing their songs. It was before Tootsie's Orchid Lounge. Roger had gotten in town and gotten himself a job at the Andrew Jackson Hotel as a bell-hop, and I'd see him over there and found out that he could play a little fiddle. So I ran down from Cedarwood's office and told Miss Minnie, "Miss Minnie, he hangs around there. I'll go down and see if I can find him."

And there he was. He was sitting in the there with his little monkey outfit on. I said, "Roger, do you want a job?"

He said, "Doing what?"

"Playing fiddle."

"For who?"

"Minnie Pearl."

"How much does it pay?"

"$18 a show. If we do one show you get $18. If we do two shows you get $36."

"For how long?"

"For three months, all out through the Midwest. Fair dates."

"Well, let me run over and give the Andrew Jackson my two-minute notice."

And that was my first experience with Roger Miller. We traveled with Miss Minnie for three months, and oh, my goodness, he'd sing them crazy songs. I said, "You'll never get shit like that cut." Little did I know!

I remember I wouldn't let him drive. Hell, he couldn't keep his mind on what he was doing. He was either thinking of songs or pussy. Oh God! He was too spastic for me, so I did the driving. We'd pull a trailer and we had a bass fiddle, and its neck went down between us.

I remember one night I was writing a song called "Indication of the Blues"—"I-N-D-I-cation of the Blues." I was humming it and he was over there asleep, and I could look over the neck of the bass fiddle and see him over there sleeping. The next morning he said, "You know, I wrote me a song."

I said, "You did?"

"Yeah, I dreamed it."

"What's the name?"

"Invitation to the Blues."

So I threw mine out the window!

After our tour with Minnie Pearl, things didn't go too well for him. Right after that he and Barbara, his first wife, moved back to Amarillo. As a matter of fact, I let him use my '55 Ford to move back. He moved back there and got himself a job as a fireman. I went through there with a little tour one time and we stopped at the fire station to see him and he was sitting there on a stool making a fiddle. He had it all finished and he was sanding it. He'd been making some records with RCA, but they hadn't caught on. One of them was "In the Summertime," and it did okay for him, but it wasn't a big hit. Then Andy Williams picked it up and had a big hit from it, so Roger moved back from Amarillo and began to get some songs cut. He wrote "Tall, Tall Trees" for George Jones and a lot of different songs after that, and then he got on Smash Records. Jerry Kennedy produced him and it just exploded after that.

We wrote one song together called "That's Why I'm Drinking," and he cut some of my songs—"I Ain't Never" and "Ruby (Don't Take Your Love to Town)." He didn't release "Ruby" then. He said he didn't know if that was a hit or not. He liked the song, but the subject of it... He didn't think radio would play it. And they may not have at that time. It was recorded by Johnny Darrell the first time around and went to number nine on the charts. But then a few years later the Kent State thing happened and they called out the National Guard. It was a Vietnam protest thing at Kent State in Indiana and several of the students were killed. And then Kenny Rogers and the First Edition recorded that song on an album. Golly, songs are timely. Maybe at the time when Roger cut it, it wasn't ready. He regretted that he didn't put it out, but he cut it.

I was with him one time in Idaho when he got the idea for "King of the Road." We were on a tour and we were in the Boise Idaho Hotel, and Roger asked the promoter if he could call and get him an appointment for a sauna bath. The promoter was Shelly Snyder. He said, "Who the hell do you think you are—King of the road?" That's where he got the idea. They got into a big fight, and I mean a fist fight. "Who the hell do you think you are? King of the road?" Roger cussed, "King of the goddamn road!" Shelly was a character too. Well, they're all characters or they wouldn't be in the business.

When I started out, I didn't have any songs. I was just out of the Air Force and went to work with my cousin. He got me a job as a fireman for the railroad for the ACL, Atlantic Coast Line Railroad, in Tampa, Florida. I would use my railroad pass to come to Nashville and see if I could get on as a singer. Well, they told me they didn't want any stuttering singers, so I said, "Well, what do you want?"

"We need copyrights."

"What's that?"

"Songs. We need songs."

"Well, I've never written a song." So, I got back on the train and started trying to write some songs and put some songs together. And I did. I put together "I'm Tired" and that "Honky Tonk Song," which were big hits and are still being recorded. "Honky Tonk Song" was just recorded by the group BR-549. I wrote songs on both sides of Charley Pride's first record—"The Snakes Crawl at Night" and "Atlantic Coastal Line."

Lyle: I didn't know that you wrote "The Snakes Crawl at Night." That's a great song!

Mel: I had bought me twenty acres in Groveland, Florida, on a lake, and I borrowed a buddy of mine's bulldozer and was clearing it off. My mother was up there visiting from around Tampa. At night time you'd have it all leveled off, pretty sand and all. I'd come out the next morning and there'd be tracks all over the place. I told my mama about it and she said, "Son, that's the snakes. Didn't you know the snakes crawl at night?" I was on that damn bulldozer and I got to comparing that to people. That's how it happened.

But those songs were mostly heart over mind. "Burning Memories," "One More Time," "I Ain't Never," "Honey Won't You Open That Door?". Shit, I wrote those songs so fast it would make your head spin. I wrote like I had good sense, which I didn't, but those were blessings in my opinion. And the same with Roger and most writers for that matter. When I came to Nashville there were only about eight or ten writers in town. There were only two recording studios—if you could call them that. One of them was a Quonset Hut on 16th Avenue, Bradley's, and the other one was over on Demonbreun. RCA was in that building.

Lyle: Did you hang out at the King of the Road Hotel at all?

Mel: You know, he'd come in town and he'd act like he owned that place. He said, "Mel, I built my dreams in concrete." But I knew they were just using his name. He was probably getting some royalties out of it or something. I remember one time Roger was roarin'—that's what we called it, R-O-A-R-I-N'—and he'd been up about three days. He could do that. He had some help, but I never did get into doing that stuff. I would drink a beer, every now and then a coke high… But I ran into him and he needed a song because he had just been covered on "Little Green Apples" by [O.C. Smith], and his version was a hit and Roger's wasn't. I was out drinking at Tootsie's or something and I ran into a fellow named Wayne Carson. He's from Springfield, Missouri, and lives in Nashville now. He wrote "The Letter," a big hit, and he was one of the writers on "Always On My Mind." He had this song called "Who's Julie?" and I said, "God, that would be a hit for Roger, and he needs one. Do you have a tape on it?" He said, "Yeah," and gave that song to me, and I went to the hotel. Roger had been up for three days and the door to his suite was open so I just went on in. He had a bed suspended from the ceiling. You know, you could swing in it. I went in there and yanked it and gave it a swing, made a lot of noise trying to wake him up. He was out, so I just got up in that bed and I straddled him. I said, "Roger, Roger, I got you a hit. Hey, Roger!" I never could get him up, so I said, "Well, fuck you, I'll record it myself." It was one of my biggest hits!

Back when he was sick, they were taking him back to where he was staying in California, and he looked out the window and said, "Mary, look, they filled our pool." The Pacific Ocean.

Have you heard the one about Roger breaking the light bulb? He just wanted to hear it pop. Tootsie's had closed and there was a big ol' trash can out in front, and they had about four or five fluorescent light bulbs in it. He went Pow!, and then here come the cops. They said, "What the hell are you doing?"

He said, "I just wanted to hear them pop." Well, they put him in jail!

I remember one time I was filling in for Frank Sinatra at Harrah's in Lake Tahoe and ol' Roger came by. He was playing across the street and had finished, so he came by my suite one night and entertained. At that time I was married to Judy. He entertained us all night long. I mean, he'd never stop. He'd do shit with his throat and all kinds of sounds, all kinds of shit. He's the best entertainer that I think I've ever known in a motel room.

One time he called me and Willie Nelson from a jet. We were at Tootsie's Orchid Lounge and he called. Tootsie said, "Melvin?"

And I said, "Yes."

"Roger Miller is on the phone. The Wild Child."

Everybody called him the Wild Child. Roger said, "Hey, do you two want to go to Tallahassee to the Governor's Ball?"

I said, "Where are you?"

"I'm 40,000 feet over Oklahoma City. I'll be there in thirty minutes. Meet me at the airport."

He picked us up on a jet! We went out to the airport and flew with him to Tallahassee. We sat in a booth at this Governor's Ball. Roger came out [on stage] and the Governor kept going, "King of the Road!" He'd do another song like "Dang Me," and the Governor'd shout, "King of the Road!" Finally Roger just stopped and said, "Please, Sir, would you let me set my own pace?" To the fucking governor! Me and Willie just went right down in our seats. Oh God!

You know, Roger was a different person off stage than he was on stage. Everybody expected him to be funny and he worked at it off stage. He'd rather entertain his peers than an audience, that's how I pictured it. He sure as hell entertained me and it takes a lot to entertain me.

Mickey Gilley

Gordy Collins

Mickey Gilley is a huge talent and a great businessman. He owned Gilley's—the largest and most famous nightclub in the world which is featured in the 1980 hit movie Urban Cowboy. I interviewed Mickey at his theatre in Branson, Missouri.

Mickey: The first thing that I think about of the times I spent with Roger was the time I did *Austin City Limits* with him [in 1983]. We got into the van to go over to the shuttle and the air conditioning wasn't working, and he said right off the top of his head, "Is it hot in here or is my career taking off again?" I just lost it! I had a picture of all of us, but when the theatre burned I lost it. I just hate that. It had his signature on it too. He was a good person and I think that he was happy the way things turned out. He had success, and of course, like all of us, we slow down when we get older and don't have the popularity in the music industry like some other people do. But we still do the things we love and that's perform for the folks.

Lyle: Did you ever record any of his songs?

Mickey: I recorded "When Two Worlds Collide" just before Roger became popular. It was produced by Ray Stevens. 'Course it didn't do anything, 'cause at that time nobody knew who Mickey Gilley was so we didn't get any play on it.

I remember some of the stories I heard on Roger. Like they'd lease a Lear jet, fly to Nashville, get what they wanted and fly back. All kinds of bizarre outings like that. Whether they were true, I don't know. Some of these guys make so much money, they do things just to get the publicity out of it. Like some of the rock groups, they want certain colors of M&Ms to be taken out, ridiculous things. I had an agent call me one time and say, "What all do you got to have?"

I said, "Just enough equipment to do the show."

He started telling me all what he couldn't get—"Well, we can't get this and we can't get that"—you know, and I said, "You think you can get me a megaphone and a flashlight? If you can get that I'll do the show." You know, I used to play in those old joints, and if I had a piano that worked I was lucky.

Jimmie Rodgers

Jimmie Rodgers' "Honeycomb" reached number one on both the Billboard and Country & Western charts in 1957. It knocked his old roommate Buddy Holly's hit "That'll Be the Day" out of the top spot and ushering in a successful recording career of thirty-eight hits that lasted through the 1960's. In 1959, Jimmie hosted his own weekly music and variety show on NBC, The Jimmie Rodgers Show. Jimmie also wrote one of my favorite Elvis songs, "It's Over."

Jimmie: Roger Miller was a brilliant writer, certainly a great performer, and an interesting cat. This guy was crazy, fun and smart. The first time I met him I was at the Statler Hilton Hotel in Dallas, Texas… Gosh, it had to be in the late fifties. Sophie Tucker, an old-time singer/comedian gal, a big heavyset vaudeville performer, was working the hotel. I opened the show, she closed. Roger Miller, who was about sixteen, came back to my dressing room. He was a little guy, kinda small, a little kid. He said, "Mr. Rodgers?"

I said, "Yeah."

"I'm a songwriter. I'd love to play you some of my songs."

I was just getting ready to go on stage and I said, "Well, I'm gonna do a show here, but when I come off stage I'd be happy to talk to you." I didn't know if I'd have time to listen to him or not 'cause usually when people do that, their songs aren't very good. I went out, did my show, came back and he was gone. And I never forgot that because, as a rule, that doesn't happen. If you tell somebody you'll meet them after the show, they wait.

So fade in, fade out, years later I was flying somewhere and Roger Miller was on the plane. We had never really talked and he came over and sat down beside me and said, "I wrote a song for you," Then he started looking in his jacket and then said, "I guess I smoked it." Then he told me, "I don't know if you remember, but when I was sixteen or seventeen I came backstage to the Statler Hilton to get you to listen to my music. I got so nervous, really scared, and when you were out on the stage, I just left."

I said, "Well, you rat, you had all those good songs and you took off and left."

Back when he had his television show we used to go out to NBC in L.A. We'd go to Roger's dressing room and help him get dressed. He couldn't get dressed by himself! He was whacko, crazy. The room was full of Coke bottles and stuff scattered all over the place, the band would be waiting. He had the show for awhile but he was so crazy that they'd have a full orchestra waiting for him for several hours before he'd come out.

Lyle: Are you buddies with Tom T. Hall? I thought he wrote the song "Me and Jimmie Rodgers" about you.

Jimmie: No, it wasn't about me. I've never met Tom T. It was the Jimmie Rodgers who died in 1933. That Jimmie Rodgers was a yodeling blues singer. He was like one of the first country guys in the business so there's a lot of stories about the old Jimmie Rodgers. Tom wouldn't have met him, but he could have been writing about a reflective idea that he had of the old Jimmie Rodgers. I wasn't named after the late Jimmie Rodgers. I was named after my uncle.

[Author's Note] In 1967 Jimmie was viciously attacked and literally had his head bashed in. He survived, but just barely, and had to undergo numerous operations, including three on his brain. He now has a steel plate in his skull. "You wouldn't believe how many people think I'm dead," he told me. He said when he does radio interviews listeners actually phone in and tell him they know the real Jimmie Rodgers is dead and that he's an impostor!

Roy Clark

Richard D. Moore

A great guitar player and entertainer, Roy Clark recorded some of my favorite songs—"I Never Picked Cotton" and "Me and the Elephant," to name just a few. Roy has headlined at some of the most prestigious venues in the world (Carnegie Hall, Madison Square Garden) and still tours constantly. Branching out from the footlights of the concert stage to the klieg lights of the soundstage, in the sixties Roy was the first country music artist to host The Tonight Show. Later he went on to co-host his own television smash, Hee Haw, for twenty-five years! He became a member of the Grand Ole Opry in 1987. Remembering one of your best friends who is no longer with you can't be easy, and reminiscing about Roger was often difficult for Roy. This interview was supposed to be only twenty minutes, but it lasted for more than an hour and a half.

Roy: Roger was as close a friend as I've ever had, especially in the music business. Him and I didn't see each other every day but there was a chemistry that started. We were introduced to each other by Rex Allen, the cowboy singer. Rex knew me and Rex knew Roger. Roger was just getting started. He had no records but he'd had a couple songs recorded by other artists. Rex said to me and to Roger independently, "You got to meet this Roger Miller/you got to meet this Roy Clark. He's as much a nut as you are." I'd been hearing some people talk about him, so we met at the Country Music Awards in Nashville when it used to be called the Disc Jockey's Convention. It used to be headquartered at the Andrew Jackson Hotel, which has long since been demolished. It was an old, old hotel then. All the record companies had suites on different floors, hospitality suites and stuff. Well, Rex Allen had a suite and he called Roger and Roger came over and walked in the door. Rex introduced us and we were together night and day for the next seven days. Never separated. I don't know why. You look back and wonder why would you pick out one guy like that and not be separated. I mean we *stayed together*. We'd lay down and get as much sleep as had to be had just so we didn't miss anything, and then get up and go. I went to his house and met his first wife. He got some clothes and we went back to the hotel. That's how it all started, and every time we were together was like, "This is the last good time we're gonna have so we gotta live it up!"

Roger lived in California and I lived in Maryland. We'd work occasional dates together, but I would see him in California or Vegas or Reno. All of our mutual friends would try and get us together. They'd say, "Roger's gonna be in town, Roy's gonna be in town, let's get together and have a party." Then they would all sit back and watch us try and out do each other. Well, one night they brought a little reel-to-reel recorder and sat it on the floor and him and I went at each other for hours. He would just do one thing after another that didn't tie in, no continuity, but you'd just be sitting there holding your gut. He [did a bit about] a big fire. It was a guy talking over this portable radio, "Yeah, we're having a terrible time down here, Chief. Yeah, the blaze, it's about a three... *(static sound)* You know the next time, what we're gonna have *(static sound)* to have here, is a pre-fire sale, because once the fire is here, all the stuff is ruined you can't hardly sell stuff that's ruined, so we'll have to have a pre-fire sale." Instead of a fire sale! And he would just do that and then it would be off to something else, just ad-libbing.

Roger saw—and I have been blessed this way too—humor in everything. Instead of saying something like, "Oh man, look at that, it's so cloudy, it's gonna rain and I was gonna play golf today," you say, "Isn't this the most beautiful rainy day you've ever seen?" You can't change it, it's gonna be, so make the best of it. Roger was like that. He'd look at anything and see the funny side of it. He was a challenge because I always prided myself on being quick-witted. I grew up in live television, where if you went on and the scene fell down on you or your guitar neck broke off, or whatever, you couldn't say, "Hold it, re-rack it and let's do the take again." You learn how to react to different things. The first time in school I didn't know the answer to something and felt inadequate, I would say something and everyone would laugh. It was a good sound and would get you out of situations. Somebody once said to me, "Clark, you're never serious. You're always a child." And I said, "That's right. I'll be old soon enough."

It's hard to describe some of the things he did that were funny because there was nothing to it. He did this one thing when we were walking along and he said "And in this corner it's Roy Clark at 195 pounds, CLARK!!"—like a guy announcing a prize fight. You know how they would repeat your name. Roy Clark…CLARK!! And with him doing it I fell to my knees. Out of the blue, made no sense, and it had nothing to do with what we were talking about.

One time… We'd known each other for years, we were playing Las Vegas and he came back to my dressing room and I don't know why I did it, but I said, "Roger, have I ever told you I love you?"

And he looked at me sorta funny and said, "Nah."

"Well, I do. When we're together we laugh and we gag and we don't make any sense. We're just always silly. I just feel like telling you that I love you."

He looked at me stern and said, "I love you too." And then he said, "But we got to keep our sillies!" That's one of the warmest memories I have of him.

Roger didn't feel all that comfortable doing television. The way he felt comfortable was letting him do something and then put a camera on him. He had a network show on NBC that I think really might have soured him. It was awful hard to structure Roger. In fact, when you tried to structure him, you lost him, you lost his magic. And they had that show very highly produced. It was, "Roger, walk over here and stand here and look at this camera and say this. Walk over here, look at that camera, introduce this guest." And that wasn't Roger, so he left. He had two shows to go in his contract with NBC and he disappeared. He just burned out. I just happened to be at NBC the day that his manager, booking agency and NBC were trying to get Roger to finish up those last two shows so they would have a season. We were doing a television show [Swinging Country] in the studio. This is like 1966, in that era… Roger came back and said, "Clark, come here." I went into his dressing room and he told me to sit down. He had a Coke—he never drank. Roger didn't drink except Coca-Colas. If he ever quit drinking Coca-Colas, Coca-Cola would notice the downward trend in sales. He had cases of them everywhere, and this is before cans. We sat back there and he drank a couple of Cokes and finally got himself together to say, "Well, let's get this thing over with." We were in one studio while he was across the hall finishing his. He made them wait. They were biding their time. That's all they could do because if he didn't do these two shows they wouldn't have a complete season. So he did it and ended his contract.

Record-wise was the same thing. Roger's first records never sold. I ran into him at the airport in Nashville one time. I was coming in to record, he had been there for two weeks and was getting ready to leave and had chartered an airplane. Back then I was flying my own plane to engagements and things, so we met there at the private FBO. We hugged and "howdied" and I said, "What have you been doing?"

He said, "I've been here two weeks recording every day and I didn't get a single cut."

"Man, if I had two weeks to come in and record I'd have a year's worth of albums. I wish I had that luxury."

Well, they tried to record him like they do everyone else. They put the guitar player over here, he's enclosed in the booth to separate him from the others so it can be nice perfect stereo. They had the steel guitar player over here. They had the background singers in the next county over there. They had the piano player over here. Then they put Roger in the isolated box. They had lost it. No heart, no magic. He couldn't communicate with these people he could barely see, so finally he walked in one day and said, "Alright, okay, all of you people here, come over here and get in a circle." So they formed a circle and looked at one another and started playing, you know, and saying, "Now, you take." That magic of spontaneity just started showing up, and that's when all of his hit records started—"Dang Me" and "Chug-a-Lug." I ran into him after that and he told me the story about what happened, and he said, "I finally recorded something—something I'm proud of."

Roger worked with a great bunch of musicians at one time. He had the best—Thumbs Carllile on guitar, Bobby Dyson on bass, and Marty Allred on drums. You couldn't get any better, but it pulled him back. Structure pulled Roger back. He lost that "I can do anything I want any time I want to" thing. I worked with him a couple of times not too long before he passed away. We played the DuQuoin State Fair. It's one of the oldest fairs in the country, in DuQuoin, Illinois. It's a racetrack. There were like 20,000 people and Roger was working by himself, just him and his guitar, and he *destroyed* them. I said, "Roger, it's taken you all this time."

And he said, "Well, it took a lot of nerve to go out here by myself."

You could hear everything he was doing. He'd just look down at his guitar and mumble a couple of things, and the audience would break up because they could hear him for the first time.

You know, I wish the world knew more about the sensitive side of Roger. When you think of Roger you think of "Dang Me," you think of "Chug-a-Lug." He was a little hesitant on showing that warm side. I said to him one time, "Roger, you know one of my favorite songs that you did was 'When Two Worlds Collide'."

He said, "That's the worst thing I ever wrote," and just put it off.

Lyle: I have one of your live albums where you sing "Smoke the Green, Green Grass of Home."

Roy: That's Roger's. I got it from him. I added a few lines to it, but the whole premise of the song was his.

Lyle: You said on that album that you and Roger used to re-write a lot of those old time songs.

Roy: Yeah, Roger was a classic at that. He didn't like repeating unnecessarily. If it hit him again he may do it, but it wasn't part of his routine. His routine was to be totally new. He wrote the musical score for the [1967] movie *Waterhole #3*. The music starts at the beginning and flows all the way through to the end of the movie. It tells the story as the movie is happening. That was the first thing Roger had ever done like that. He played me some of the first demos of cuts that he was working on and he was really proud, like, "Hey this is coming together. I didn't know I could do this." It really pleased him because it showed off a side of his creativity that wasn't obvious. And all of a sudden the world was saying, "This guy is pretty bright. He is not only talented, he is extremely bright."

[After he did *Big River*] He said to me after that, "I have to write another Broadway play."

I said, "Why is that?"

"To prove to those turkeys that this wasn't a fluke."

Lyle: Did you ever hang out at the King of the Road Hotel?

Roy: Oh yeah, that used to be our gathering place. Roger had no money in it. The money people got together and used Roger's name "King of the Road." In all actuality, it was a terrible hotel. It had the worst smell, it was musty. It wasn't that old but it smelled like it was two hundred years old and had never been cleaned. Roger had a falling out with the people, he felt he was being used. They didn't follow through on the deal they made, and he tried and finally did get out of it. He had a contract for them to use his name but as soon as it was up, he bailed. I think—and don't quote me on this— well, you can quote me on this because I'm just saying what I think—I think Roger stayed in another hotel when he was in Nashville. He wouldn't stay there. I don't recall him ever going there. Not with me. If we went somewhere we'd go somewhere else.

Roger used to carry an attaché case filled with pills. One of those times, when our friends got us together in L.A., he walked in and had a double-size attaché case, opened it up and said, "I'm gonna straighten my act up. I'm taking way too many pills. I'm staying up too long, and I'm not getting enough rest." He'd gone to a doctor for a visit. I don't think he had any health problems, but he went and had a complete physical and to see some kind of a specialist. He told that guy about all the pills he had been taking. He took pills to sleep, pills to wake up, pills to perform. I bet he had 10,000 pills in that attaché case! All herbs. Herbs and herbal Chinese roots. All of this stuff was supposed to take the place of the barbiturates that he took. He made a serious attempt at it. I can see that like it was yesterday. Everybody wondered why he was carrying this beautiful-looking leather attaché case, because he wasn't that business-minded. He sat down on the couch, put that case on his lap, opened it up, and *my God!*, there was about 10,000 herbs and roots and powders and all the voodoo remedies to break the habit of these pills. And all these herbs would replenish all the things his body was lacking.

The last time I saw him was in Nashville. I had heard that he had throat cancer, but it was like they weren't sure that it was….They thought they could get it. We were in Nashville doing a tribute to Minnie Pearl. I ran into him backstage, him and Mary. He looked great, he looked good to me. I said, "Hey, how you doing?"

It was obvious to him that I didn't know.

He said, "Well, they cut me."

He had a little thin blue line, almost like a cosmetic scar, very, very unnoticeable. It wasn't like a great big jagged thing. They took out one of his vocal cords and had put in what they called a false vocal cord so he could make a sound.

He said, "I have to put my head down to the side like this to talk."

I said, "You look like a mobster. Why don't you get some gangster songs to record?"

He smiled.

I thought he looked great for someone who was supposed to be sick. But I saw the tape [of the show] played back and he was standing in the back. He couldn't sing, but he was mouthing the words when we were all on stage together. And I saw the age. He'd aged fifteen, twenty years. And that's when I knew, when I looked at that, I knew he was sick.

I didn't keep in touch with him or Mary because I knew everybody else was. But one of our mutual friends, David Huddleston, who's an actor and lived in Sante Fe not far from Roger, called me and said, "Roger is not going to be with us long." And that's when….I guess I wasn't accepting it. I thought Roger was indestructible, he'll get over this. David said, "Roger's on his way to California to see a specialist to try some kind of new procedure. It broke my heart to see him. He's not gonna be with us much longer." And it wasn't three weeks later he called to tell me that Roger had passed away.

Don Bowman

Don Bowman, born in Lubbock, Texas, is an accomplished singer/songwriter/comedian, recording for RCA songs like, "Chet Atkins, Make Me a Star" and "Hello, Mr. DJ." Don co-wrote "Just to Satisfy You" with Waylon Jennings. A long-time character and musician of the Nashville scene of the sixties, he even had Waylon and Willie singing back-up vocals for him! Don was the host of the American Country Countdown radio program from 1973-1978, and for many years was Willie Nelson's opening act. Elvis Presley was known to be a big fan of Don's albums and used to play them over the PA system at Graceland.

Don: Everybody loved Roger. Everybody. Nobody disliked Roger. Everybody looked up to him because nobody could keep up to him. Nobody could out ad-lib him, nobody could out-funny him. The funniest mind. Good God Almighty, he had the fastest mind I've ever known in my life! He was the only person on earth I couldn't top. The shit he said....

"Chickens are the only animals that can gain weight and never show it in their face."

"If you get to thinking you're really important, stick your finger in a glass of water and then take it out. If it leaves a hole we can't do without you."

Once he was on one bus and I was on another bus. We left Dallas and were going to Houston. He said, "Hey, if you get to Houston first, draw a line. If I get there first, I'll erase it," which means absolutely nothing, but at the time I thought, Goddamn! that's funny....I think! I'm not sure what the hell it meant, but damn, he was the funniest man. He'd go on stage and sing a song, tell a few jokes, and then he'd just sit there and clean his fingernails 'til he thought of something.

"So what'd you do last night?"

"I paid $15 to watch Roger Miller clean his fingernails!" People would laugh their ass off!

The stupidest thing on earth is to be a heckler and try to out ad-lib Roger Miller. I mean, you might as well stick your head in a combine. What a dumb-ass thing to do. He would sit there and wait on a heckler. Some dumb-ass with about three beers in him would go, "Blah, blah, blah," and Roger would put his guitar down and say, "Okay…" and do about twenty minutes [on the guy]. When he was done, the guy was about one inch tall. He'd eat a heckler live!

In 1965 I was making a movie in California with Ferlin Husky [Hillbillies in a Haunted House] and we were staying at Gene Autry's Continental Hotel. We had like a thirty-day schedule. I mean every day for thirty days, and the only day off was Thanksgiving. Ferlin and I had no family or anything, we were just stuck there making a movie, so we were gonna go downstairs and have Thanksgiving dinner or call room service. About noon somebody knocked on the door. It was Roger. He said, "Hey, what are you doing for Thanksgiving?"

"Well, me and Ferlin are gonna go downstairs."

"No, come have Thanksgiving dinner with me."

"Well, it's kind of late Roger."

"No, don't worry about it. Let me use your phone."

So he called home and you could tell it just didn't go over well at all. "Well, come on God Almighty! They're friends of mine."

You could tell his wife was not ready to have two people come have Thanksgiving dinner with them, so Ferlin backed out. I didn't want to go, I didn't want to get in the middle of this shit, but we got in the car. I was driving and he was sitting in the passenger seat, all the way to Coldwater Canyon, down to Ventura Boulevard and out to the Valley where his house was. Thanksgiving Day, no traffic, it took thirty or thirty-five minutes, and he was humming and tapping on the dashboard. He didn't say a word all the way there. We got there and he got out and walked in the house, picked up his guitar and sang "Husbands and Wives." He had written the entire song over that fight they had over the phone!

Lyle: When he wrote a song like "Husbands and Wives" was it pretty much done the minute it hit the paper?

Don: Yeah, if he wrote it down at all. I went to the recording studio with him the night they did "England Swings." He sang the first thing and then he sang the bridge, then they did a turnaround, then he sang the bridge again.

This A&R guy said, "That's not enough, Roger. That's a minute and eight seconds long, we need another verse." Roger picked up a yellow pad—I swear to God—wrote a verse on it, signed it 'Roger,' and handed it to me and said, "Here. Frame this and pray."

I've got it framed somewhere in all my stuff—somewhere. It's the second verse of "England Swings." I got that in his handwriting, signed and dated. By writing it down he already knew what he'd written down. He never looked at it again, just stepped up to the microphone and sang it.

Once Roger was driving down the road about ten miles outside of Indianapolis. He told me this story a hundred times. Right outside of Indianapolis there was a billboard with a hobo [on it]. He saw it...the thing went by like that, you know, driving sixty miles an hour...and by the time he reached Indianapolis he had "King of the Road" written. It just rolled out in ten minutes.

When we were all broke everyone called him Roger the Dodger. God, he hated that. This is back when we were bumming cigarettes and borrowing fifty cents anywhere we could to buy a pack of cigarettes. Then all of a sudden he had "Chug-a-Lug" and "Dang Me." He came by the office one night. I was over at Harlan Howard's. I wrote for Harlan's publishing company. Roger called me over and said, "I'm not bragging. I'm not blowing smoke up your skirt. I just want to show you this." And he had this check for like $140,000! It was the first check he had from Tree Publishing for "Dang Me" and "Chug-a-Lug." It's not even for "King of the Road." We haven't even got into "King of the Road" money yet, which is eight times that. It was the first check he had gotten with commas in it. $140,000. He just came all the way over there and said, "I just want to show this, Don, I'm not bragging."

I said "Goddamn! Ain't life good?"

He said, "Yeah it's fine."

Do you know what old yellers are?

Lyle: Those are uppers, aren't they?

Don: Yeah. They're made by the SE Massengill Company. All they made was douche powder and Overdream, which is speed, and they were the same color, so you never knew if you were real high or real clean. But anyway, that's what old yellers are and we took a lot of them. A lot! The first tours that were twelve or fourteen days we never went to bed. Of course, we were twenty-two or twenty-three. We probably wouldn't have gone to bed anyway. We stayed up six days one time and he said, "Drive me out to the airport. I got a Lear jet and am playing Jacksonville, Florida tonight."

So I drove him to the airport and he said, "Have you ever been in a Lear jet?"

"No, never been in one."

"Park the car and come on. Let me show you this."

I got in the jet and he went to the back and said, "Look back here at all this stuff."

I'm in the back looking and he slammed the door and he said [to the pilot], "GO!"

I went, "WAIT!."

I had a show the next day in Des Moines or some freaking place. He went "Go!" and we took off in the Lear jet. My Thunderbird was left right there on the runway and he's there on the radio saying, "Somebody has to get out there and get that car off the runway." We were in Jacksonville in two hours, did the show, and came back the next day. He finally decided to go to sleep after eight weeks.

We stayed up six days and seven nights one time just to see how long we could stay up without just falling down and going *boom*. On the seventh morning Ralph Emery had a TV show at six a.m., one of those "Good Morning Nashville" things. So we went out there after we'd been up…I couldn't even speak English, just mumbling…and finally got through this show, and Ralph said, "You guys need to go back to the hotel. I mean you guys really need to go lay down or something."

We got back to the hotel, got on the elevator and Roger just dropped right there in the damn elevator in the Stonewall Jackson Hotel! He weighed 175, 180 pounds, even back then when he didn't eat for weeks. I picked him up, got the door open, was going down the hall carrying him, and he started giggling. I said, "You son of a bitch!"

He said, "Damn you're gullible!"

Ralph Emery [hosted a TNN version of] *The Tonight Show*. This was before cable, way back there in the sixties. Ralph had a morning show and a night show and was on vacation or something, and Roger was hosting it and had to do a live commercial for Goody's Headache Powders. He was reading the telecopy: "This is the strongest headache remedy you can get without a prescription," and he looked at whoever was sitting right next to him and said, "Yeah, right! I know other stuff that you can take that will cure a headache and it has nothing to do with Goody's Headache Powders!"

God Almighty! The advertising agency called—Mr. Goody himself called—and Roger had to go on the next night and apologize. They damn near lost the whole account!

I think he was talking about old yellers. They'll cure a headache. If you had one you couldn't find it with both hands. Simcoes, made by SE Massengill Company. Right in the middle it said SE MCO—Simcoes, S.E. Massengill Company. They also made speckled birds, which were the same thing, Overdream, only they were time-released things and were twice as strong as the little yellow things. The little yellow things weren't but five mg, and you were supposed to take like three a day. We'd take sixty or seventy! We always had thirty or forty in our pockets. Just take a handful, never even look, never count them. We were only twenty-three, twenty-four years old, you know. Shit, you're 5' 6" and bullet-proof!

One time I was living out in one of Willie Nelson's condos and Roger was staying in one of them. They had recording studios out at this end and were recording an album up there at the time. Roger came by my condo at nine o'clock in the morning and he had this vial of coke. So he gave my wife a buck and he gave me a buck and he took a buck. Afterward he said, "I'll just leave this for you."

"Okay," so he left. We tore that goddamn condo apart! He didn't leave the goddamn coke there. It took us forty-five minutes before we realized it. He had said, "I'll leave this here for you," but he didn't leave shit there! He took it with him. He did it on purpose.

Let me tell you something. This has nothing to do with Roger Miller, but while I'm thinking about it, everybody in Nashville took those damn things, because it just got to be "the thing". There were no buses back then, you didn't have a driver. If you had a show one night in Lubbock and the next night in Houston, the only way you could do it was to take them little pills 'cause we didn't have the bus to get on and have the driver drive you.

Everybody had a station wagon or a Thunderbird or a Cadillac and everybody took 'em. Cash.. Good God, Cash took 'em! We all took 'em. Waylon, Willie, all of us would take them by the handful, day after day, and stay up for days. Except for Bobby Bare. Bobby Bare is the only human being I met in my life who'd bite them in half. I mean they're five mg, good God! You take six of them and your eyes barely even blink. But Bobby would bite them in half. That's just Bobby. He gives a whole new meaning to mellow. Just he and Chet together on a three-hour recording session, and Chet would say, "Hmmm...."

And Bobby would say, "Hmmm...."

And Chet would say, "Hmmm...."

And Bobby would say, "Hmmm...."

That's it! That's Bobby—just level. No highs, no lows—just right there. The world could end and he'd just say, "Hmmm...."

Now, Lyle, don't go writing a whole bunch of stuff about speed and stuff and say I'm the only one who mentioned it. I don't want to be the only one. We were all doing it, every one of us. Everybody knew it and everybody used it. If you ask the next person you interview, "Did you do speed in the sixties?" Damn right they did! If they say, "No," they're lying.

We bought it by the case and we took it by the pound. It's a matter of record. There was a doctor called Dr. Snap. Everybody seen Dr. Snap. It looked like a goddamn Grand Ole Opry meeting every Monday morning in his office. Faron Young, Webb Pierce—every country music singer in Nashville was sitting out in his lobby waiting to see Dr. Snap. You'd go in and he'd say, "Yeah, you're fine. Blood pressure? Yeah, okay. Pulse? Yeah, you got a pulse okay here." And he'd write you a prescription. Then we'd all go to the pharmacy that Dr. Snap owned. He made fourteen million dollars and ended up in prison, because pretty soon it was so obvious. Yeah, he wound up in prison. I never paid him a dime—I recorded for RCA.

Lyle: Do you have any live performances of Roger recorded on tape?

Don: I do, but I don't. I've been married five times, Lyle, so that means I've got five ex-wives and five storage lockers in five different cities. They've got all my CMA awards, all my tapes, my Roger Miller stuff. Nah, I don't have anything.

I got on a plane one night in Nashville going to L.A., sitting in first-class. I just got on, didn't look behind me. We got to Memphis and landed. The stewardess came up and said, "Sorry, Mr. Bowman, but we're going to have to bump you."

And I was doing a show that night in L.A. I said, "Bullshit! I have a first-class ticket and I've had it for eight weeks."

She was trying to keep from laughing. Then I hear these noises behind me and I turn around and it's Roger. "Gotcha!" Son of a bitch! He had the stewardess come up and tell me I was going to get bumped in Memphis. "Gotcha!"

He was just the sweetest man in the world and I just loved him to death. I thought the music from *Waterhole #3....* God, I thought that was just genius, just freaking genius. You listen to the words and think, "God Almighty!" And he wrote it just like that. Just as fast as he could move a pencil. He was like nobody else. I've been in this business for fifty years and nobody I ever met was like Roger Miller. Nobody could top him, nobody could cover him, nobody could keep up with him. There is nothing negative. When you think of Roger Miller you just think of happiness and funny, and great, great songs that just came out of the man like, *Whoa!*

Buck Trent

Buck Trent is renowned for his skills on the five-string banjo, guitar, steel guitar, mandolin, dobro, and the electric banjo, which he invented. He played on the original recordings of Dolly Parton's famous singles "Jolene" and "I Will Always Love You." In 1975 and 1976 he was named the Country Music Association Instrumentalist of the Year. In the sixties he was a regular on The Porter Wagoner Show, and, in the seventies, on Hee Haw. He now has a morning show in Branson, Missouri.

Buck: Roger Miller was the Robin Williams of country music. He was unbelievable. I was on a forty day tour out west with Dolly Parton and Porter Wagoner and we had a couple of days off in Fresno. Roger come up and got me in his Lear jet—me! gee-wiz!—and we went back to his house in L.A. We partied around for a couple of days. He took me to Rex Allen the singing cowboy's ranch and that was unbelievable. We went to Hoyt Axton's house. That was an experience. We met some actors and things like that. Roger was friends with everybody. We was taking pills and staying up. Glen Campbell would come over to Roger's house. I taught Glen Campbell how to play "Foggy Mountain Breakdown." It wasn't long after that Glen was playing for Merle Haggard's "Bonnie and Clyde." Roger flew me back up there and I joined the show again with Porter. It cost him a fortune to come get me and just buddy around awhile for a couple of days.

Shot Jackson, who made my electric banjo and all my music stuff, had Sho-Bud Pedal Steel Guitar Company. He got me a ukulele. It was bigger than a small ukulele. He put a fifth string on it and banjo strings on it, and I wrote a lot of instrumentals on it going down the road on the bus. Roger called it the "Buck-ulelee" and a lot of people wanted one, so I got him one. It's like a banjo but it's small. Roger also named me the "Five-String General." Roger came up with an invention about putting strings on a guitar, where you just put the string on and pull a lever down and you got it on. In other words if you broke a string on stage you could put one on in a second.

Lyle: How did you first strike up a friendship with Roger?

Buck: I went to Nashville in '59 and went on the Grand Ole Opry with Bill Carlisle. Then I was with Porter Wagoner from '62-'74. That whole time there in Nashville everybody wanted to know everybody and everybody wanted to be friends with everybody. Back then we had a place called Tootsie's behind the Opry. We'd do a spot and then run like crazy across the alley there. Roger would be there and Willie Nelson, Faron Young, Webb Pierce, all the guys on the Opry. Here I was twenty-four and it was my life-long dream. We just had a ball.

Back in those days diet pills were flying like grass seed—everybody's taking those diet pills to stay up. You could get fifty of them for five or ten dollars. We had a great time. At least they said we had a wonderful time. I quit drinking in '83 and ran into Roger out there on Music Row and told him, "I quit, and I'm getting straightened up here. How are you doing?" He said, "Well, I take a little just to keep the chill off."

Roger got me some stock in the King of the Road Hotel. I got in at the ground floor for buying stock. It was real cheap and then it tripled right away. Of course I didn't sell it and then it went bankrupt. We could of sold probably when it quadrupled but we didn't. He told me about it and said, "You oughta buy some stock in this place 'cause I think it's really going to go up." And it did for awhile. It was really something, it was so far ahead of a lot of places, because Roger had his own ideas. We used to do some partying on the top floor there. You can't believe the people that was there. It was a meeting place—everybody that came in town went there.

I learned a lot from Roger as an entertainer. I learned to not just play the instrument. After you learn to play the instrument you gotta know how to perform for people. He was a performer too, he wasn't just a musician. Like Roy Clark. I went with Roy Clark in '74 and I seen where Chet Atkins is getting $5,000 a day and Roy Clark was getting $40,000 a day, and I said, "Well, I better start telling jokes. I better start being funny and start entertaining people rather than just play." That's the way I do it now—entertain people, not just play an instrument, and that was Roger. He was one of the first to entertain and play tunes and sing and write all that stuff. He was an all-around entertainer, musician entertainer. I think he was the first one I heard play the guitar and do the harmony part with his voice [referring to "Dang Me"]. He went on The Tonight Show the first time and he just killed 'em. Talked about his socks he had on. They couldn't believe it. He was really something. Not many like him come along, they don't.

Tom Brumley

Great steel guitar players are highly prized in country music, and Tom Brumley is counted among the very best. Now a living legend, he was one of the original Buck Owens' Buckaroos and played with Ricky Nelson for ten years. His father, Albert E. Brumley, wrote hundreds of gospel standards, including "I'll Fly Away".

Tom: I first met Roger Miller back when I was working with Buck Owens. He came up to Bakersfield in '64 to a homecoming thing that Buck had every year. I knew Thumbs Carllile really well. Thumbs was one of my best friends. Of course, he worked with Roger for a long time. Roger would fire him and then to get him back, he'd have to give him more money. Thumbs never got the credit that he deserved. Incredible—he was always playing. As soon as Thumbs got in the dressing room he'd get the guitar out and start playing. He'd be talking to Roger and playing at the same time. It was something to see! He could sit there and play and hold a conversation with you.

Everybody knew Roger was on bennies and stuff for a long time. I worked with Rick [Nelson] for a long time, about ten years. We were doing an album—it must have been middle seventies sometime—and Roger came by one day and said, "You know, I quit all that stuff and I haven't written a song since. I'm afraid all my ideas are coming from that." He was quite honest. He totally quit and I got to see the real Roger, which I very seldom saw before. He was a great guy and I really admired his work too. My gosh, if I could write the songs that man wrote…where he was coming from. I don't know, but his talent wasn't that benny, I'll tell you that.

Roger was great and all those stories should be told… The problem you're going to have with your book is a lot of these guys won't be able to remember a lot of stuff. Some people say your memory changes after a while. The guys who did that stuff hung around together—Roger, Waylon and Willie—and that's why they got together, because they did the same thing. But Waylon straightened up completely a long time ago. In fact, anybody who drank or did anything in his show got fired. Nobody could even take a drink. He not only straightened out, he wouldn't have anyone with him who wasn't straight. I took a half a benny one time in my whole life and that's it. I wish I didn't take that. I was awake for three days and had no idea what it would do. I was with Buck. I was gonna drive from Hackamore, Washington, to New York City to do *The Jimmy Dean Show.* I was told that half of one won't do anything, it will just keep you awake while you're driving. Three days later I was still awake in New York City! My wife met us and said, "What happened to you?" I guess I hadn't eaten, hadn't slept. I only took half of one! I can't imagine what somebody would do takin' a handful.

Jim Owen

As a songwriter, Jim Owen has written hits for many of country music's most famous stars, including Crystal Gayle, Mel Tillis, Jerry Reed, Conway Twitty, Loretta Lynn and Roy Clark. As an actor, he's well known for his portrayal of Hank Williams in two television movies.

Jim: I wrote for Tree Music for a while and Roger was Tree's greatest writer ever. He was a genius. He was like many geniuses—very little self-control. Much like Hank Williams… I'm talking about the drugs he did and the drinking he did, smoking three packs a day knowing it would kill him. It's very devious because it doesn't kill you with one shot, it kills you very slowly. And eventually, he died of cancer. Except as Roger got older he attained discipline and began to show what talent he really had by, in his forties, writing *Big River*. Most writers burn out, and Roger burned out for a while. And then he came back stronger than ever. He didn't direct it toward country music, he directed it toward the stage.

He would have had a great television show if they had left him alone and let him do what he wanted to do, but they thought they had to write it for him. It was a network show on NBC. He had the hottest show of the year in 1966. Tremendous show… Except as the show got hotter and hotter the executives hired writers. When they were letting Roger do what he wanted to do it was fine, but then they started to write it. It killed it. Roger had to be spontaneous, like Dean Martin. In the first six months it was the hottest thing on TV. They killed it off by writing it for him. If they had left him alone he would have been on TV for ten years.

He was very funny even up to his death. Johnny Cash called him and Roger was almost gone and Johnny said, "How are you doing?" He said, "My luck is running bad. I need a new liver and California refuses to repeal the helmet law."

I went to dinner with him and some other people and a guy just came over and handed him some song lyrics—just words written down on paper, no tape, no music, no nothing. He just handed them to Roger kinda like somebody shy might do. He had his head down and just put them in Roger's hand, and Roger said, "I can't use this, somebody scribbled on it."

We were at the King of the Road Hotel, in the dining room upstairs on the top floor. At that time that was a fabulous hotel, the showpiece of Nashville. The chef would cook you a steak, but first he would come out and present you the uncooked steak to make sure this is what you wanted. So Roger ordered a T-bone, or whatever it was, and the chef came out with this big silver platter like a turkey platter. He presented it to Roger and Roger said, "I'm sorry but he doesn't look a thing like you," and we just fell out on the floor! I wish someone had taken down every one-liner because it would be a better book than Will Rogers's.

Lyle: Do you know much about his songwriting habits?

Jim: He wrote in bunches. He would write for hours and hours and hours, he wouldn't write just one song. He'd write one song and a line from that song would give him a line for the next song and he would go to the next song. I was there when he was working on "Old Toy Trains." He just blew me away with his talent. First time I heard "King of the Road" I didn't know Roger then. I was driving somewhere up in Illinois and I just pulled over to the side of the road and listened to the song. I'd never heard a Roger Miller song before and I just pulled over and listened because at that time I thought I was gonna be a songwriter someday, maybe. It was amazing, the lyrics and how he painted pictures. I could see this hobo sweeping up this hallway of a motel so he could go in and have a bath and sleep for a couple hours. I could see that in my mind. It's a great talent to be able to do that. He could do something that most songwriters cannot do. He could sit down with his guitar at one of the several little bars right there on Music Row, and he could sit there and just make up a verse quicker than anybody you can imagine. Some of them turned around and turned into real songs. "One Dyin' and a Buryin" was from a line he pulled out then, and it became a hit song within minutes. Not many people can do that.

Roger was a child with a man's brain. He did what he wanted to. It cost him two wives... He found real happiness with his last wife.

Jean Shepard

Jean Shepard cut her first record for Capital Records when she was only fifteen years old, and over the years she has recorded more than twenty-five country music albums. The Grand Ole Opry cites her as a woman of many firsts: the first woman in country music to sell a million records; the first to overdub her voice on record; the first to make a color TV commercial; and the first female country singer to be with the Grand Ole Opry over 40 years (a member since 1955).

Jean: Roger was a very outgoing person, very outgoing. He had his quiet moments, but I think that Roger was just born to be an entertainer. He was a fairly good musician. I think he played fiddle, played a little drums, but Roger wasn't meant to be a musician. Roger was meant to be up there in front. When he hit the stage, let me tell you, it was front and center. He was there and you *knew* he was there.

We were up in Ohio one night and we were playing the American Quarter Horse Association, the A.Q.H.A. I was up there with my band and we were playing for about three thousand people. It was a big dance. Well, Roger had played a show somewhere around there and here he come by. He said, "I'm gonna play drums with you." He hadn't been behind a set of drums in twenty-five to thirty years! And I'll tell you, he got behind those drums and it sounded like an Apache raid on a Chinese laundry! I said, "Roger, come sing. Just get off those drums!"

I loved the Walt Disney *Robin Hood* cartoon. I watch that little silly animated cartoon because Roger is in it.

Even with Roger's weird sense of humor he had a very tender side. Our friend Skeeter Davis got cancer very bad and Roger would call Skeeter and ask her how she was doing. Any of the people that Roger knew he would check on them, because this was his family.

Roger was gonna leave Nashville to go to California and he called me and said, "They're gonna have a party for me at Dottie West's house," a going-away party. It was kind of a sad time because we were losing a member of our family, so to speak. I hugged him and said, "Roger, oh, I'm gonna miss you."

And he said, "I'm gonna miss all y'all, but I think this move is the best for me."

And it was. It turned out good for him. [After that] he would come to Nashville quite often, and of course, every time I would get to see him. When they found his cancer he came to Nashville and I was in the dressing room, and he came and spent an hour with me. I felt his pain, but he held up very good and we just loved on one another and hugged one another. I told him how much I loved him and that we were praying for him. He said, "I'm doing good." It wasn't too long after that he left us…a few months later.

I didn't go [to his memorial service at the Ryman Auditorium]. I don't think I could have handled it. I just sat around that night and thought about my times with Roger and remembered a lot of stuff we laughed about, and shed a few tears.

I look around, Lyle, and I'm sixty-seven years old, and I thank God for my health every day. So many of my friends are not with me anymore. I'll be at the Grand Ole Opry forty-six years in November [2001], and Little Jimmy Dickens and Bill Carlisle are the only two that are still there. So many of my friends are not around and it is a very sad thing. I'll tell you, there are certain characters in this business that you miss a little more than others, and believe me, Roger is one of those characters that you will miss because there was always something funny going on if Roger was around. Some little silly something was going on and you knew he was right at the head of it. He was the one who instigated whatever was going on.

Let me say in closing that I'm proud to have been associated with Roger and I'm proud to say that he was a friend—and not just in "the business," but a friend that you really loved. And I truly, truly loved Roger Miller. And anybody who didn't get a chance to know him, gosh, you missed out on something. You missed out on something.

Buck Owens

Buck Owens is a country music legend. He was the co-host of Hee Haw from 1969-1986, and is a member of the Country Music Hall of Fame and Nashville Songwriter's Hall of Fame. He is a respected business man who has successfully owned and operated booking agencies, publishing companies, nightclubs and radio stations.

Buck: Roger was the most unusual, uncommon, unique human being I've ever met. I've never seen anybody like him. He'd come into a room and instead of saying "Hi, Buck," he'd say, "How are you doing, sucker?"

Roger Miller and I were playing St. Louis, Missouri, way back in about '64 or '65. He had "King of the Road" and I had "Tiger by the Tail" and both of them were just red hot. The record company wanted us to do a big autograph session at this big record outlet. So we sat down there beside one another, and Roger—if you knew Roger he was always on, he was never off—Roger said, "Do you ever notice, Buck, that these people come along and you sign their albums. They say, 'How are you doing?' and everything, but they don't hear what you say?"

And I said, "They don't?"

Roger said, "I'll show you what I mean. Watch this now."

This woman came along, he signed her album and he said, "Thank you ma'am. Fuck you very much."

I nearly fainted! And this is a true story! Another ten or twelve people came along and every time he would say, "Fuck you very much." Nobody ever said a word, they didn't hear him.

I said, "Roger, now stop that now. You're gonna get us in trouble."

So he said, "Okay, we'll do something else."

The next lady came along with an album, Roger signed it and she said, "Boy, we sure enjoy your albums."

And he replied, "You know, my grandmother died last night. She was eighty-three. We've always been so close and God, how I hate to lose her."

And the lady says, "Thanks a lot!" She didn't hear one word he said.

Roger was one of these "under the breath" guys. He'd say something out loud and then say something under his breath. Once you caught on to his humor he was one of the funniest guys and had one of the most brilliant minds. Roger Miller and Sonny Bono both reminded me of one another because they were always on. Their humor was a lot a like, a lot of it was subtle. They were very smart and very quick. I always thought that the world has lost a couple of guys here and there is no way to replace them.

Here's another story: I was traveling with Faron Young in 1957 or '58. I had to be part of the band in order to be in the show. That's the kind of things we did then. We would have one band that had four or five acts and everyone played for one another. Everyone had to take turns driving. Well, Faron had this big old Oldsmobile and we pulled an old trailer. It was snowing everywhere you looked. We would just plough along. Faron wasn't with us, he took the plane. Big Ben Keith was driving and he looks back at Roger. Roger's sitting back in the far right on the seat and I was sitting in the middle right by him. We're all trying to sleep but Roger was still up. He was still going, he'd still rattle with anyone who would rattle with him. Ben said, "Roger, you'd better get some damn sleep. It's your turn to drive next, you know."

And Roger said, "Hell, sleep! What's that? I'm not familiar with that."

After about an hour Ben pulled into this service station to fill up with gas and he said, "Come on, Roger, get your ass out here, it's your turn to drive."

Roger said, "No way, man. I'm too sleepy now, I can't drive. I'd kill us."

Ben said, "Get the hell up here."

Roger looked over at me and said, "I'll be right back."

He gets up to the driver's seat and Ben gets in the back. So now we're driving along and all of a sudden the car gives a jerk to the left and it shook everyone up a little bit.

Ben was very nervous and said, "Roger! Roger, God dammit! Are you awake? Are you asleep? What's the matter with you?"

And Roger would sit up straight and say, "No, I'm fine, I'm fine. What's the problem? What's the problem?"

Ben said, "God dammit, don't go to sleep."

So in another couple of minutes all of a sudden there's another big jerk and Big Ben came unwound! He says, "God dammit, Roger! I know you're falling asleep!"

And Roger said, "I promise you I'm not sleeping."

Now what Roger does is he gets settled back and closes his right eye, the one that Ben can see from the back seat. He can't see that Roger has his left eye open. So Big Ben jumped up and grabbed a hold of Roger and yelled, "What the hell's the matter with you?!"

Roger says, "Man, I'm not asleep."

Ben says, "Stop this goddamn car right now!"

Roger pulled over and Ben got back in the driver's seat. When Roger came in the back and sat down next to me he looked at me and gave me this great big wink.

I met Roger on that tour. You see Roger was starving back then and Faron said, "Anybody should be able to play boom-chuck..." That's drums, you know. Faron went down and bought this set of drums and said to Roger, "You're going to be my drummer, so learn how to play these drums." Roger was a very, very talented musician. He could play fiddle, guitar, bass, he could play a lot of things. He never played drums but he could play them all right. He learned them just a little bit. Johnny Paycheck was playing the bass, Glen Stewart was playing rhythm, I was playing lead guitar. We were all acts trying to get started. What we did was we acted like Faron's band and we'd all get to sing two or three songs of our own records. It was a way to get started. That's the way we did it in those days, and it worked.

Lyle: Do you recall any times when Roger Miller was on *Hee Haw*?

Buck: Well, he just came on whenever he got ready. If he was supposed to come in at a certain time, he would. He could sit in any time because he listened to the radio a lot and knew everybody's songs. He used to play the fiddle in George Jones' band. He was one of the great songwriters of our time...of any time. If you look at some of the songs he's written, like "When Two Worlds Collide" or "King of the Road"... He's written four or five big standard songs.

Let me tell you about the last time I saw Roger. I was at the Academy Awards in L.A. at the Universal Theatre. They happened to seat Roger and me next to one another. My wife was sitting by me and she said, "Oh my Lord!" They watch your seats because they know where you are and they want to film you whenever they want. And whenever someone would be called up to the stage, Roger would have something funny to say every time. My wife would say, "Shh! They're all looking at you!" Clint Black walked out on stage with Lisa Hartman—this was before they got married—and her dress was slit all the way up to the hip on one side. She had everything covered up but you could still see her leg and parts of what was up there. Somebody sitting in front of us said, "My God, look at that poor Lisa." And Roger said, "Poor Lisa? Poor Clint!" And what he meant was he's gotta take care of this woman. That's the way his mind ran. He was absolutely just a remarkable mind.

But as we stood up to go and it was all over my wife and I knew that he had the cancer and I said to him, "Roger, how are you?" And he said, "They tell me I'm doing fine. I just got me a bus and a band and we're ready to go back out there and do the honky-tonks."

About a week and a half later I couldn't sleep one night and I turned on the television. I was watching *The Tonight Show* and I noticed that they were talking to Roger. They said, "Roger, if we gave you a guitar, would you give us a little bit of 'King of the Road'?"

Roger said, "Sure."

I noticed he was in a hospital gown, he was in the hospital.

I said, "I'll be damned, Roger's back in the hospital. He told me a week ago that he was just fine."

So he starts singing "King of the Road" and they faded out the credits, and right after that the announcer's voice came in and said, "We are sorry to bring you the report that Roger Miller has just passed away."

I talked to his wife Mary later on and she said that the doctors and everybody decided that there wasn't anything that could be done about it and there was no sense in telling him. So he got to live a little better, a little longer.

Waylon Jennings

Richard D. Moore

Waylon Jennings was one of the coolest guys I ever met. I spent some time with him and his crew over a weekend in July of 2001 at a casino in no-man's-land, North Dakota, and it is one of the best memories I have. Waylon was "on" all the time, very friendly, very funny—and very fast. He invited my girlfriend and me to have brunch with him, he told some great stories, sang bits of some of my favorite rare Waylon songs [like "Willie and Laura Mae Jones"] and hit on my girlfriend (now wife)—a lot. It was all in good fun. She thought he was a bit of a dirty old man, but I thought he was a genius. I later ran into him in the hotel hallway and he asked me, "Where's that pretty girl you're with?" I told him she was in the shower and he responded, "Well, what in the hell are you doing out here? You tell her that I said a pretty girl like her doesn't have to shower."

Waylon: It's an endless story about Roger. He was one of the cleverest people I've ever met in my life. He never was lost for words, never, and he was always funny, always funny. His best audience was Mary, his wife. She laughed better than anybody. I think he loved to make her laugh. I never [let time] go by without thinking about Roger or something he said. I loved Roger Miller. One time his wife came in the house and went upstairs and he said, "Where have you been?"

She said, "Well, I've been downstairs shooing flies."

And he said, "Boy, I bet those shoes are little, ain't they?"

That's the way he thought. He thought in reverse, as the way I see it. He thought of the basics first.

Lyle: A few years back I became a big fan of Roger Miller, and the more I got into his music, the more I wanted to know about him. But I found that there just wasn't much information available on him. You have your autobiography and have made it in every country history music book out there. But with Roger, just the basics are mentioned, which I find weird because he was so loved and had such a unique personality.

Waylon: You know, that's funny what you just said there, because if there was ever anyone lost in between something, Roger was lost in between the rock field and the pop field and country field. They didn't know what category to put him in because he hit in almost all the fields.

Lyle: How did you guys first meet each other?

Waylon: He came to a radio station in Lubbock, Texas, and tried to get my job. Now he was a big songwriter in them days, but in them days they didn't make nothin'. I'm talking back in '59. I'd never seen anybody that funny and energetic. He was just bouncin' around all the time. I didn't see him again for a couple of years, then we got to running around together and we both were drug addicts at that time. We were harmless, the thing we were hurting the worst was ourselves.

Lyle: I must admit, whenever I thought of drugs in the music industry, I'd think of Jimi Hendrix or Jim Morrison, not "The King of the Road".

Waylon: Roger Miller could do more drugs than anybody! Me and him, well, we'd stay up for days and days at a time. I don't know that Roger completely got off of 'em. I know he was better but I thought he might have dabbled a couple of times.

Lyle: In your autobiography, you mentioned that Roger used to carry around a briefcase full of pills, but I was told by someone else that it was when he was trying to get off the pills he had a briefcase full of Chinese herbs.

Waylon: Chinese herbs? I never heard of that. It could be. He was very addicted to [drugs]. He thought he couldn't write songs, couldn't do anything without them. And I know what that's like because I felt that way too. When I quit it took me six or seven years before I could even write a song again. You get so dependent on them, and you think that you've got to be high before you can do anything. I tried herbs and all that stuff and that didn't work either, for me. But I never went back once I quit.

Lyle: One of my favorite video clips is of you and Roger singing "Old Friends" together and you looked at him and said, "We should have rehearsed this."

Waylon: Ya, we did a television show together [a tribute show on TNN, *The Door Is Always Open*]. We both knew this woman—in fact, everyone on that show knew this woman—called Sue Brewer. She was kinda like a house mother to all the guys around there, the hillbillies and everything. I gave her a place to live the last few years of her life and Roger helped her along. He'd come by and see her, you know. She had a kind heart, always laughing right 'til the end. We had this song, "The Door Is Always Open," and that was Sue Brewer's house. Any time day or night you'd go up there and play poker, and you'd find Roger Miller and you'd find me and you'd find just all of the hillbillies, all the singers up there. You'd sit there and you'd write songs up there. Kris Kristofferson lived up there for a little while. It was like a place where everybody was on equal footing. The biggers, the haves and the have-nots could hang around together. Roger spent a lot of time up there. We had a great time at Sue's.

Lyle: Did you guys ever share the stage at all together?

Waylon: I guess on TV was our only time. I don't remember any other time. I think I was on the road with him one time and went out and sung with him a little bit, but you're taking your life in your hands trying to sing with Roger. He'd play a trick on you. He's the best phraser in the world, you know. He knew what he was doing.

Lyle: Do you recall anything from Roger's TV show?

Waylon: I remember he was too fast for the world. He was just too fast. He'd get up there and start rolling and people would just, you know, their eyes would just cross because he could be so fast and funny.

Lyle: Here's a question that I've been dying to ask you. Who started the "Whoop whoop" and what does it mean?

Waylon: Roger Miller started it. He was imitating a rock going across the water, "whoo, whooo, whooo, whooo!" You don't want to know what I was imitating. I got it from Roger, but I called it something else—pussy finder. That's what I called it. That's too many pills!

Lyle: I love your version of Roger's song "I've Been a Long Time Leaving (But I'll Be a Long Time Gone)." On the *King of the Road* videotape you hosted, you said that you liked it so much that you recorded it twice, but I've only been able to find the one version.

Waylon: I don't know about twice, I think that was it. I recorded it in waltz time [*sings part of it*]. Roger did it and wrote it in 4/4 time [*sings the way Roger did it*]. And I did it in 2/4 time. No, I probably got that wrong… Yeah,

I did it in waltz time. I even changed the melody a little bit. That's still one of my favorite songs to this day.

Lyle: Were you ever around Roger when he wrote songs?

Waylon: No, I don't know of anybody that was very often. Roger was really private about that. He couldn't write with ya. He could give you a piece of a song and say, "Here finish this," but he never did that with me. But that would be the only way he could write with anybody, because if he ever had somebody there, he would write the song bouncing off of them, you know—and the walls. Co-writing was not his thing at all. You could tell where Roger stopped and they started. There was a couple of songs that he had that had other people's names on them, but I don't think they had much to do with them 'cause there ain't nobody that had the cleverness that Roger had.

I asked him one time, "Damn, how are you so funny all of the time?" And he said, "Let me tell you the truth. When I started, my Momma used to call it 'showing out,' because when somebody comes in I'm afraid that they're gonna leave so I'm gonna try to keep 'em happy and keep 'em laughing. That's when I'm the funniest 'cause I don't want them to leave." I thought that was such a gentle and sweet thing.

I remember he could rattle off a song, just start singing something, you know, like, he'd get an idea for a title and then he'd start rattling it off. I'd ask him, "Did you write that?" And he'd say, "Yeah, just then."

I remember the funniest damn thing. Me and Roger checked into this hotel in Nashville. We had our rooms next door to each other and had the door opened between 'em. I had my gun, a 22 magnum. Roger came up to me and I'm aiming my gun at the ceiling, clicking it and clicking it. I didn't know that there was a bullet in it and I shot a hole in the ceiling! And this little gooky guy come down there jumping up and down like a turkey, and he's hollering, "You're crazy, you're crazy! Get out of my hotel! Get out!!" And we're both doing like this [*covers his ears with his hands*], because we're both in a room with a gun, a magnum, which is really loud. It almost deafened both of us. You know, we were harmless to other people, but we were pretty rough on ourselves.

Lyle: I understand that Roger went through a dry spell with songwriting. Do you know any reasons behind that?

Waylon: I can tell you what I think, but I don't know if this is true. Roger could talk himself into things, you know. But if he went though a dry spell he was trying to get off of drugs, and once you've been a drug addict—and I can testify 'cause I have been one—when you quit you think you can't do anything without 'em. It takes you a long time to get over that. That might have been his dry spell. But Roger never had a complete dry spell. He could write something all the time 'cause it just came out. He couldn't help but be a great writer. It was part of his psyche, it was part of his being, part of what kept him alive.

Lyle: Do you think he was happy with the way his career way going, with his reputation?

Waylon: No, he wasn't happy. He was like a comedian. Comedians all want to be taken seriously. Sometimes Roger would be happy with it but I don't think he realized how great he was. I don't think he could get to this point of what Roger Miller did best, and just do that. He always wanted to stretch out in other ways. If there ever was a genius, he was. He was a genius. His moods, his psyche, everything like that. You look at some of these guys who invent things and it's like Roger. He had a dark side, I tell you, that comes with that genius in him. His highs were higher than anybody else's and his lows were lower. He could get in a bad mood and in a depressed mood just like anybody else. It was rough to get along with him sometimes. He could make you madder than an old wet hen, you know. He'd be pissed off at ya, and hell, you wouldn't know what he was mad about, but he would say something to piss you off. His mood swings were so drastic. He'd get down and out, then he'd be in a happy mood. Either very high or very low. He could be in a bad, bad mood, and all I'd do is get away from his ass when he got that way with me.

Lyle: What can you tell me about the King of the Road Hotel?

Waylon: I tore that thing up pretty good! He wouldn't like it 'cause you see, I'd make 'em give me his room. He had this suite up at the top of that thing, and I'd say, "I want that room," and [the hotel clerks] weren't gonna say no to me. I'd get up there and we'd party. And then me and Tompall Glaser stole the books one time just to see how much money he was making out of it. Looking at all that stuff… It was one of the watering holes.

Downstairs they had this one guy playing guitar, and we'd get some guitars and start playing and stuff. Then they had this band upstairs. That's were I first met [Ronnie] Milsap. He was playing there and we'd go up and hang out with him, sit in with the band and play, have a good time. It was a fun and a musical time back in those days. Nashville's not like that much anymore. Now, it's control music.

Lyle: When was the last time you saw Roger?

Waylon: I saw Roger just before he died, and he didn't look very good. I remember the last thing he said to me was, "Why don't you go home and get some sleep? You look terrible."

He was the cleverest man I'd ever met, and when he died it really hurt me. I just couldn't picture the world being without Roger Miller.

Lyle: You mentioned you and Tompall Glaser hung out quite a bit. Have you talked to him lately?

Waylon: If I never talk to Tompall Glaser again, it'll be too damn soon! He's the worst son of a bitch I ever saw in my life! You never know what his mood's gonna be. He has these big mood swings and he'll call you one time and be real friendly and then he'll call you the next time and want to tell you off—and he couldn't tell off a rock. And you can go ahead and put that in your book!

[Author's Note] I had to include that last bit as I've always been interested in that ongoing feud from the seventies that he and Tompall had. I was playing at a music festival in Zurich, Switzerland when I heard the news of Waylon's passing on February 13, 2002—it hit me hard, he was my hero. Waylon was a superstar in every possible way.

Tompall Glaser

J. Clark Thomas

Tompall Glaser co-wrote with Harlan Howard the 1966 hit "Streets of Baltimore," charted high in 1975 with "Put Another Log on the Fire," and wrote and recorded many great songs in between. In 1969, Tompall opened a recording studio in Nashville, known around town as "Hillbilly Central", that became an important outpost for the Outlaw movement of the seventies. But what may be an even more interesting fact, reported in Waylon Jennings' autobiography, was the ongoing feud between him and Waylon from something that started in the seventies. I tracked down Tompall's phone number in Nashville, rang him up, and asked the man who answered if Tompall was in. "Who's this and why are you calling?" came the reply. After explaining my Roger Miller book and chatting for a few minutes, I casually mentioned that I had interviewed Waylon and that he had said something about Tompall and him stealing the books from the King of Road Hotel. Immediately, the man spoke out in a melodic tone, "This is Tompall..." and started asking what Waylon had said about him. I told him I preferred to meet him in person to do an interview and he replied that he'd rather do a telephone interview, unless I took him out for a nice supper. When I told him I was on a popcorn budget, he cussed a bit and said, "How about lunch?" This turned out to be the most memorable lunch I ever had.

Tompall: So Waylon was talking about the King of the Road?

Lyle: Yeah, he said you guys took the books one time to see how much money Roger was making off it.

Tompall: The damn fool! They might still be looking for them. It was the mob. I was stoned. I don't know where Waylon was. I went in and picked up my messages at the King of the Road Hotel and laid my briefcase down on a pile of stuff. I was all stoned on cocaine—which, for the record, I quit in 1978—and I didn't notice until I laid everything down in the room and started looking at it that it was the books for the lounge upstairs. The mob was running the business. This happened somewhere in July and that book was filled out to the end of the year, how much they'd made every day. That's what the amusing thing was!

Lyle: Was there a Nashville mob or were they from some place else?

Tompall: No, *The Mob*. [*Please see pages 4 and 219.*] They're the ones who built [the hotel] in the first place. Roger was getting a cut out of it. But they lost money every day! Well, I don't think they really did but that's the way those books were filled out so they wouldn't have to pay no tax. I was laughing about it to Jack Clement and he said, "Tompall, you better get rid of those damn books and shut up about it. The Mob owns that place. They wouldn't think that's too funny." So when the maids weren't looking, I ran down the hall to a room with its door open and stuck them in the bottom drawer of a dresser.

I had a lot of fun at the King of the Road Hotel. Vic Ames worked there, he was one of the original Ames Brothers. The Glaser Brothers idolized the Ames Brothers. He ran the pub there and he'd fix me up. Whenever he saw me doing good with a young lady, he'd get me a key and a room with champagne and flowers, right across from the elevator. I'd say to the girl "Have you ever been to the bar downstairs?" She'd say "No..." I said "Would you like to?" She'd say "Yeah." So I said "Let's go down." When we got on the elevator, I'd press floor five—the door would open and she'd say "What's that over there?" I'd say "It's yours." She'd say "I thought we were going to the bar downstairs," then she'd say "ah, what the hell, why not."—Frank Sinatra style!

Lyle: Were you living in Nashville at the time?

Tompall: Well, I was getting a divorce. Or I should say I wanted a divorce but my Catholic wife at the time didn't want to do it, so I moved out of the house. I didn't want to buy another house and have her get that too. I was stoned anyway, so I just lived in a hotel. Sometimes I'd double book! I'd have a suite in one hotel, forget about it and then check into another one. Waylon and I had a suite up at the Hall of Fame motel. We paid for that [with money from] Baron, our publishing company.

Lyle: What's the first thing that comes to mind when you think of Roger Miller?

Tompall: Well, Roger came to Nashville after I did, so I've known him since about '59, I think, or whenever he got here. He was hanging out at Tootsie's. Most of my time around Roger was at Tootsie's. Tootsie thought he hung the moon, that's for sure. He was always such a clown and I wasn't. I was serious. He always had a bunch of little "coatees" around picking up on his humor. They were probably getting ideas for songs. He wouldn't leave until closing time and Tootsie would stick him in the ass with a hatpin. That little crowd would stand around like they was never going to leave and she would stick them with the pin. I don't know if anyone ever got any dreaded diseases. Well, there wasn't any AIDS back them. There wasn't a lot of fear, just a lot of pussy. Everybody was getting pussy. Those girls liked gospel singers and hillbillies. They would come to town, sneak out and fuck you, and nobody in their hometown would ever find out about it. You'd be gone. It's like a traveling salesmen. I didn't realize that women loved to fuck that much when I was growing up on the farm. That ain't the way my mamma told me. She *misled* me.

Old Faron Young hired Roger as a drummer. Willie Nelson was playing bass. I think he just picked him up at Tootsie's and went out on the road. Roger didn't even have a set of drums, I don't think he even played drums. If he did, he never did it for a living. Everyone around town was laughing about how Roger and Willie were discovered. I heard Willie say a lot of times that Faron [who committed suicide in 1996] was his idea of a hillbilly, he was exactly how they should be. Pretty true, but Faron, like me, didn't like this getting old shit.

[In those days] there was this old guy who's dead now, Bill Hall. Bill had a little record company and he'd come to Nashville and go down to Tootsie's and hire us guys for twenty-five bucks a song to go out and sing the latest hits out at Starday Records. Roger went out there one night, then the guy came back and got me, and I went out there four or five times. Roger did too. We'd net twenty-five bucks. I went up there to do Jim Reeves. I'm sure I didn't sound much like him!

Lyle: Why would they do that back then?

Tompall: They'd steal all the time. That's the fucking business. All these crooks in it. The bottom feeders got to make a buck. They're guys that don't got any talent. They'd go out there and steal [songs] until somebody found out about it. I don't know that it was really illegal but it was sure chicken shit. But I didn't know any better 'til I got a record deal and then I didn't want anybody stealing mine.

I came to Nashville with a record deal. Marty Robbins had started a record company, then he sold our contract to Decca. I stayed on Decca for a while, then I went over to MGM. MGM was putting shit out on us right and left with Jack Clement producing them. We had a lot of top ten records and didn't have no contract. Another mob outfit! MGM changed presidents three times in about a month and a half. I had gone to New York and signed with the president at that time who was from England. He was the president of Polydor and he signed me just like that. Then another guy came in and usurped my English guy, who then just disappeared off the face of the planet. I was getting ready to have a meeting with the *new* president when my secretary says "a guy named Mike Curb is on the phone, the new president of MGM. He's coming to town with his whole staff and would like to come into the office and meet you." I went into that appointment and there he was, the boy wonder, with seven guys all lined up in a row like a military inspection. And he was twenty-four fuckin' years old! He looked like a baby. I was older than he was. I told him, "You know I don't have a contract with MGM."

And he said, "What?? Well, you're putting records out!"

"Well, how 'bout that? I wonder if there is a lawsuit in there somewhere."

"I've got this movie I'm working on called *Tick Tick Tick*. I need a new soundtrack for it. What will you charge me to put a new soundtrack on it?"

So I socked it to him for the money and the contract! He put his name on it as song supervisor or something, and I got myself an "in" with Hollywood. Waylon did a movie where he wrote a bunch of tunes for the soundtrack and overdubbed the voice kind of like *The Dukes of Hazzard*, so I charged them! They agreed to the charge but they never paid it. I heard the movie was going to come out and open in Waylon's hometown, Lubbock, Texas. My lawyer at the time was Dick Whitehouse. I said, "What can I do? How do I get my damn money?"

And he said, "We'll shut them down."

So this little hillbilly from Nashville shut down a fucking movie company until I got my check. They couldn't do any openings! I heard the sheriff walked up to the theatre and closed it down.

I made some good moves then. I bought Waylon's publishing company for $10,000. He didn't have nothing in it but "Good Hearted Woman," and that's the one I wanted to record, but he jumped on it with Willie and begged me not to put it out. I shouldn't have listened to him. I didn't think I could do any fucking wrong, like it was all going to come into my lap. I felt like I didn't deserve [the money pouring in] and just couldn't waste it fast enough. I'd like to have a little of that now. I had twenty-five percent of the publishing on "Gentle On My Mind." We had 350 cuts of that around the world.

Lyle: Do you still have the publishing on that?

Tompall: No, I had it for 25 years. God, it's terrible to get old!

[The last time I saw Roger] I ran into him at the 1982 Academy of Country Music Awards and he was hawking me about being an Outlaw, which I never did quite understand. He said, "Hey Tompall Outlaw!" Whatever the fuck that was all about.

Lyle: So that kind of pissed you off?

Tompall: Sure did! I mean, there was a lot of people that thought I was coming down here because of civil rights—I had a lot trouble—when all I ever wanted was to be on the Grand Ole Opry. I didn't know what their problem was. Roger was an Outlaw himself! Do you think he was mainstream country?

Lyle: No, not at all.

Tompall: So what the fuck was he ragging me about? This was at the Academy of Country Music Awards party, the year that Alabama won and we didn't. It was in '82. His wife was with Kenny Rogers and the First Edition. She was the girl singer and they did their last album up in my studio. It never really sold anything but it was a good album. We had some memories up there. Glaser Sound Studio *Incorporated.* Hazel Smith worked for me. I hired her for promotions after we started promoting Waylon. She had a column in that *Country Music Magazine.* She still writes for them. She called her column "Hillbilly Central," so everybody thought that the studio was called Hillbilly Central, but it was Glaser Sound Studio, Incorporated.

At one time I had seventeen corporations and thirty-some employees. I had a talent agency, four or five publishing companies, a production company, a photography company. It was a tough road. I hadn't learned yet, but you got to let other people make money or you wind up owning one hundred percent of nothing. Everybody has to make a buck. I made my biggest money with a smaller percentage. As an artist I got two percent of the *Outlaw* album. It sold nearly five million copies and was the biggest selling album for a long time. Neither Waylon or Willie did that good on their own, I don't believe. It set the town on its ear. The way it happened was Waylon and I couldn't stand the offices because we were doing that coke and we'd go out and play pinball and watch the lights flash and talk business, and they'd bring papers over and I'd sign them while I played pinball! One time I spent seventy hours straight playing pinball, just a-shootin' and a-cokin'.

I put Waylon up there in the studio and said, "There ain't no clocks. Forget the clocks. Get in there with your band until you get a sound." I started out producing him, but I soon realized that that was not going to help him get his sound. I helped him with those six songs on the *Honkytonk Heroes* album. I should have stayed involved in it. But there was money everywhere! I didn't need to be smart. I needed to be dumb. All the money I ever made was by being dumb. God, in its heyday my studio was making $260,000 a year! I'd just pop my feet up. I'd give [Jimmy Bowen] a little piece of it for managing my studio. Then he decided he wanted to clean up the sound of the town. He wanted to build a studio and wanted me to just get out of it and let him sign the checks. I don't think so!

Everybody knew Waylon was going to be big someday, too distinct of a voice. Waylon was married to Jessie [Colter] and Jack Clement was married to Jessie's sister. Well, Jesus!! One time we were up in New York to attend the Grammys—course they gave the hillbilly Grammys out in the afternoon, which pissed us off—and Jack was there with his new bride. We were at this fancy restaurant and she fired the waiter right off the bat. So they sent us another one and she fired him. She fired seven waiters and the maitre'd. Jack got up and disappeared and I thought I'd better go see where he is. I looked around on every floor. I finally found him. He was walking around in little circles and looked like he was ready to jump off a balcony or something. Saying something, pace, pace, mill, mill, pace, pace. He was thinking about getting rid of that girl. She was nuts! Everybody left the table. I don't know if we ate anything. She just ruined it.

Lyle: I understand that you and Waylon haven't spoken in a while.

Tompall: You know, I don't forgive very easily. Waylon pissed me off so bad. I probably should have let it slide. If he ever apologizes to me I will. But he called me a son-of-a-bitch. He was mad and he meant it. I never got to know him when he wasn't stoned. That's the unfair part. I don't know what we would have been like together straight. We were wearing our cowboy hats and vests and beards and they wouldn't let us in to some restaurants. They made us take our cowboy hats off, so we wouldn't stay. Then they started that movie down in Texas, the one with John Travolta, *Urban Cowboy*. When that movie came out and the *Outlaw* album came out, we went back to that same restaurant and it was full of cowboy hats! I will never forget it. There were cowboy hats on all the men at all the tables.

Roger's television show could have been good, but I think he was coking then. It ruined a lot of people. People hid behind it. I know that's what I did. Now Waylon could work on it—except the third day. The third day he couldn't do nothing. He'd have to try to go to sleep and his body would just twist and jerk. It was terrible to see. I liked doing cocaine but when I quit I didn't have any withdrawals. Cigarettes are what gave me trouble and I probably drink too much to this day. Ah, I can always quit later.

Captain Midnight

J. Clark Thomas

Captain Midnight (Roger Schutt) was one of the most famous DJs and all-round characters around Nashville. In the seventies he had an apartment in Glaser Sound Studio and was there during the whole Outlaw movement, even going out on various tours with the Outlaws. Captain Midnight did the voice over for the King of the Road Video. Captain surprised me now and then with a phone call and I spoke to him a just few days before he passed away on February 8, 2005.

Lyle: How did your friendship with Roger begin?

Captain: I was working for a magazine called *Music Reporter* doing freelance stuff. It was before I became Captain Midnight, actually. *Music Reporter* was the third biggest trade magazine. There was *Billboard*, *Cashbox* and then *Music Reporter*, which is created here in Nashville by a guy named Charlie Lamb. Charlie Lamb hired me to do a bio on Roger Miller. He said, "His manager will pay you. Roger's going to be here at nine o'clock in the morning. Could you meet him here?" So I did. I was pretty fresh. I hadn't been in town but a year or so and I had been a news reporter for WSM, a writer for radio and television, and I was going to Belmont College, a Baptist college. I didn't really know what was going on. I was pretty naive and pretty innocent.

So Roger met me about nine o'clock in the morning. He picked me up in his Cadillac convertible and two days later he says, "Do you want me to drop you off at Charlie's or do you want me to take you home?" He kept me up for two days and two nights!

Consequently, I wrote the bio and Roger never paid me. He said, "My manager will pay you," and I called the manager and he said, "Roger will pay you." Well, as life played out, two years later I became Captain Midnight on the radio, from midnight till six at one of the local stations, and Roger had just started getting hot. I'd play a Roger Miller record and I'd say, "Here's Roger Miller, who owes me twenty-five dollars." This went on constantly for three or four years.

So one night—it was the night of the [1965] Grammys—Roger won five Grammys. He won everything except best female vocalist. Marijohn Wilkin, who wrote "Long Black Veil" and published all of Kris's big hits like "For the Good Times," she signed Kris Kristofferson when he first came to Nashville. So Kris and Marijohn and I, after the Grammys, went to this joint just down the street and across the road from Tootsie's Orchid Lounge. They sold food, supposedly, but the hillbillies just hung out there. So we walked in and I saw Roger sitting in the back with a newspaper. I said, "There's Roger Miller sitting back there reading his reviews."

Kris said, "That's not Roger. Let's just get a booth."

I said, "Roger Miller!" And Roger looked up and came and sat down with us. I was seated beside Kris and Marijohn was sitting next to Roger. I said, "Roger, this is Kris Kristofferson. He's a writer who just came to town."

And Kris says, "Glad to meet you, Roger. When are you going to pay Captain Midnight that twenty-five dollars you owe him?"

And Roger, he didn't bat an eyelash, looked right straight at Kris and said, "Captain Midnight can take that twenty-five dollars and shove it up his ass!" And that's the way Kris Kristofferson and Roger met.

Roger Miller did [*The Roger Miller Show*] and it only lasted one year. Roger's manager got him this deal with NBC. The deal was that Roger's first show would run after the Super Bowl, where there's like a billion people watching, just a major audience. Millions of people watched it, so it was far from a non-successful venture on Roger's part. I mean, how many of the hillbillies had a goddamn television show of their own? When all the interviews were done for that Roger Miller video [*King of the Road*], there were three or four guys who said that Roger really screwed up. "He had a network TV show but he was too screwed but blah, blah, blah...." Roger did not do a bad thing with that television show! He got criticism from his best friends. They were just jealous. He had a show for a year. Jesus Christ! What do you have to do to impress somebody? Jimmy Dean had a TV show and he did more for the hillbillies than any other person I can think of. I say hillbilly because that's what we call ourselves. It's an inside term.

Roger preceded the Outlaw years. The Outlaws came middle to early seventies, I guess with that Outlaw album. Outlaw is a misnomer, it's just something that caught on. Waylon, Willie, Tompall Glaser and Jessi

Colter—that's when the Outlaw thing began. Roger Miller was so far ahead of that. He was ten, fifteen years before that. He wasn't part of the Outlaw thing, he was the Outlaw! Roger was the original outlaw because he did everything on his own terms.

All the hillbillies, we were like a brotherhood, because the city didn't claim us. I was in radio and Roger was in music, and it was all the same thing to them. If you were in the entertainment business in Nashville, you paid one hundred dollars deposit for a telephone instead of $25 like a civilian. And the bank wouldn't loan you money unless you were Johnny Cash or Eddie Arnold. And if people rented to you they upped the rent. A lot of times they wouldn't even rent to you!

The town didn't accept us, so we really hung together. I remember Mel Tillis had been on the road and was home for three weeks but he hadn't been home at the house. I just happened to be at this little joint on 16th Avenue and he called his wife and his wife is trying to give him hell for not being home. He says, "Did you get the dogs in? Jesus Christ, you didn't get the goddamn dogs in? What the hell's wrong with you?" And he'd been out roarin' for three weeks! He got down on his wife because she hadn't put the dogs in. That's very typical of the lifestyle.

You know, the cocaine came because the government put the lid on prescribing diet pills, except in extreme cases. Ninety percent of us in the hillbilly community were getting our speed from legitimate doctors. Dr. Snap was the most famous one. But there were other doctors that prescribed. You didn't get arrested for driving under the influence of speed. You didn't get busted for dealing. There wasn't any kind of a crime about it. It was a very creative time in the city's history. There's a big difference in the time of Roger Miller and today in the music business. The music business today, the business men are running it. In Roger Miller's day, the talent was running it. Roger Miller could not have survived in today's climate.

Roger never had one or two people that he hung with all the time, Roger was everywhere. People would say, "I spent two days and nights with Roger out roarin'." He hung out with everybody. He had some best friends. If you said that you hung out with Roger all the time you're a liar, because you didn't. He was a real loner but he was always around people. And he was never overtly a ladies' man. I'm sure he had his share of the ladies, but he was low-key with that.

In the late sixties I was at a real low point in my life. He came up to me and said, "Captain, you gotta get a hold of yourself." I had a tooth that was missing and I needed a hair cut. He said, "You need to get your hair cut and get that tooth fixed and dress up a little bit, because you are an embarrassment to yourself." He was instrumental in me getting my act together because I could have really gone down the tubes. Roger was one of a kind, one that we will never see again. I'm proud to have known him.

Bill Anderson

Richard D. Moore

"**W**hispering Bill Anderson" has been a member of the Grand Ole Opry since 1961, and of Nashville songwriter's Hall of Fame and the Country Music Hall of Fame. He has been a game show host, a soap opera star, a television host, an author, a singer/songwriter and co-writer with Roger Miller of the song "When Two Worlds Collide." Bill Anderson was the first person I called when I arrived in Nashville. After I got off the phone with him I told my girlfriend, "Okay, I just got us backstage passes to Saturday night at the Grand Ole Opry." I never thought those words would ever come out of my mouth!

Bill: Roger only had, I think, an eighth grade education, but he was the closest to a genius I've ever known, because he could do things with the English language that were just almost unbelievable. Like take "The Last Word In Lonesome Is Me." My goodness, who would have thought of that?

Roger and I met each other before either of us came to Nashville. I knew him probably before anyone here with the possible exception of Sheb Wooley, who was married to Roger's sister at one time. Roger and I met when Roger was in the army in Atlanta. He was stationed at a place called Fort McPherson in Georgia, right outside of Atlanta, and he was playing fiddle in a country band they had there called the Circle A Wranglers. The emblem for the third army was the letter A with a circle around it, so the band was called the Circle A Wranglers.

I don't actually remember meeting him. It was one of those things where you don't remember ever not knowing him. [But we probably] met at one of the country shows that came to Atlanta, one of the Grand Ole Opry shows or something. They would bring shows to Atlanta every couple of months or so on Sundays. I was working as a disc jockey at a small station close to Atlanta, and Roger and I would meet each other at these shows at the old Tower Theatre in Atlanta. We would hang out backstage and talk about our dreams. We wanted to go to Nashville, we wanted to write songs, and we wanted to perform. He was a couple of years older than me so when he got out of the army he came to Nashville first and had a little bit of success. And then when I got out of school and was free to come up here he opened a lot of doors for me. He introduced me to a lot of people. We were really good friends.

We toured together quite a bit. As a matter of fact, the first tour I ever went on out of Nashville, there were three unknown singers on the tour—Bill Anderson, Roger Miller and a guy named Donny Young, who later changed his name to Johnny Paycheck. Nobody knew who any of us were and we were out traveling around the country together with George Morgan. Roger and I did a lot of concert dates together up until the time he hit big. Of course as soon as he hit big, he went off and left all of us in the dust.

I remember working a show with Roger one time in Hammond, Indiana, just outside of Chicago. That's where the country shows used to play back in the early sixties. I remember standing in the back of the auditorium. I think I had already performed and I wanted to watch Roger perform, and I stood in the back of the room and the people just didn't catch on to what he was doing. They just did not understand his humor. I said later, "You know, Roger, I was standing in the back and it was like I could see those words coming out of your mouth and go right over the heads of all the people in the audience until they got to me . And I'm back there dying laughing! I'm the only person in the room laughing. It's just totally over their heads, like it's bouncing off the walls." But eventually they caught on to what he was about and then they tuned in and laughed right along with him.

Lyle: What inspired the song "When Two Worlds Collide"?

Bill: There was an old science fiction movie from the late fifties called *When Worlds Collide*. It was Roger's favorite movie and he kept telling me he wanted to write a song called "When Worlds Collide." I said, "Roger, you can't do that, that's the name of a movie. It would be like writing a song called "Gone With the Wind." You can't do that."

And he said, "Oh yeah? Well, I want to do that."

[Weeks later] I said, "Ok, you want to write that so bad, let's call it 'When Two Worlds Collide' instead of 'When Worlds Collide.'" We were driving to San Antonio, Texas, in his station wagon and there was another guy with us. We put the other guy behind the wheel, Roger and I got in the back, and we wrote that song between here and San Antonio. It was totally finished [by the time we got there]. In those days we didn't have these little tape recorders like you have now, so we had to stay up all night singing it to each other, all the way down there, so we wouldn't forget it. We got there the next morning and Roger called a friend of his from the radio station and he came over to the hotel and brought a tape recorder and we put it down on tape. But we were afraid we'd forget it, so we just kept singing it to each other.

Lyle: What was it like writing with him? Did you guys have a ton of ideas and then cut it down to a couple of minutes?

Bill: No, not with Roger. Writing with Roger... Well, number one, he was a wonderful writer, just a fabulous writer. A lot of times when Roger would write by himself he was not disciplined. He would write a verse, or a verse and a chorus, or two verses, and then it wouldn't hold his attention long. He had a very short attention span when it came to this kind of thing. He'd be on to something else. A lot of times other people would have to finish his songs for him. "Half a Mind" that Ernest Tubb recorded, Ernest wrote the last verse. Jim Reeves, I think, wrote the last part of "Billy Bayou."

Lyle: Do any memories stick out from times spent at the King of the Road Hotel?

Bill: I have a wonderful story about the King of the Road Hotel. My wife and I went down to the King of the Road to have dinner with Roger. She was working for a man who was running for governor of Tennessee at the time, whose name was John Jay Hooker. My wife had been out on a campaign visit with John Jay Hooker that afternoon and she walked into the lobby of Roger's hotel wearing a ribbon that said "Hooker," that's all it said. Of course people in Tennessee knew it was a political thing, but a lot of other people didn't. Roger had never met my wife and he walked up to her and saw her standing there with that ribbon hanging down and said, "Oh, so they're advertising now."

Lyle: Do you remember what kind of music he listened to at all?

Bill: Oh, he listened to country music in the days I was around him, early in his career. He was a big fan of western swing music and a big Bob Wills fan. He grew up in Texas and Oklahoma and grew up on western swing. Bob Wills was his hero. I sat behind Roger at the CMA awards the night that Bob Wills was inducted into the Hall of Fame. Roger was the first person in the audience up on his feet and he had big ol' tears running down his face. He was so happy that Bob Wills made it into the Hall of Fame.

I almost killed Roger. He almost became the late great Roger Miller before he even became famous. He broke into my apartment one night and I didn't know it was him. I was in the bed asleep. He didn't think I was home. The window was right there by my bed, I'm lying in bed, and all of a sudden I hear the window go up. And then I see this hand reaching inside. It's a good thing I didn't have a gun because I would have shot him. I thought he was a burglar. Then he got his face in the window and I pushed a pillow right up against his face to try and push him back out the window and all I heard was, "Hey, Bill! It's me, Rog." But, it's frightening to think of what I would have done if I had a gun. I would have shot him!

One time Roger and I took our wives—we each had one young child at the time—and we went to the beach together for a vacation. Of course Roger was very, very thin. I had a movie camera and was taking some pictures of him, and he put on his bathing suit—he was real skinny—and walked up to the camera, pointed down to his legs and said, "My legs always swell up this time of the year." And they were about as big around as toothpicks!

Buddy Killen

Gordy Collins

Buddy Killen was a very instrumental part of Roger's life and the lives of many other writers and artists. He was a musician on the Grand Ole Opry for years and managed and eventually owned, Tree Publishing Company, selling it in 1989 to Sony/CBS for thirty million dollars. Buddy was personally involved with and responsible for some of the greatest music ever recorded.

Buddy: I don't think that Roger has ever had his just dues. OK, they put him in the Hall of Fame, which is nice. OK, they had a TV show special on him. That's nice. But there's more. There is so much more to Roger than I think they've come up with. He never seemed to garner the respect that he should have even with all the great songs he's written. He was such a unique talent, absolutely a superstar in many ways as an entertainer. He did it all—even wrote a Broadway musical that had unbelievable acclaim. His peers loved him.

When he first came to Nashville, when I first met him, he would go to these parties because he was the eternal partier, taking those pills, rockin' and rollin' and having a good time. Writers would follow him around waiting for his droppings. I tell you he spoke songs. Everything he said was a song title. So many of the writers in those days, in the late fifties, wouldn't steal, but just take ideas that Roger would speak without even knowing that he had done it because he was a creative type of talker. When he talked he came out with metaphors and all kinds of creative lines and stuff because he was always trying to be funny. He would have little twists to what he would say, and any good writer is waiting for that as you know, waiting for that little thing so he could write it down.

Lyle: How did it all begin with you working with Roger?

Buddy: I came here right out of high school and worked as a bass player on the Grand Ole Opry. I worked with all the different stars and had an opportunity, in the early part of 1954, for $35 a week to go to work for a brand new publishing company called Tree Publishing Company. I continued making my living as a musician working at the Grand Ole Opry. I didn't even have an office until later. When I first started I worked out of my car, and then we got this little office up on Seventh Avenue at the old Cumberland Lodge building in 1957. Between shows on Saturday night at the Grand Ole Opry, I'd play a show and then go across the alley over there to what is now called Tootsie's Orchid Lounge. In those days it was called Mom's. It became Tootsie's after Mom [Upchurch] sold it to Tootsie. We all would hang out between shows. Go on…do a fifteen minute segment…and then you might not go on again for another hour or two later. The Opry was there at the Ryman Auditorium and across the alley is where Mom's was. I was going through a miserable break-up of my first marriage and was very unhappy and always looking for something to take my mind of my problems. So between those shows I'd go over to Mom's and stand at the pinball machine putting in money that I couldn't really afford. I was really wasting my money and so forth, but it took my mind off of my problems.

So I'm standing there one Saturday night doing that, and this little guy comes up and starts talking to me. I didn't really want to talk to him, I just really wanted him to go away because I was sort of standing there in my miseries. But he kept talking. He said, "My name is Roger Miller and my sergeant suggested I come to Nashville. I'm a fiddle player and I want to get a job playing fiddle." I listened to him and he finally gets into something that piqued my interest. He said, "I'm a songwriter."

I said, "Well, I work for a new publishing company called Tree Publishing Company. I'd like for you to come up and see me Monday."

We kept standing there talking and he said, "I have a place to stay but I don't have any money to eat."

I had $5 that I hadn't put into the pinball machine and I said, "Here take this." His wife was Barbara at the time, his first wife, and I said, "At least you guys can have something to eat tonight."

He comes over to my office on Monday, sings me some songs, and just blew my mind. I said to myself, "Wow, this guy's real good!" So I called Jack Stapp, who was the president of the company and president of WKDA, which was a rock and roll station in those days. He spent all his time down [at the station] and turned the publishing company over to me from the beginning, gave me $35 a week and said, "Go!" I called Jack and I said, "There's a guy up here, he's really good. I'd like to sign him. But he wants $50 a week to sign with us."

"Fifty dollars a week?!!"

"Well, let me see if he'll take $25." So I said, "Roger, will you take $25?"

"Well, Okay," Roger said. Twenty-five dollars, let alone fifty, was a whole lot more money then than it is now. I signed him and started trying to get his songs recorded, and I got him a deal with Decca Records.

Roger wrote for me for thirty-three years. The first song I got recorded that became a top ten for him was "Half a Mind," [recorded by] Ernest Tubb. About that time, late '57, early '58, he did a record for Starday Records, "Poor Little Fool," or something, and "Invitation to the Blues." Ray Price covered "Invitation to the Blues," so all of a sudden Roger had a hit with Starday. Then in 1958 he had "Half a Mind," so he was beginning to create some noise.

He didn't like pressure, he always resisted it. He'd write all night, stay up all night long and sleep all day. But I kept pushing him. Somewhere deep inside he had to appreciate it. But he resisted it, you know. Stallions are like that. Normally, if you just lay that rein on his neck, he'll go. But if you start pushing him he'll rare up on you. He just wanted to party. Anyway, he came in one day and I said, "You written anything lately?"

"Uh, I've written this little thing that Skeeter Davis likes." He was working with Skeeter Davis on the road playing fiddle or drums.

"Sing it to me."

He sings, "In The Summertime."

It was only a verse and a chorus. I said, "Wow, that's good."

"You've got to be kiddin' me."

"No, no I'm not kidding. I think it's great. The problem is you've got to write another verse."

So he wrote one and I did a demo session with him. I played this song for Chet Atkins and said, "Chet, I believe this is a hit song."

He listened to it and said, "I think you're right. Who do you think would be good for it?"

I told him that I though he should do it with Roger.

"Well, can we?"

"Well, let me call over and get him off of Decca." So I called Owen [Bradley] and said, "How about turning Roger loose?" He said OK, turned him loose, and I put him on RCA. Well, they did "In the Summertime" and that became a top ten record for him. Andy Williams did it and it became a big pop hit.

So from 1957 and the two years following, he was beginning to make some noise, but he never had his big hit. I think Jack Clement produced him. Chet was awesome to be around for a musician or a singer, but Roger was not comfortable with Chet. One day when Roger first came to Nashville he had an audition with Chet. He hit the key of G and started singing in A, or something, he was just so nervous. Roger was sort of like Willie Nelson— he never could fit right into the typical boxed-in pattern that Nashville tends to always want to do. But then Roger started doing *The Tonight Show.* He'd get up there and sing those little silly songs, just bits and pieces. But Nashville still wasn't paying any attention to him record-wise.

About 1963 he and Barbara had broken up and Roger wanted to move to California and needed some money to get out there. I went to Shelby Singleton who ran Mercury Records and Smash Records and made a deal for Shelby to sign Roger for $100-a-side advance. We did three sides to try to get a single and none of them really came off, so they set up two three-hour sessions back to back. We cut twelve songs in six hours—"Dang Me," "Chug-a-Lug," "You Can't Roller Skate in a Buffalo Herd." All of those little songs. Well, they put the album out and all of a sudden out of that album "Dang Me" just exploded. So that was the beginning of his real career as a writer, performer and singer. From then on, it was unbelievable.

Back before he happened, though, he was always needing money. He came up [to the office] one day and said, "I need $300 bad!" We had just bought him a Cadillac, paid $9,000 for it. He said, "But I need $300. Boy, I'm desperate for it."

I said, "I can't get you any more money. You already owe me more than the company is worth, and you haven't wrote a song in six months."

"I'm not in the mood to write a song. I don't want to write a song."

"Well then I can't get you any more money. I'm not going to ask Jack to approve it unless you write me another song. Go in there and see what you can come up with."

He stomps off into a little office over there and twenty minutes later comes out and says, "Okay, I've got this and see what you think about it. It was a song called "Home."

I said, "That's really good. I think I can get it recorded."

The next day I did get it recorded by Jim Reeves and it became a number one record. I called Jack and said, "Jack, Roger needs $300. I know we just bought him a $9,000 Cadillac, I know he owes us money, I know all that stuff, but he's desperate for $300."

Jack said, "Okay."

So I said to Roger, "You got your $300. You can go down there and pick it up, but before you go, why are you so desperate for $300?"

"Buddy, there is this riding lawnmower that I saw and I just got to have it!"

So he went and got that riding lawnmower and drove it home eight miles down the road! He probably cut the grass once.

One time Roger wanted a motor scooter, so he got one, had a wreck the first time he got on it, and they put him in the hospital. The next day they let him out and he immediately goes back to the hospital because he had a wreck a second time! He was really accident prone.

Lyle: The first time he came to your office with some songs, do you recall what they were?

Buddy: It was probably songs like "My Ears Should Burn When Fools Are Talked About," and those things that he did with Owen Bradley on Decca.

I'll tell you something: At one point in the late sixties, after we hit with "King of the Road" and "Dang Me" and we did a few albums, Roger had only written 135 songs and I'd gotten every one of them recorded. Every song he had I got recorded! Of course he recorded many of them himself, but I mean, those songs... We were getting people to record them all over the place.

Lyle: Who chose what songs were to be recorded?

Buddy: Well, Jerry Kennedy became his producer for Smash. We had worked very closely, Roger and I. I was his publisher, I was his mentor, and

I was trying every way I could to be a part of it. We'd all go into the studio and he'd show Jerry what he had and we'd cut them. I'd get out there and snap my fingers to "King of the Road" and whistle to "England Swings" and "Walking in the Sunshine." I did whatever—play the tambourine on the side... I was always a part of everything that he did, but Jerry was his producer. The three of us together sort of shared the selecting and decision-making.

Lyle: Was Roger prepared in the studio?

Buddy: Rarely, rarely. The only time Roger ever raised his voice to me was one day in the studio, and he cried when he did it. What happened was, we got there and he wasn't ready. We set the session up, got there, and his songs were half written. I said, "Roger, you gotta go down and finish up a couple of songs."

Well, he had probably been out the night before and had been roarin', and he didn't like pressure. He yelled, "You always want me to do things!" And then immediately he grabbed me and hugged me with tears coming out his eyes and said, "I'm sorry. I didn't mean it."

I said, "I know you didn't, you're under pressure."

He'd go down there, take a pill, and finish up his song. When he'd come back up, many times those pills would change his voice. It wasn't wonderfully deep and resonant, but [instead] a high up-in-your-head vocal sound, especially when he got really bent. He finished so many of his songs right there in the studio.

Lyle: In the studio, what kind of input did Roger have on the arrangements of the songs?

Buddy: He had a lot. Roger was always more than just a songwriter and a singer. If you listen to his stuff there's syncopation, like in jazz. [*Buddy sings first line of "King of the Road."*] He had so much in him, and when he'd write some of these songs he sort of knew where he wanted to go with it. It was always away from the traditional music. If you had tried to do Roger's songs like anybody else's they wouldn't have come off. We tried that. His first three songs we did for Smash and all the stuff that he had done before was typical Nashville music. When he was allowed to sit on that stool there with four or five pieces around him and just do Roger Miller, that's when we captured him. I mean, it was unbelievable. Yes, he had tremendous input in what he wanted.

If there was something special he wanted or something he didn't like he'd immediately say, "I don't like it." But like I said, it was a community effort on the part of everybody. Once you got to get the feel for what the deal was, you knew it had to be very sparse, not this big wall-to-wall sound cascading down on you, because it was not what Roger Miller was. Simplicity was Roger Miller. If you think about "Dang Me," you would think of it as a funny song, don't you? But tell me what is funny about this: [*Quotes the first verse of "Dang Me."*] Now what's funny about that? Roger Miller is what's funny about that. The lyric itself is not funny. It's delivery and all the things that are around it; if you just break it down, it's not funny. "Chug-a-Lug" was funny. But "Dang Me," there's nothing funny about those lyrics.

Lyle: I'm just blown away with all that Roger could do with his voice. He was an instrument himself.

Buddy: Yes, he was. Vocal gymnastics. He liked to do all that phrasing. Whether it was in tune or out of tune, he didn't care. He tried everything. He was a unique performer, and he never sang it the same way twice. You better get him pretty quick because his uniqueness is up front. Once he starts getting into the same old pattern, you're losing it, it doesn't work.

Lyle: Was there an expectation of funny material from him?

Buddy: Well, yeah, because people starting thinking of Roger as being funny. When he was on stage he always wanted you to laugh at him. He wore me out! I mean, he tried to be funny, funny, funny, and I'd laugh until my face was breaking, then he'd do one that wasn't so funny. It was a break for me so I could let my face relax. He would say, "Well, you didn't laugh." And I'd say, "Roger, my face is already cracking. What do you want me to do?"

He needed that acceptance. He always needed to feel that you were responding to what he was doing, especially in the early days. He became a little cooler with it as he became more mature and sure of himself. But in those early years, he was a tough one sometimes.

Lyle: Was there was an expectation from the publishing company for Roger to write more humorous type songs?

Buddy: No, I was too smart for that. You know, you can't keep going back to the same well. You write what you write, you record what you record. The worst thing you could do is get into a pattern. You do that, you're dead. Roger was too unique for that anyway. Just because he wrote "Dang Me" today didn't mean that tomorrow he was going to write another "Dang Me." He wrote what he wrote, and it was like he wasn't writing because he had to. He was writing because he was wanting to. Rarely would I have to change one of his songs. Most of the other writers, I would change some melodies, change the lyrics, give them ideas, and do this or do that. Not Roger. He had it all.

Lyle: When he wrote songs did he have other artists in mind or did he intend to release them himself?

Buddy: He just wrote them. I don't think he ever said, "I'm going to write a song for somebody." It would surprise me if anyone could ever tell me that he wrote a song for them, because he wasn't that disciplined. He just wrote when he wrote.

Lyle: Personally, I think of Roger Miller as one of the greatest singers of all time, but most people think of him as just a songwriter. Why do you think he wasn't known more for his singing?

Buddy: Roger was not a great singer, he was a performer. He performed his songs, he did not sing his songs. He was blessed with a voice that had an edge. He could go low and he could go high, but if you listen to him, many times he was singing out of tune. He didn't have that smooth timbre to his voice, he had a unique timbre to his voice. It was more of a performance as a creative rendering than it was as a singer. If you put him against some of the real great singers you will find that he was not that great. Up against a great singer he wasn't considered a singer. He was more the funny guy, Roger Miller, who performs this unique thing. And yet he'd knock your head off with "Husbands and Wives" and some of those great songs.

Lyle: Did he consider himself an artist or a songwriter?

Buddy: I really don't know what Roger considered himself. He was just Roger Miller. I really just think he knew he was a songwriter, he knew he was a performer, he knew he was all the things that he was, but I don't think he ever had a clear picture of who Roger Miller really was. I think he was just living his life.

Roger had an ego the size of Shea Stadium—he really did. I think that he certainly wanted respect from the world, but all of us have our moments where we don't think we get credit for all we've done. He had that television show and he never shot one of them that he wasn't stoned high as a kite on those pills. You can't do that. You just can't do that. You've got to be in command of yourself if you're going to last. Maybe he was nervous or insecure with what he was doing, but I was out there on the set with him when he would be doing some of those shows and if you do pills, you don't exercise patience with other people. You do stupid things, you go off into things that you shouldn't be doing. You just do all kinds of things when you're not stable. And when you've got that kind of show and that kind of pressure on you, you better at least have some semblance in your mind of where you are. There are times I thought he went a little bit too far. The show only lasted thirteen weeks, but he was so hot he could have really pulled it off.

Lyle: Do you know what caused his dry spell in the seventies?

Buddy: Everybody has a dry spell, I don't care who it is. Harlan Howard had a ten-year one. Curly Putnam had a big one. Creativity is a funny thing. You start, you're energized, you do it, you do it, and then all of a sudden all of the distractions come in. Overindulgence in alcohol or drugs, overindulgence in women, or whatever. You have almost too much. And along with that comes all the pressures and the problems of life. You lose your direction, you lose who you are. The smart ones go home again. They go back to their basics and say, "Wait a minute. Out there there's the public persona, but inside of me I'm just a human being. I'm just a little guy and the same guy that I was."

Roger went through personal problems. He went through all the drugs, he went through excesses of everything you could think of, and he lost sight of who he was. He started screwing up. People stop trusting you and stop thinking that you're the horse to bet on, and the more people treat you that way the more you withdraw. Roger went through an awful lot. It wouldn't do no good for me to get into that because that's his personal life. But he had his ups and downs. The only real stability that happened with Roger was when he met Mary. When he met Mary he was down on his butt. I mean he was *down*. That was a really bad time. He was out there playing little clubs and things, trying to make it. I think he and Mary started singing together. I re-recorded all of Roger's greatest hits. We did twenty songs for a TV package and I could tell that he had been misusing cocaine because his voice was just off. I couldn't get a performance. He just wasn't into it. He went through a long, long dry spell until Rocco Landesman came along. He always loved Roger Miller and he came up with the idea about him writing the music to *Big River*. They negotiated, I guess, and Roger agreed to do it, I think with Mary's prodding. And then he sat on it for ever and ever. He wasn't getting anywhere, wasn't trying, and I think finally Mary just said, "You're going to do it." She put the heat on him to do it. He started writing. It took him a while to do it, but, let's face it, it was a score.

Lyle: Some of my favorite songs that Roger recorded were done in the early seventies. How did it come about that he recorded so many Dennis Linde songs?

Buddy: He did a lot of stuff by Dennis. He was the first to record "Little Green Apples" by Bobby Russell. Because he wasn't writing any [songs of his own], he had to do other people's. He did Kristofferson's "Me and Bobby McGee." He did a lot of things that were written by other people because he'd hang out with those writers, they'd play their songs for him. He had access to them so he would do them, [but] he wouldn't have hits with them. Somebody else would come along after Roger would do them and have hits with them. During that time Roger was really hitting those pills. Songs like "Me and Bobby McGee" became big by Janis Joplin and "Little Green Apples" by O. C. Smith—just huge hits. Roger had opportunities to really have big hits, but he didn't strike because they weren't Roger Miller. His songs were Roger Miller. Nobody else's made it with Roger.

Lyle: Did Roger regret losing his television show?

Buddy: Oh no, he never talked about it. I'm sure it would have been nice if he had kept it going, but I just didn't feel like Roger was ready. He was in over his head for that. He needed to have a little more time to settle down. It was too much for him too soon. Don Williams and Allan Bernard were his managers. They got the deal for him, but I think it was premature. One time I was out there while Roger was on *The Tonight Show* and he said to me that he wanted to sign with a big agency like the William Morris Agency. A guy by the name Bernie Schwartz had been after Roger. I said, "I think you're making a mistake." This was before he really hit it. I said, "I see that you are determined to sign with them, but put a clause in there that says if they don't book you something within ninety days the contract is null and void."

That was one of the smartest things I ever did. Ninety days later Roger still had not done anything. *The Tonight Show* stopped calling him because he had signed with an agency. Apparently the agency was making demands that *The Tonight Show* didn't want to do so they stopped calling him. Six months later he still hadn't done anything, hadn't even played his first gig, so he got out of that. About that time we did "Dang Me" and it exploded. For months before I was trying to get in touch with Bernie to see why he wasn't doing anything with Roger, and he didn't return my calls. When Roger hit, Bernie called me. He said, "Buddy, you got to help me out man. You got to get Roger to re-sign the contract because it's going to make me look awfully bad."

I said, "Bernie, you looked bad a long time ago. There is no way Roger Miller is going to re-sign with you! There is no way I would ever go to bat for you. You wouldn't even take my calls. Sorry, Bernie, you lose."

Lyle: What can you tell me about the King of the Road Hotel?

Buddy: The King of the Road Hotel was a disaster. We all lost on that one. They sold stock in it, I bought some. Roger got a piece of it [so they could] use his name, basically. I don't know that he put a lot of money into it. He probably didn't. In those days, Nashville was red hot for franchises. Tex Ritter's BBQ went under. Hank Junior had a place that went under. Minnie Pearl had fried chicken that went under. Because of the name value, Nashville became this entrepreneurial Mecca, and people bought into it because it was a great way of using the hottest names in country music. The sad part is that none of them put anything together that was worth having because none of them knew what they were doing. Every one of them went under.

Roger Miller had one of the brightest minds I've been around. He did not need drugs to be Roger Miller. He had the God-given talent to write those songs. Possibly drugs took the edge off of him so he could expand his mind a little bit, because sometimes that gives you a little freedom to bring out what's already in there. But he was just a great talent he didn't have to have it. I remember he'd go on *The Tonight Show* and say, "You know, I don't mess with drugs anymore. I don't do drugs anymore." Why did he even mention it? Was that an excuse for not having written anything in a while? Was that an excuse for not creating any excitement out there?

I never believed that he had to have drugs to be creative. He just had talent and he was always the fastest mind in town. You'd say something and he was on top of it in a second, responding with some funny kind of thing. He was doing a television show one time when a fly landed on his thumb. He did a whole routine for the camera with that fly sitting on his thumb. That's Roger.

Marty Stuart

Marty Stuart is a great singer and songwriter who owns one of the largest private collections of country music memorabilia. In Marty's early days he used to play guitar for Johnny Cash, and at one time was married to Johnny's daughter Cindy. He has been a member of the Grand Ole Opry since 1992 and is currently married to fellow Opry member Connie Smith.

Marty: Roger was just one of those unexplainable, once-in-a-lifetime, God-sent phenomenas. He was so fast, his wit was so fast, you didn't have time to get to a tape recorder. You know, it's hard to get a tape recorder when you're laying on the floor laughing. You can tell those stories, you get a giggle and a respectable laugh, but it just ain't the same without Roger telling it. The thing that was so cool about Roger was he was like a shotgun, you never knew what was going to come out of his mouth. I think he blew himself away as much as he blew the rest of us away, and when he got on a roll and got you laughing, he was like Muhammad Ali: he just kept punching, you know, until you wet your pants. That was his biggie, to get you down and keep you choked until you couldn't take anymore. One laugh led to another.

Lyle: How did you first meet Roger?

Marty: Well, the lady that was managing me at the time was named Bonnie Garner, and she was also managing Roger, with her partner Mark Rothbaum. I recorded my first album for MCA, the *Hillbilly Rock* record, and was in that dead zone between album being done and album coming out. I was stuck basically summer to fall with nothing to do except wait for a release date. Roger for some reason had decided to change his musicians around and Bonnie recommended that I go play with him. I really didn't want to go to work with anybody else until my record came out, but I was really kind of hurting [financially] and there wasn't a lot of work coming in. The way Roger got me to come in and play, he said, "Look, there's buzzards circling your career, so why don't you come over here and play until you become a star?"

So I went out [on tour] and spent a couple of rounds with Roger. I remember the first time I ever saw my first commercial video come out on TV. We were playing Notre Dame University. In the Green Room Roger stood next to me and we watched my video together. We were standing there watching that video and he said, "You ain't going to amount to shit. You may as well just stay here."

It was a wonderful time. It was so intense and I savored every moment of it. I knew it was a special time and it wasn't going to last long so I drank it in and totally committed myself to it. It really was one of those kinds of life-changing experiences to be around such an original person. There was a lot of comedy up front, but the well ran deep, and just to be around the wit and wisdom of Roger Miller really was a transforming kind of thing.

Lyle: Did he give you any advice about songwriting at all?

Marty: Well, he was really stern about songs. He knew that was his game and he was flat brilliant at it. He made no apologies. He spoke of simplicity and talked about it in kind of the same way his songs are laid out—basically, get to the point real quick and make it as clever as possible.

[One of] the more touching things I remember is that day I was at his house in New Mexico and he took me upstairs and showed me all of the manuscripts that he did for *Big River*. I took it that he was really proud of that one and I was proud that he shared it with me. There was something about *Big River* and what Roger had accomplished that he kind of treasured.

Lyle: How would you describe a Roger Miller concert?

Marty: Well, it would be like riding a roller coaster with no seatbelt and your hands in the air. You never knew what was going to happen. The songs were always brilliant, it was a fun ride, you took a memory home with you, and at the end of the evening you just had to look at the guy and go, "Great entertainer, knock-out songs, total pro, flat brilliant, just flat brilliant." The public fell in love with him for certain songs and they kind of held his feet to the fire to play "Dang Me," "England Swings" and "Husbands and Wives." You know those are the kind of songs you never get tired of playing. They were good the first go-around and they're still good today.

Lyle: When you were growing up, what influence was his music on you?

Marty: Obviously I was touched by "Dang Me" and "England Swings" and "King of the Road." Who wasn't? I just knew they were great songs. But when I finally got in his presence and saw how fast his wit was and what kind of quasar-like mind he had, it meant a whole lot more.

Lyle: Was he writing at all while you were on the road with him?

Marty: He wrote a song, or half-way wrote a song. It was called, "Preserve the Wild Life, Don't Tear the Honky-Tonks Down." He had little bits and pieces of it, but that was kind of a work-in-progress.

Ever the rebel… We were in Canada one time, and Roger said, "Ah, you know, I'll see you on the plane, I'm gonna hang back."

There was a [Canadian] Mountie that came on the plane and said to me, "Mr. Miller will be detained."

I said, "Is he sick or something?"

"No, he'll just join you later."

That's all I got. I found out later that Roger was busted for pot—had a joint in his cigarette pack. And you know, he got out of it. He grinned his way and charmed his way out of it. I think he played them a fiddle tune or something.

[One day] he came to Vanderbilt [Hospital] when they diagnosed him with cancer and I remember Bonnie Garner and me went to his hotel room to check on him and Mary. Everybody was optimistic and I said, "Roger, how do you feel?" He said, "I feel like a shotgun that's been in a corner for twenty years that hasn't gone off and it just went off today and the shotgun wonders what the hell's going on." That was a strange description, but I understood it.

You know, I found out Roger really was a Hush-Puppy and cardigan guy in a leather society. He was the cardigan sweater guy on the edge of town. He had a take on all of us that none of us had on us. He really was in every sense of the word just a normal Midwestern kid that grew up and did good.

Lyle: When was the last time you saw Roger?

Marty: At the ACM [Academy of Country Music] Awards. I guess it was the year he passed away. I knew he wasn't feeling good. I was just about to have my first gold record, called, "This One's Gonna Hurt You," in the spring of the year he died. The Thanksgiving before I had been at his house and just hanging around him inspired me to write songs. By the time I got from Santa Fe to Albuquerque I knew I had to write "This One's Gonna Hurt You for a Long Long Time." It just bowled up in my heart and mind, and by the time I got to Salt Lake City, I wrote that song, on the Salt Lake runway, in about five minutes. It really came out in about five minutes.

I knew I had a good song and I knew I finally had a song that I wasn't ashamed of or afraid to play Roger. But by the time it came out he was starting to get sick. The record was about to tip over gold and I wanted Roger to have the first gold record, so I called MCA and asked if they would go ahead and print one for Roger, 'cause I wanted him to have the first one. They did and I sent it to him. I missed it by just a few days. He passed away before it got to him, but Mary got the first one.

Afterwards, his son Dean and I decided to write songs one day. Dean came out to the place I was staying at and brought one of his dad's guitars, and we wrote a little bit, set the guitar down, leaned it up against the wall and were sitting there talking about his dad. While we were talking one of the strings just snapped out of nowhere. We just looked at each other and broke out laughing, you know, 'cause he never goes away.

Lyle: The only clip I've ever seen of Roger's memorial service, was of you telling a couple of funny stories there. His service seemed to be very unique. Can you tell me anything about that?

Marty: They had two services—one in California, in Beverly Hills, and one in Nashville [at the Ryman Auditorium]. The one in Nashville was just pretty much the Nashville gang gathering up telling Roger stories. It was basically a big old storytelling session, and everybody showed up and brought their best Roger memories. It was a great send-off. I remember leaving there. Me and Waylon and Jessie walked over to Tootsie's and just shook our heads. There wasn't much to say. It had already been said on stage that night. But I remember wanting to be a better person, be more like Roger.

Bobby Braddock

Bobby Braddock has had over thirty-five songs in country music's top ten charts and at least fourteen number ones.

Lyle: Did Roger Miller ever cut any of your songs?

Bobby: Never did. We talked about co-writing quite a bit but it never happened. He had a title that he kept, and every time I'd see him he'd say, "We gotta write this song." It was "The Hero and the Heroin." I always thought that was a great title, but we just never got around to writing it. My favorite Roger Miller song was "Husbands and Wives," which is a great exercise in the economy of words. There's not many lines in that song but every one of them is just wonderful.

I met Roger at Tree Publishing. I was a new kid in town, playing piano for Marty Robbins and looking for a place to take my songs. I knew that Tree Publishing had just become the biggest publishing company in Nashville, that they had Roger Miller and that he had just left Nashville and moved to the West Coast. I thought that'd be a good place to go, so I did. Buddy Killen signed me to Sony Tree and also got me a record deal. I think he had it in his head that I could be the next Roger Miller because I had a knack for writing offbeat songs. Well, I never thought that and nothing could've been further from the truth. I ended up with five different major record deals but I don't think anything even got into the top twenty.

One thing I heard Roger say that I always thought was funny was, "Your karma ran over my dogma." I think Roger is probably the funniest man in the world, funniest person I've ever known. Roger was a great entertainer and had a great deal of charisma too. He had all that stuff it takes to be star and I never had that. I couldn't stand being on the road. I like either being in Nashville or in front of the ocean, one or the other.

I remember one time we were down in the recording studio in the Tree building. There was a girl in there and she talked pretty country. She got up to leave the room she said "I think I am gonna get a drink of wahr-ter." When she walked out the engineer said "I didn't know water had an 'r' in the middle of it." Without missing a beat Roger said "Well if it didn't it our-tta have."

Jack Clement

Gordy Collins

Ever since I got hooked on Johnny Cash I wanted to meet Cowboy Jack Clement. He has produced some of the best records in music history and wrote many of the all-time greatest country songs, songs like "Ballad of a Teenage Queen" and "I Guess Things Happen That Way." Producer and songwriter notwithstanding, Jack for a time was an engineer and session player at Sun Studios in Memphis, working with the legendary Sam Philips to record and produce artists of major importance, like Jerry Lee Lewis and Johnny Cash. This interview took place at his studio/home "The Cowboy Arms Hotel and Recording Spa."

Lyle: I understand that you were a performer before you got into producing.

Jack: I started off real young as a performer playing the guitar and stuff. I played in high school, used to get up and play at assemblies. I went in the Marine Corps when I was seventeen. I'd been in high school for three years and hated every minute of it. I was flunking everything you possibly could, so my father treated me to a trip to New Orleans for a couple of weeks right after school was out. After I got out of boot camp I was able to get a guitar, so I always had a guitar and was able to entertain the boys around the barracks.

I never wrote a song 'til I was about nineteen. I started writing songs on guard duty there late at night between twelve and four in the morning. I was stationed at the Marine barracks in Washington, D.C., a very historical place. The Marine Band rehearsed and played there. I was on the drill team and played in the band, what you call a Hollywood Marine. We were there to be on display, we did funerals, weddings, everything. I was about nineteen, there was a lot of work, we did a lot of marching.

After I got out of the Marine Corps I immediately got a band together. I had bought a guitar that is sitting right here and we were going to crash the Grand Ole Opry. This would be in 1952. I bought the guitar in 1951. This guitar has played on a lot of records—"Ballad of a Teenage Queen," "I Guess Things Happen That Way," "Big River," several Waylon tracks, Charley Pride's first two or three hits... That guitar has been to a lot of places and could write a story. Sometimes I think about when I'm writing my book that I should let the guitar write it: "I was sitting in this big music store in Washington, D.C., when along come this handsome young Marine, picks me up and says, "I'm going to marry you."

Lyle: Do you have a name for it? [*At this point Jack passed it to me and let me play it, probably one of the most famous guitars in country music history next to Willie Nelson's Trigger*]

Jack: Sue… It's a girl. It's a great guitar. It's for sale. Put you into it for a million three. I had that guitar since I was twenty.

Well, I had this band ready and we were going to get out there and strike it rich. We did pretty well. We'd play joints around Washington, D.C., got to making a fairly decent living. I'd have to borrow money from my father every once in a while, but that's alright, he didn't mind. We tried to crash the Grand Ole Opry but we didn't get in. First we auditioned as a country, harmony, bluegrass kind of thing, and they liked it but said they already had that, they needed a comedy thing. So me and Buzz went back to D.C. and got some joke books, magazines, some costumes, and we went back and tried again. We got on as a kinda Homer and Jethro thing. We did that for about six months.

I got a job teaching dancing at Arthur Murray's in Memphis and after a while I decided I wanted to go to school, so I went to Memphis State. I studied everything except anything to do with business or chemistry. It took me a long time and a lot of mistakes to learn that debit is left and credit is right. Anyway, after two and a half years of school I was interested in construction, so I got a job at this building supply place in the hardware department, which I hated.

That's what I was doing when I went in to see Sam Phillips. By this time Sun Records is doing pretty well, Elvis is rockin'. If you had a tape and wanted to get it mastered, Sam was the best place to go. He was still doing that himself even though he had sold Elvis and got all that money, had the big hit with "Blue Suede Shoes" and [Johnny Cash's] "I Walk the Line." He was rocking by then, but you could still hire him to go in there and cut your record for four dollars, like Elvis did! He really liked to do mastering, he took a lot of pride in it. I'd been in to see Sam before. I went and auditioned for him and he sat and listened to me for a long time and said I was too good, too slick for him. I was into Marty Robbins and some bluegrass but you can't stand up and do bluegrass by yourself.

Anyway, when I was working at the building supply place, we'd cut this record and I wanted to get it to Sam, so I took it down to him on Wednesday afternoon and left the tape with him. The next Wednesday I went back to pick up the master so we could get it pressed. We were going to put it out for sale. I walked in and Sam Phillips said, "I really like that record, that's the first rock and roll anybody's brought me around here." Everybody by then was trying to do Elvis stuff. Then he said, "Maybe you oughta come work for me."

I said, "Well, maybe I should," and two weeks later I did.

That was June 15, 1956. I was there for close to three years, played the guitar and ran the board. Within the first four months I had a hit with Jerry Lee Lewis' "Crazy Arms." It wasn't a smash hit but for a first record it was great, sold about a hundred and forty thousand [copies]. The next record was "A Whole Lotta Shakin' " and that sold well over a million. I played on a lot of sessions. Sometimes I would get Sam to run the board but most of the time I ran the board. Then I taught Billy Riley and Rollen James how to run it so that I could play on some stuff, overdub. We could overdub mono to mono. We would have to have three tape machines to do it though.

I had been [at Sun] for about three years, then I tried to be in the record business for about a year. By then I was making some pretty good money from songwriting royalties. I had written "Ballad of a Teenage Queen," "I Guess Things Happen That Way," the B side of "Whole Lotta Shakin'" ("It'll Be Me"), and many others, but I didn't really make any money in records. I started Summer Records and messed with that for about a year, put out about three singles. It wasn't happening [money-wise] so I went to work for Chet Atkins as his assistant. I was like a consultant, so I could continue to live in Memphis. I commuted [to Nashville]. At the same time I had a little studio in Memphis, but we never cut a lot of stuff there. Chet would let me produce all the things he didn't want to produce, anything he didn't want to mess with, he'd dump them on me.

While I was working with Chet is when I first met Roger Miller, hanging out with him a lot. Suddenly there was this guy named Roger Miller and he's a real nut and everybody loves him and he's funny as shit and he's a genius, sorta in a class by himself. Sorta a loner in a lot of ways. What a mind! It was always a party. Whatever time of day it was, he was always on. If he wasn't on he'd stay home. Any really good ones have to be on to be on, whatever that means. Very musical guy, funny guy, very original.

I produced his last session at RCA. I don't remember what it was. It never was released. It was going to be his last go-'round. This was in the sixties when I was in Beaumont. I came up to Nashville do it. We were going to do "Dang Me," but for some reason we didn't do it. The session just wasn't a real success. If we'd had some more time and I could have worked with him more, then we probably could have pulled it off.

There's one thing that always sticks out in my mind: Back then he was into pills. I don't know what kind of pills because I was never into pills, but he was into pills and he always had some around. [Once] he was staying at a hotel in town and he checked out but he forgot his pills, so he called somebody down there in housekeeping and said, "This is Mr. Miller from room such and such. I think I forgot my medicine." Then he went down and got it.

Lyle: I hear there was a lot of medicine back in those days.

Jack: Yes. My partner Bill Hall sorta managed him for a period of time. Roger used to come through Beaumont every once in a while. One time he left a bunch of pills in Bill Hall's filing cabinet. Bill was thumbing through it one day, and under D for 'dope' he found a file full of pills.

The last time I saw Roger was when Frances Preston had a party at her house in his honor because he had that hit Broadway show. Now that was pretty surprising to all this friends, that he actually finished such a thing, retained that kind of level of concentration. I told him I was proud of him and he said "I'm proud of you too."

Lyle: Can you tell me anything about what inspired your song "West Canterbury Subdivision Blues"? I always found it interesting that the title of that song doesn't appear in it anywhere.

Jack: You remember the *Canterbury Tales*? Chaucer, kinda risqué stuff, tales of adultery and fucking around? I just thought that might be a name of a mythical subdivision. We lived in West Canterbury, so I borrowed that from Chaucer. I borrowed "Miller's Cave" from Mark Twain's *Tom Sawyer*... There were no caves in Georgia. Hell, there's no hills in Georgia. Can't have caves without hills.

[Author's Note] Well, this interview was a good history lesson about music and the life of a legendary producer/songwriter. As I sat with him in his office, there was music being played in the background. I didn't realize it was live music from the upstairs recording studio until Jack grabbed his microphone (just like a classic school principal's) to tell them to redo a certain line. I didn't realize it at the time but he was producing that session right in front of me. He was one of the nicest guys I met, no ego at all for all that he has accomplished. He showed me around his studio and he played some of his songs including an incredible version of "Guess Things Happen That Way," which is title track of his long-awaited CD, now released on Dualtone.

Billy Arr

Gordy Collins

Billy Arr is a singer/songwriter and producer. He had a number one song called "Looking For Tomorrow" with Mel Tillis in 1975. More than eighty of Billy's songs have been recorded by country music artists including Roy Rogers, Mickey Gilley and Tom Jones. Roger called Billy "Thumbs" because he's missing two fingers. This interview took place at The Idle Hour on Music Row in Nashville where Billy is a fixture.

Billy: We had a professional club here in Nashville in the sixties called Wally's Clubhouse, where you had to earn at least half of your income from the music industry in order to be a member. It was a place where you brought your own bottle and they mixed your drinks for you and would keep your bottle behind the bar. They'd have a piano there and some guitars, a poolroom, and serve food and drinks. Mostly guys would sit in the corner and write songs or play their songs for each other. I would run into Roger there, but I met him once in L.A. before that. After a night of going hard, we would gather there and drink 'red beer'—beer, tomato juice, salt and pepper, and Worchester sauce. One time we were having what we called a 'sick call,' in the morning, around nine a.m. Roger came in and said, "I got a great idea. I'm going to open a three-minute eye-wash."

All the guys at the Clubhouse used to sing and I would play piano for them. Faron Young would sing a couple of songs, I'd sing a couple, and then Webb Pierce [would come along], and by the time he was drunk we would have done his entire catalog! Webb would just sing, sing, sing, all day. He'd just keep calling out songs one after another. I'd ask him what key it was in and he'd answer, "The original one." Webb never knew what key he sang anything in. [One time] Roger came up to me and said, "I want you to stop playing piano for him. He's driving us insane! How much is he paying you to play?"

"Nothing."

"Well, I'll pay you more than that to *not* play for him."

Roger and Faron Young would take shots at each other a lot. Faron would call him a "West Coast son of a bitch," and Roger would always say to him, "Congratulations on your new pop crossover hit, 'Four in the Morning.' "

Faron would get pissed off. He was a good imitator too and he'd imitate Roger, "Dang me, they should have taken a rope to your ass!"

Faron had the foulest mouth in Nashville. He never really got pissed off at Roger, they were just jiving, mostly back and forth one-liners. They loved each other to death.

Roger would always say, "Sheriff, you're going pop." He'd accuse him of sounding like Dean Martin.

Faron would just say, "Fuck you."

There were a lot of 'fuck yous' flying around back in those days. That was then. We don't have the same camaraderie here in Nashville anymore. Everyone is business, going here and hiding there. Back then all the stars and writers hung out together.

Roger wasn't a big co-writer but he'd love to jack around with you and say that he would. He'd come up with these weird ideas that he knew damn well wasn't a song and get these younger songwriters thinking on them. They'd think, 'If Roger thought it was a good idea, then it *must* be.' But they sucked! Then Roger would say, "What if I said I'd co-write with you on 'You Can't Roller Skate in a Buffalo Herd'? Would that excite you?" So he got them thinking that maybe what he said *was* a good idea for a song. He liked to jack with people's minds. He was one of the worst in the world to start something and then get up and leave. He'd start a conversation about something, get everyone thinking weird thoughts trying to think like he did, and then he'd get up and say he had to go to the bathroom and just leave.

Roger used to say he wished he had a pill the size of a tractor wheel, and that every time you took a bite out of it, it would grow back.

One time I was in California with Roger backstage at *The Johnny Carson Show* and Don Rickles said to Roger, "You know, you'd be more successful if you converted to Judaism like Sammy Davis, Jr." Right off the top of his head Roger said, "I couldn't pass the physical."

He would call himself the Screwdriver. If he heard you writing a good song, he'd say, "You need that tightened up. Let me put my screwdriver to it."

One time Mickey Newbury, Roger and I were at the Holiday Inn Lounge on West End and Faron Young came in. Faron was going through a divorce with his wife and he came up to us and said, "Son of a bitch! I just got out of the courtroom with that ex-wife. She sued me for more alimony. I told the judge when I got a chance to speak that she didn't need no more damn money, she's already eaten too well. She's got more chins than a Chinese phonebook!" Roger came unglued!

Roger loved to quote W.C. Fields, "Alligators are smarter than people. They eat their young."

Every time the phone would ring Roger would say, "Get that. It might be the phone."

Scotty Turner and Ted Harris

Scotty Turner holds a very interesting place in music history. Originally from Nova Scotia, Canada, he was a professional athlete who ended up writing songs and playing lead guitar for Tommy Sands and the Raiders. He is one of the few people who co-wrote with Buddy Holly. Scotty's songs have been recorded by dozens of artists, from Roy Clark to Dean Martin. He's been a record label executive for a number of major labels and signed Waylon Jennings to his first record deal. He was a close friend with war hero Audie Murphy, and, in fact, they co-wrote many songs together. Ted Harris is an accomplished songwriter who had a big hit recorded by Charley Pride in 1967, "Crystal Chandeliers." I met Scotty and Ted in Nashville at a breakfast club of music industry legends that meets every Wednesday at 7:30 am. After that we met twice a week for about a month to talk about Roger and the old days in Nashville.

Scotty: I did the music for Roger's last television show in 1988, the one he did on the Mississippi Queen steamboat here in Nashville. Roger did a couple of songs from his Broadway show and he had special guests like Lyle Lovett. I had to record the tracks without Roger there. He later sang to the tracks. It sounded great, but don't let anybody ever fool you—those tracks were real inventive. On some of them we'd go from 3/4 to 4/4. The musicians even said they'd never realized [how hard they were to play]. Roger said, "I don't know how you did it because those are not easy tracks."

Lyle: How did you become friends with Roger?

Scotty: Dorsey Burnette was a real close friend of mine. I was going over to Dorsey's to write. I had gotten there and fifteen minutes later in comes Roger Miller. Dorsey asked him, "How did your session come out?"

Roger said, "I got this piece of junk I cut."

Dorsey said, "Let's hear it."

It was "Dang Me." I said, "You're kidding aren't you, Roger?"

He said, "No man, I really don't think it's going to do anything." He really didn't believe in that song at first until everybody started telling him, "Look out. You got yourself a monster!"

[Later] I went to work for Liberty Records and Roger would come by because he had friends there. I'd be in the middle of a big meeting and the door would open and there would be Roger. One time he stuck his head in the door and said, "I've had it up to here with Jimmy Dickens," (*motions Roger putting his hand up to his stomach*) and then he closed the door and walked off.

We used to go out to the Palomino in L.A. quite a bit. I was with Billy Graham, Glen Campbell's bass player. We used to do some writing together. This one night we had gone out to the Palomino and Roger was there. He got a little ripped so we took him home, out to Encino. We walked in the house and everything was gone. Leah had moved everything out. Roger had no idea. Billy and I knew we couldn't leave him there. Just down below was Goober, George Lindsay's, house, so we took Roger there and said, "Here, George, here's Roger," and took off. I saw Goober a few years later and reminded him of that night and he said, "Ah well, it turned out all right."

The next day Billy Graham came into my office and played me a song he had written the night before, "It's Going Home Time (Gee, I Wish I Had a Home)."

On a Fourth of July weekend I drove up to Las Vegas to see some shows, and I'm checking into a hotel and these two hands come down over my shoulders. It's Roger. He said, "Scotty! What you doing here?"

I said, "Oh, I just came up to see some shows."

He gave the bellman $10 to take my bags to the room and then we went up to his room. [Later that night] we went down to Roger's show, and after the show Roger said, "What you doing tonight?"

"Roger, I'm here in Vegas. I came to relax."

"Fly back with me to L.A."

"Why?"

"I gotta pick up three suits."

I said, "Roger, you can go down to the tailor in the lobby and buy three custom suits. It's cheaper than the jet."

"No, no, no. These fit me."

So I'm on an airplane, this chartered jet, on the way back to L.A. at two o'clock in the morning! He had just bought one of the first VCRs. We spent the day watching Roger [on TV] and then got back [to Vegas] just in time for him to go to his show. That night Roger bought about $500 worth of fireworks and we drove out to the desert and had our own little fireworks display. Man, he was lighting skyrockets and these big bangers and there was only myself and Marty Allred and I think Buddy Emmons was there. So after that I had to get back to L.A. and I hadn't even been in my room in Vegas!

I think the best night of our lives was when Joe Allison was having a party at his home. I invited Audie Murphy and we went over there. They were all very honored to meet Audie. Roy Clark and Roger Miller were there. They started with the one-liners back and forth. Audie sat there and his mouth hit the ground. He never laughed so hard! Roger was incredible with his one-liners and Roy was just about as fast. That night Roger and myself and Audie went back to Audie's house. The Browning Rifle Company, when they'd come out with a new model, would give one to Audie, so he had a gun rack in his home that was incredible.

I met Audie through Guy Mitchell. I said, "Boy, I can't wait to hear about the war."

Guy said, "Oh no, no don't mention that. That's bad memories. If he brings it up, then okay."

One night [later on] Jerry Reed was in L.A. with Chet Atkins and they invited me out to dinner. Jerry Reed said to me, "I got to meet Audie Murphy."

I said, "Well, when do you want to meet him?"

He said "Tonight."

So I'm driving Jerry Reed over to meet Audie and Jerry said, "Man, I can't wait to hear about the war."

I said, "Jerry, I've known the man for six years and if he brings it up, then okay."

We get over there and Jerry starts doing some of his tunes and Audie's on the floor cross-legged with him, roaring. He was doing "Guitar Man," all of his novelty type of stuff, and Audie was going nuts. Jerry did about an hour concert for Audie and I'm sitting on the couch and Jerry lays the guitar down and said, "Chief, Scotty told me not to but I'm just an old country boy from Georgia and I've got to hear about the war." I could have died!

Audie looked at Jerry and said, "Where would you like me to start?"

Jerry said, "At the beginning."

"Well, you better go and take a seat because this is going to take awhile." He went through the entire war. I wish I would have had a tape recorder that night, it would have been priceless.

Ted: Roger was hands down the most creative articulator of words that we ever had in Nashville. The man could run the gamut of wonderful smooth pure country ballads all the way to "England Swings" or "Dang Me." That is very rare. Nobody else ever approached the cleverness with which he could handle a subject. He was really an expert of our language as the common man understands it, which is a very important facet. You could be very intellectual but you could be so far above the people that they don't ever understand or appreciate emotionally what you're trying to say. But Roger could really hit the bull's-eye every time when it comes to an emotional quotient in his songs or an entertaining quotient in his songs.

I remember one morning we were brainstorming—Roger, myself and Ted Daffan, who was my publisher. There was a lull in the conversation and Roger said, "Boys, I gotta go. I oughta be out borrowing money right now." Those were really slim days, but nobody would have thought to say a thing like that. But Roger did.

[At one point] this kid kept following Roger around. Every time he'd see him at Tree or wherever he was at the time he would almost attack him and say, "Come on, Rog, write a song with me. Come on, Rog, let's do one together." Roger was a very patient and decent individual and he certainly wouldn't just quail anyone's ambition for no reason, but this went on and on and on. Finally Roger turned around and said, "Look, Hoss, Picasso didn't co-paint." What an answer! Only Roger could say that.

Nashville has changed. They're hiring a lot of young people who really don't know our heritage. They haven't been here long enough, they haven't lived long enough to know the art form we have in Nashville, and they certainly don't know the older song catalogues. I had a friend of mine who did an independent session and on it he re-recorded "Crystal Chandeliers." He took it to one of the major labels here in town and the person they had in charge of A&R, this young lady, listened to the tape. When they got to "Crystal Chandeliers" she said, "Now there's a song! Where did you ever find a song like this?" You know, they tried to book Jim Reeves for ten years after he was dead in South America.

Scotty: [Once] a new artist in town was looking for songs and he ran into Roger somewhere and Roger said he'd meet him up at Tree. Roger would play him a song and the guy would say, "Geez, that's pretty good, but that's not a hit." You don't say that to Roger Miller! So he'd play him another one and the guy would say, "That's good but that's not a hit." Finally, after about six songs Roger said, "Why in the hell don't you cut 'Stardust'?! *That's* a hit!"

Lyle: I notice in today's music industry a lot of artists and songwriters view each other as competition. Was there much of that attitude back then?

Scotty: We never looked at Roger as a competitor.

Ted: It wasn't that way in those days. I can explain the difference between Nashville then and now real easy. Back then we were art-driven. The publishers published, record companies did records, writers wrote. There was no competition, we had a mutual admiration society. Everybody was art-driven. Now the question is: "Who owns the publishing? Do I own the artist? How much can I make out of this song? Can I get half of that?" The quality of the work and the art form in that has taken second place—or last place, if you will. Now the whole business is greed-driven rather than art-driven. We were doing it because we loved it. Roger wasn't a competitor, he was a friend. We all really were genuine friends. This town was just an absolute pleasure in those days. Anything could happen.

The greatest publisher was Fred Rose. Chet Atkins told me that Fred used to walk through the studio when someone was cutting a session and they would always ask him, "What did you think of that, Mr. Rose?" And he'd say, "You oughta change the third word of the second verse to so-and-so." And they would do it. There was no ownership involved in anything. This was Einstein telling people how to do the damn theory of relativity. That's the kind of town we had. We all miss that. Now it's a greed game filled with cast-iron secretaries, voice boxes, e-mails, code-a-phones, and security guards where you can't get in.

Scotty: You can walk into a major record label now, shoot a shotgun, and not hit anybody creative. It's all secretaries and attorneys.

Thom Bresh

Gordy Collins

Guitar player and one-man band, Thom Bresh is one of the few people who can do a great Roger Miller impression. Thom had a famous uncle named Merle Travis. When Thom's dad passed away, he found out that Merle Travis was his real father. This probably explains where he got some of his talent.

Thom: Roger was a unique, complex character and I'm glad somebody is delving [into his life]. I always lovingly referred to him as the Idiot from Erick, Oklahoma. Roger was just a crazy man, a wild man, but so loaded with unique talent and a bizarre way of looking at everything. That made him Roger Miller... This brilliant mind... You'd think there'd be stuff everywhere, tons of books on him.

I was brought up in show business. My dad was Merle Travis, who was a writer and a guitarist, and Roger was a big fan of his. I ran into Roger when I was about sixteen or seventeen in '64-'65, that era. I was working with a guy named Hank Penny. I replaced Roy Clark [on guitar] 'cause he had a chance to open for Andy Griffith in the main showroom. Hank was a big entertainer in Vegas, Tahoe, Reno, a big lounge act. Roger was a big fan of Hank's and would come around. I knew all of Roger's songs, and when we were with Hank we did this Roger Miller medley: "Dang Me," "Chug-A-Lug," "Can't Roller Skate...," "My Uncle Used to Love Me (But She Died)," "England Swings," and end off with "King of the Road."

Hank had a lot of people start with him. Thumbs Carllile worked a lot with Hank, then he went with Roger. Marty Allred used to play drums for Hank Penny and Marty became Roger's drummer and road manager.

[One night] when I was playing at the Mint Hotel in downtown Vegas with Hank, a napkin was passed up on stage that said, "Hank, have Bresh do me," signed Roger Miller. They had me do this Roger Miller medley. After the show Roger came backstage and gave me a big hug. He said, "I want you to meet the funniest nigger that's ever lived. This is Richard Pryor, this is Thom Bresh. I call him nigger because that's what he calls himself. He's opening for Bobby Darin down on the strip."

I said, "Wow, I love Bobby Darin."

"You want to meet Bobby Darin?"

"Yeah!"

So, Roger took me—I'm about seventeen at this time—and this black man that I just met, Richard Pryor, outside and there's a limousine sitting out there. Roger bangs on the window and it comes down and there sits Bobby Darin in there. Roger said to him, "This is one of the most talented kids I ever met right here and you're a big idol of his and I want him to meet you. Thom Bresh, this is Bobby Darin."

Darin stuck his hand out through the window and said, "Hi, kid," and then the black window went right back up.

Roger was one that loved shock value of any kind. He just seemed to love anything that was totally left field and would just drop your jaw and shock you like, *What?* I'm sure you heard the story of him bringing down the curtain at Harrah's Club forty different ways. Roger and I got to talking about it one night and Roger was just laughing like hell. He said, "There's like a five-year period of time I was taking too many pills and there's about a five-year chunk that I only hear stories about. I'm not proud of that, but that's part of what I was. Usually if I'd hear the same story two or three different times from different people that I trust and know, I figured, well, it must be a true one."

The way I remember it, they used to introduce Roger at Harrah's in the main show room. This was pretty much in his wild days, and as you know by talking to anybody, he had quite a wild destructive spell there for a while. They'd introduce him, "Ladies and Gentlemen, Harrah's proudly presents the King of the Road, Roger Miller!"

The band would start playing and he would come out. They had this gigantic gold lamé curtain that went across the entire stage in the showroom and the curtain would come up. Well Roger, on this particular night, was up on top of the catwalk up there on the curtain and when they announced him he was just going to grab the curtain and slide on down when they brought it up. However how he had it figured in his head didn't quite work out, because as soon as he jumped on it the curtain rings just started popping and he came down to the stage, but so did the curtain! Half of the curtain was hanging. He was real thin at the time. When he grabbed it, he used his weight and he just came on down. The band was dying laughing. This was probably a $100,000 gold lamé curtain hanging halfway down! I believe Harrah's fired him on the spot, or it might have been his last night there, but that kind of ended his Harrah's career. I remember he didn't play there anymore.

I don't ever remember seeing him drink except for Coca-Cola. One night he had his Coke and he was talking to some people. It was a business conversation going on and they had their cocktails, 'cause it was at sort of a formal event. Roger is standing there all dressed up nicely—he always had those nice three-piece suits with the vest and tie—and his voice never changed during the conversation. He took this Coke like he was going to take a big drink out of it, and he put it right in the middle of this forehead and just poured it. It went down the side of his face, down the front of his shirt and suit! He dumped the entire coke. All he said was, "Hell, I thought I was taller than that!" And then he went right back into his conversation. The people were dying around him but he never ever drew attention to it or anything. He just stood there dripping, finished his conversation and then walked off. It was one of the funniest things that I ever saw.

[Another time] Roger was walking down the street with a bunch of people and all of a sudden there's a parking meter. He stopped at the parking meter—he had loafers on—and kicked these two loafers off, immediately dropped onto the loafers with his knees and grabbed that parking meter. Now he looked like a little short guy with the two feet coming out of his knees. He grabbed that parking meter like it was an old-time microphone, started patting it, and sang into it. Then he stood up and started down the street again.

We were in Reno one time and he said, "Are you writing any songs, Thommy?"

I said, "Yeah, I got this one I'm working on now, 'Reno Lady.'"

"'Reno Lady'? What's it about?"

"Well, it's about this guy that comes to Reno and always loses his money. But this time he comes and sees this woman across the way, and this time Reno's not going to take his money. It's going to take his heart."

"OK, I got your line: 'I made a mental bet and almost lost my mind.' Free of charge from Roger Miller. I'm giving away lines today. You can have that one."

"Really?"

"Yeah, but remember songs that are topical like Reno, people in Wisconsin don't give a shit about 'em unless there's a reason for it. Like 'Kansas City Star' is double entendre with Kansas City star being the star of this little TV show and the newspaper *Kansas City Star*. That's why that's clever. You can have that line. Hope you can make it rhyme and work."

Lyle: Did you use it?

Thom: Oh sure. If Roger Miller gives you a line, you're going to figure some way to use it. It was probably the best line of the song.

Lyle: Can you tell me anything most people wouldn't know about Roger?

Thom: He got an allowance—$2000 a week—and [yet] he would always borrow from the musicians. On payday he'd say, "Okay, everybody divvy up." They would give him money and they would have to turn in a slip that said, 'Roger borrowed $500 from me.' So the next week there would be an extra $500 on their check, at which time they would turn *that* over to Roger. They would always be $500 behind.

Lyle: Did Roger ever give you advice on your career?

Thom: The only thing he told me is just be honest in what you do. He said, "I would love to help you, Bresh. I think you are a star. You won't understand this now and I hope you will later so you won't think badly of me, [but] I can't help you 'cause you would be direct competition to me. If I were to help you, you could possibly take away something that should have gone to me if you get big enough. You'll understand it when you get older."

But anytime he could help, he did. [One time in Vegas] he said, "Everybody's going to be at my house. I'm going to pick you up and take you out to the beach house. You mill around with these people—all the stars from Reno and here that are going to be there—and I'll get you to play." And he did. I mingled with everybody. He'd come in there with his guitar and say, "I want you to hear this kid. Thom, come over here and do them a couple of songs." He'd give me the guitar and everybody would just shut up. He [told me later,] "You'll never know when that'll help." So that was his way of helping.

I understand now what he was saying. I don't agree that I would've been in direct competition, but I understand what he was saying. Like he would help Thumbs Carllile because Thumbs was just a guitar player so he's going to endorse him. There's no way Thumbs is going to take anything [from him] but I do impressions and I do his songs and I do my songs and I'm a guitarist. I'm all of these things. To him a sixteen-year-old wouldn't affect him in any way. But maybe five years down the road at twenty-one, maybe I would. In his mind that was his reasoning.

Roger was always really nice to me. I never saw him throw any fits. I'd see him do crazy things and say off-the-wall stuff. I think his mind went a hundred miles an hour because that's just the way his mind worked. It was just *on*. He'd get on the stage and say, "I want to write a song. I need a topic. Anybody, anybody!"

I remember one night I was sitting there watching 'cause I loved this part of the show when he makes something up. Some guy hollered out, "Half and half!" I'll never forget it 'cause I wrote it all down at the time. Roger sang, "There's three things you can't get from a calf. Buttermilk, sour cream and half and half." And he went on for a whole song right off the cuff.

Years later we were talking about the five year period that he really doesn't remember much from, and Roger said, "That time period we were all together, it was new and I was wild. I'm taking them pills and everybody's taking pills around me. I was up for days, sometimes a couple of weeks, from those damn pills. You could hear it in my songs. How else could you think of things like 'You Can't Roller Skate in a Buffalo Herd,' 'My Uncle Used to Love Me (But She Died')? Oh boy, was my mind in a weird place! But I'd have these fits of depression and you'd get things like 'Husbands and Wives.' You'd get 'One Dyin' and a Buryin'.' It's not good for you. I'm telling you I did it. I'm telling you first-hand. I'm just trying to straighten myself out now."

I did hear at one time, and this is hearsay, but it came from Thumbs. I said, "Thumbs, how does Roger keep going with those pills?"

He said, "Do you know how many pills he's taking a day? Those black beauties?"

"No."

"He's built up a tolerance to almost eighty of them a day."

Now that could have been an exaggeration. If it was twenty a day I'd go, *What?* But he said, "We've all built up pretty heavy tolerances to that stuff."

Thumbs would come over to my room every once in a while and beat on the door and ask me if I had a necktie. I'd say, "A necktie? It's three o'clock in the morning. Where are you going?"

"Man, I just gotta close my eyes and put the tie around there so it'll keep my eyes closed. I gotta try and get some sleep." The eyes just literally didn't even blink! They were just open all the time.

Roger was hosting the Academy of Country Music Award shows out in L.A. There was a girl that had a hit TV show at the time and she was on. Her name was Joyce Bulifant. Roger came out from backstage and he was really wrecked during this show. You could see it, you could hear it. It was being taped so it wasn't like it was live, but Roger would come out very professional but totally letting himself go. I remember he came out and said, "Our next presenter is a lady currently with a big hit television show called such-and-such. I've never watched it personally, but I don't watch much television. Please welcome her. Her name is Miss Joyce Bullshit. What the hell does that say? Stop the tape a minute, I can't read that." And Joyce comes on, she's kind of embarrassed. Roger said, "I'm sorry honey. Bullshit? What is it? How do you say it?"

Joyce said, "It's Bulifant."

So Roger said, "B-U-L-I-F-A-N-T. Okay, I'll do it better this time… I'd like to introduce a lovely lady I never heard of before but they tell me she's a big star. Ladies and Gentlemen, welcome Joyce B-U-L-I-F-A-N-T."

The director, comes out, "Roger, can you give us one more? A little nicer, please? Just read what's on the cards there, Roger, please."

You can tell by the tone of his voice that he was getting a little irritated. They'd have to go find him a couple of times and there'd be a big stage wait. Joyce Bulifant started to come out a second time and she had to turn around and go back. Then the third time he read what was on the card, "There's a big television show right now. Here's the star of that show, Miss Joyce Bulifant."

He didn't trim himself a lot, he could but he didn't edit himself in any kind of a situation. That's kind of what he was all about. I'm glad he didn't. That's what made him Roger.

Sheb Wooley

Gordy Collins

Songwriter, recording artist and actor Sheb Wooley was born in Roger Miller's hometown of Erick, Oklahoma. He acted with such movie greats as Errol Flynn (Rocky Mountain), Gary Cooper and Grace Kelly (High Noon), Elizabeth Taylor and James Dean (Giant), and Gene Hackman (Hoosiers). From 1959 to 1966, he played the role of Pete Nolan in the television series Rawhide. As a recording artist, he's probably best known for his big hit, "Purple People Eater." He died in September 2003, and his obituary, as written by Country Music Television, included this fact: "Wooley was a major musical influence on Roger Miller, who was related to him by marriage. Miller was only 11 when Wooley gave him his first fiddle."

Sheb: I was real proud to be a part of Roger's life.

Lyle: You were married to his cousin, weren't you?

Sheb: Yes. When Roger was three years old they lived in Fort Worth and his father died. They had three boys and his father had three brothers. His mother said she could not take care of those boys. This was back in the depression when times were petty hard. So Elmer Miller of Erick, Oklahoma, took Roger, and the other brothers took a different boy and went to California.

We lived out in the country in a farm ranch operation. The first time I ever saw Roger I rode my horse out by where Mr. Miller was farming, and well, Roger was sitting up on the wagon driving these mules. He was four years old, dressed up in a cowboy outfit with a red handkerchief around his neck, the cutest little devil you ever saw. A few years later I started dating Melba, who was his cousin really, but he was raised with her being his sister. They raised him like he was their own boy. As a matter of fact, they didn't even like for his mother to come around. By the time Roger was about eight or nine, we married. We were still working for Mr. Miller in the cotton fields, hauling cotton. Roger was about ten. He was there out on the field with us, but when something would fly over like a plane he would watch it as long as he could see it and stand there and daydream. I would yell, "Roger!" and he would jump and start working again.

His dad had a bunch of grazing land, so I went down to Oklahoma City and bought a bunch of cattle, forty head of steer. We brought them up there and had to fix a lot of fence... I had an old black horse named Nig and I'd jump on the horse and Roger would jump on behind me, and off we'd go fixing fence. We would spend the whole day together and just got to be real pals. He's nine and I'm eighteen or nineteen. He's always been like a little brother to me. But I got the bug to be an artist, a singer.

Lyle: What was your first calling, to be an actor or singer?

Sheb: A singer. I came to Nashville first, spent a year and couldn't get a job on the WSM or the Grand Ole Opry. I went over to the WLAC, which was another fifty thousand-watt station here, and said, "Hey, I'll work for free," so they gave me a test. They put me in the room with a microphone and I did a fifteen-minute show, and they came out and said, "Okay, we're going to do it." They started me off at four-forty-five in the morning. That went on for a while, then another slot opened up, four-forty-five in the afternoon. So I had two slots a day, two fifteen-minute shows, and I'm getting known around the town a little bit, playing for the politicians, making a living, selling a song with a picture on the back of it for a quarter. You should have seen me with all those quarters! I made thirty or forty dollars a week. I had to make a living. I was living at a boarding house.

In the meantime, Roger was growing up and he says, "I wanna be like Sheb." He never wanted anything else in life. I gave him a three-quarter-size fiddle when he was about twelve, thirteen, and he learnt to play it. He would say, "I can play the fiddle better than you can." And he could too! I went down to Fort Worth and got a network radio show for General Foods and Roger was listening in all the time. Then Roger went into the service, he was in Korea. He would send me songs. They had a little merit, but they weren't ready. I was able to watch him grow in his songwriting, year after year, a little better, a little better.

Well, when he came back he went to Nashville. By this time I was in Los Angeles with an MGM record contract, and I would meet my producer in Nashville and record here. I would come to town and Roger would come and meet me, and we would talk. One time he came in and he played me a few songs. He started this one, [*Sings the first verse of "Dang Me"*].

I'm getting ready to record and I said, "Well, Roger, if you write another verse I'll record that."

He said, "Oh well, I'll finish it sometime on the way to a session."

He wanted to do it himself. Then he went back and wrote [the rest of it] and it was a smash hit for him. The whole dang album was a hit. He was rolling. That was about the early sixties. I was really pleased that I had seen him develop all the way. And he just surpassed me, I'll tell you that. He got to be a fantastic writer. "King of the Road" I think is one of the best-put-together songs you'll ever find.

Long before Roger hit he was known in Nashville as the clown. Every day he had a different saying. He told me, "I don't get up until I've figured out something to say for the day." I could kind of identify with that. He was so clever with words. One of my favorites is [when] he was standing on the beach in California watching the most beautiful sunset and he says, "Just think what God could have done if he'd had money."

Lyle: Everyone refers to Roger as a genius. I don't think anyone could be taught to think the way he did, but I was wondering if you knew where his wit came from?

Sheb: I think from his mother. She was pretty clever. I didn't know her that well, but I believe it was from his mother. And he might have learned a little from me. He went back to the old barn where we used to sit and kibitz. I had said to him years before, "Roger, when I get famous this is the way my autograph is going to look," and I wrote on that old barn in big letters. And he took a saw and sawed that part out and took it to his Beverly Hills home after he got famous and moved to California. I was always flattered. Like I say, he was like a little brother.

One time I was going to teach him to be a cowboy, so we went out to the corral. We had big old milk pin calves, like half-grown bulls. I put a loose rope around one of those things and I put Roger on there and I said, "Hold on tight." Well, it threw him off. There was an old metal water trough there and Roger hit his head on that metal and it knocked him out cold as a wedge. He's laying there in the corral and I said, "Oh God, I've killed the kid." At about that time Mrs. Miller came out the front door and started down that way, so I grabbed my hat and poured water on his face. He comes sputtering up and was on his feet by the time she got down to the barn. But I sure thought I had killed him!

Somebody [once] asked him, "Did you do anything for your folks when you got rich?" and he said, "Ya, I paved the farm."

[Once] he was riding along on the back of this car, with some old boy and he's done doing shows and he's driving all night, and he woke up and said "Hey Carl, you get sleepy up there you just howler, that oughta keep you awake."

Lyle: Did you guys ever talk about co-writing together?

Sheb: No, I don't think we did. We never did write anything together. I've written a lot of crazy songs.

Lyle: Your crazy songs came out before Roger's did. That must have made an impact on him.

Sheb: Ya, it might have. I had "Purple People Eater" in 1958, which sold several million. He didn't really hit until a couple years after that, some time in the early sixties. I'm sure it meant something to him. If I did nothing else, it was that I showed him that a guy picking cotton in western Oklahoma could make it to Nashville and Hollywood or wherever the heck he wanted to go. I showed him that it could be done. When I was at that stage my dad said, "You'll never make it." Well, I guess I'm the type that says, "I'll show you, you old turkey." I did my best and had a very good career. That, I'm thankful for. A lot of luck. The best things that happened to me were not my preparation—meeting somebody, saying he's a nice guy and not knowing where it's going to lead. I had recorded once a couple of sessions for MGM when I was down in Texas. Then I went to California and a fellow I met down there [named] Jessie Kay. Well, he and I hit it off real well and we started recording. I was with them for twenty-seven years. That was MGM. Most people haven't stayed with a label for that long, but they just kept me around. Sometimes I wasn't hitting, but then I could come up with something that would sell a whole bunch for them.

Lyle: Did you ever do any singing together?

Sheb: Back when he was nine and I was nineteen, and we would ride that old horse together, ride out across them prairies, singing them songs. He had a nice voice when he was little kid. He was on pitch too. He had a sense of humor even back then.

Lyle: Are there any stories you could share from times you spent at the King of the Road Hotel?

Sheb: Well, it's too late for them to arrest us for smoking pot. We'd get silly once in a while.

Lyle: Did Roger hide his use of pills when he was around you?

Sheb: No, I knew he took them. He'd slip me one once in a while, but I never habitually took pills. I used to drink alcohol. He never liked to drink, he would just fly around on those pills.

Lyle: Did he talk to you about his pursuit in acting?

Sheb: Yes, I think he did some. He always wanted to be like a Will Rogers. Roger was humorous, but not like Will Rogers. He had something different, he was just so darn sharp. If you can capture that and get the audience hooked, you're going to sell a lot of books.

Lyle: Do you recall the last time that you saw him?

Sheb: I talked to him on the phone. He was down in Houston taking treatments for his cancer and I said, "Roger, I hear you're in trouble."

He said, "No, they did surgery, they got it all."

I said, "Great man, great."

Then a few weeks later he was gone. Certainly if there ever was a genius in the music business it was Roger Miller. Even when he was sacked out taking the pills he was still clever. Everyone had a great respect for him.

[Author's Note] Perhaps that knock on the head on the metal trough is what woke up that genius in Roger Miller. After the interview, Sheb asked what else I did. So I told him besides writing the book I'm a singer/songwriter, actor and I'm writing a screenplay. Well his eyes lit up and said that I did all the same things that he did. I asked him about his screenplay that he's been working on and the coolest thing happened; he got out of his chair and acted out the movie for me, playing all characters from the comedy Mexican western he wrote. It was one of the highlights of my life! Just a couple of weeks before he passed away I received this email: "I can hardly wait to see your book....I know it will be successful. Stay in touch. Your friend; Sheb Wooley." Unfortunately, he was right about the first part.

George Lindsay

Gordy Collins

Dr. George Lindsay is an actor best known for his role as "Goober Pyle" on The Andy Griffith Show. For twenty years, he was a regular on Hee Haw and has acted on many television shows and films including The Twilight Zone, The Alfred Hitchcock Hour, M*A*S*H, and Gunsmoke. He has an honorary doctorate from the University of North Alabama for his many humanitarian achievements.

George: Roger and I lived about five blocks apart in California. He had a black woman that cooked for him. Boy, she made the best cornbread and white beans in the world. I was eating up there all the time. We met at the CMA awards in Nashville and discovered that we lived five blocks apart in California, so I went over to see him one day and we became friends. I loved his singing and he liked my acting. Roger wanted to act and do serious roles in television. I'm so covered up with that Andy Griffith Show and Hee Haw that people don't know I did The Twilight Zone, The Rifleman, Gunsmoke, and Hitchcock and stuff. Roger really had a respect for my acting and I think he was the best damn singer there ever was. He's the fastest humorist in the business. He thought I was funny and I thought he was funny, so we spent a lot of time falling down at each other, laughing at each other. I'd just go by Roger's house and pick him up and we'd go eat lunch or we'd go drive out to Santa Barbara or someplace. He felt like he could come over to my house any time and I could come over to his house. He used to roller-skate in his backyard. I'd go up there and he'd be roller-skating.

Lyle: Did he talk to you about getting into acting?

George: No, you don't talk to another actor about that. They can't hire you.

Lyle: Are you a singer as well?

George: I made a lot of albums and singles and I still have them, mostly in the garage. I did have about an eighty thousand sale on one record I did. I did two musical and one comedy album for Capital, but it's pretty hard for an actor to become a singer and vice versa. I always thought Roger was the funniest guy in the world—next to me.

Buddy Emmons

Gordy Collins

Buddy Emmons is a legendary musician best known for his talents on pedal steel guitar. He is notorious in the country music industry as a real character. He's been a member of many famous bands including Roger Miller's, Ernest Tubb's, Ray Price's, Little Jimmy Dickens' and The Everly Brothers'. He's appeared on hundreds of songs as a studio musician for artists like Gram Parsons, Rick Nelson, The Carpenters, and Willie Nelson. I lucked out and met Buddy Emmons at one of his rare performances with Johnny Bush at the Midnight Jamboree in Nashville.

Lyle: How did you first start working with Roger?

Buddy: I was working a club in Printer's Alley and Roger came in. I was having a particularly hard time getting work then and he asked if I would be interested in playing bass for him. He asked me if I'd like to come out and see if I liked California first, so he flew me out there for a few days. I looked the place over and it felt pretty good, so I told him I'd be glad to and that was the end of it. I moved from Nashville to California in '68. I believe I came back here in '74.

We had the same sense of humor. We didn't have to say a whole lot of words to understand each other. We were very close and very parallel in our thinking. Once in a while he would call me up to see if I wanted to go to a club where he could get a chance to say hello and sit in for a couple of numbers. One time we ended up in north Hollywood somewhere and he was whipping out one liners every fifteen-twenty seconds, feeding off whatever the neighborhood gave him, reading signs, billboards and whatnot. We passed this one street called Moorpark and he said, "Moorpark spelt backwards is 'crap room.'" That same night we were going in a northerly direction and he saw a motel sign that said 'Heated Pools' and he said, "My pools aren't heated, but my suits are." Ridiculous stuff, but it was funny at the time.

Lyle: I'm really intrigued by the way some of the things he said seem to make no sense, but after you think about them for a while they make perfect sense.

Buddy: Yes, that was the thing that we thrived on. It appeared not to make any sense, just goofy things. It had some meat to it and hooks and depth. If you really thought of it, it was there.

Roger loved little gadgets, little mechanical things...locomotives, steamboats, things of that nature. We were in Australia one time and he had a steam engine that he bought in Sydney that was on a flat board. He had taken it up to his hotel suite. I walked in and he was playing with it.

Some of the good times we had were before he even got successful. His roots were very country. He was quite a Hank Williams fan. He came to town as a songwriter but he made his living for a while as a musician. He was drawing fifty dollars a week down at Tree Publishing. In the meantime he would take various sideman jobs. We became close back then because he loved musicians and he used to come to the jam sessions Jimmy Day and I would have. He'd sing a few and play a few, played fiddle. [One time] we were sitting on the front porch at my house in Madison, Tennessee, and neither one of us had a pot to piss in. We were kinda looking off into space and he said, "If I had your talent..." I can't remember what he said after that, but I was sitting there thinking the same thing. I thought, "If I had your talent I wouldn't fool with this guitar for one minute." Our minds ran parallel at that particular moment and it was pretty much that way ever since.

Back in the times when none of us had anything, Roger and a DJ named Ed Hamilton came over and they said, "Well, what do you got to eat?"

I said, "I don't have a thing. Maybe some cold water in the fridge."

So they said, "We'll be back."

They came back in about forty minutes. They both had long coats on at the time, and they pulled their coats open and started unloading canned goods and milk and stuff that they had walked out of the store with. So we all had a nice meal that night.

Roger was into Lear jets while I was working with him. Him and Glen Campbell and myself were up in his room in Vegas and he decided he wanted to go back to California to his neighborhood and shop. So he rented a Lear jet and we all piled in at about one in the morning and flew down to California, and he went on this shopping spree at one of his favorite places.

Lyle: Back in those days were Lear jets readily available?

Buddy: As far as I know they were. I heard of other people in the business using them. He always seemed to have access to one. I remember one story Carllile told me about Roger hiring a Lear one of those times when he wanted to take off in the middle of the night. He put the phone down after he had made the arrangements and fell asleep. It sat at the airport until somebody called and said he wasn't going to be there.

Lyle: He must have been very wealthy back in those days to afford those Lear jet ventures.

Buddy: Oh, ya. When we first went to his house he was opening the mail—I guess it was royalty check time—and he got a few checks and was reading them over and said, "Aw, seven thousand dollars... I didn't even know that was out there." It must have been one of his lighter tunes. Ya, he made a tremendous amount of money. He invested a million dollars one time in some glass manufacturing company as a write-off. The first year after he invested they made a profit. He wasn't happy about that. Well, he acted like he wasn't happy because he was doing it as a write-off and ended up making money off it.

Lyle: Did you keep in touch with Roger later in his career?

Buddy: He would call me when he came to town. We went down to a hotel he was staying at one time and talked about the old days and the band. By that time our drummer, Marty Allred, had died, and the guitarist Thumbs Carllile. He looked at me with this somber look and said, "I guess it's just you and me." About a year or two later he called during Christmas and I had a week of family things going down here at the house and I couldn't get down to see him. But he told me he was in town to check on a lump in his throat. He more or less laughed it off. It wasn't long after that I heard he was gone. I could have seen him then and I regretted that, but you never know.

Fred Foster and Glenn Martin

Fred Foster started Monument Records, his own independent record label in Nashville and signed artists like Roy Orbison, Kris Kristofferson, Willie Nelson and Dolly Parton. Not bad for an independent label. He's the ultimate producer. Listen to those songs he did with Roy— they are masterpieces! I met Fred backstage at the Opry during the Musicians' Union's 100th anniversary concert. He invited me to his office, where I met him and his partner songwriter/musician/producer Glenn Martin. Glenn has written/co-written many hit songs including "(Is Anybody Going To) San Antoine" and "If We're Not Back In Love By Monday."

Fred: Roger was such a humorous guy. If you ever notice people who are really funny, even though they may be heavily talented in other areas, they don't get the recognition in the area that they deserve. For example, look at Dudley Moore. He was an excellent pianist but nobody ever paid much attention to his music. Roger was always right in your face with his humor, and [because of that] I think most people didn't realize the depth of this talent. That's sad. He was such a brilliant writer. The way he could turn phrases... The first song I ever recorded of his, I did with Rusty Draper. It was called "You Don't Want My Love." [*Sings the first verse of "In The Summertime"*]. In that one line he captured all those colors and painted the picture of summertime. It was amazing.

We had a party one time out on the West Coast. I was out there to do some recording. I ran into Roger. Gene Autry owned the old Continental Hotel then, and that's where most of the music people stayed and that's where I was staying. I was also out there to rehearse Robert Mitchum. We did an album on him, had a couple of hits on that, oddly enough. Roger said that we needed to go out and have some fun. He had all these pills of course and I never had taken any, but shoot, four days later we're still roarin' around L.A.

[That night] Roger said, "We gotta quit worrying about songs. The real money is in commercials. Let's write a hit commercial."

I said, "Okay, I'm game. What do you want to write it about?"

"We gotta pick a big company, you know, one that's got a lot of money. We can't go with a little company. Think of a big company."

I was standing at the window looking out and this huge Ford truck drove by and I said, "How about Ford?"

"Fantastic! Let's write one for Ford."

We worked on that thing a day and a night, and it was to the point I had forgotten what we were trying to do. I wasn't quite myself. So finally I said, "Why are we here?"

"We're writing a hit commercial."

"Oh, yeah."

In desperation more or less we had our legal pads out that we had been writing on, and they were just covered up with scribbling. So I wrote F-O-U-R-D, and I held it up to him and he said, "I don't know what it is but I love it. What is it?"

"That's you in a Ford."

"We've done it! I'm calling J. Walter Thompson," and he tried for two hours to get somebody at J. Walter Thompson. We never did do anything with that.

Lyle: Were you hanging out with him in Nashville at all?

Fred: Yes, we would go out. He didn't eat much, of course, but we'd talk and tell stories. He loved telling stories, he loved the history of the business, and I was sort of a history buff. He knew a lot. He could tell you a lot about Bill Monroe, for example, the Carter family. He'd ask me a lot of questions or tell me a story about Grandpa Jones. He loved Grandpa. Grandpa was an amazing human being and he thought the world of Roger, too. He thought Roger was very clever in the way he talked. "He's dead clever, ain't he?"

He also hung out with Kris Kristofferson a lot. I had just started Kris' first album for Monument—this was like '67—and I had picked four songs of Kris' that I thought were potential singles: "Me and Bobby McGee," "Sunday Morning Coming Down," "Help Me Make It Through the Night." In the midst of working on this album I signed Kris for what in those days was a very healthy draw. Well, during the process of doing this album I went in for my annual physical and they did the rectal exam and found a little growth. They said that this is not good, it may be nothing but it may be something, you can't leave it alone, it's got to come out. This is about two inches up the rectal tract. So the doctor operated on me and took a plug out of me the size of a silver dollar. "Just to be safe," he said. God, and they packed me with a roll of gauze the size of an ear of corn, and it had all this medication on it that I was allergic to. I had a hell of a time. I was in bed for about three weeks. The only way I could survive was on a hot bath, a 'sitz' bath they call it. About every fifteen minutes I'd sit in it. Otherwise, I'd be climbing the wall.

So Kris walked into my bedroom one day at my house and he said, "Man, I feel pretty good. I'm going to make some of your money back."

I said, "Oh, how's that?"

"Roger Miller has just cut 'Me and Bobby McGee,' Ray Stevens has done 'Sunday Morning Coming Down,' and Sammi Smith has done 'Help Me Make It Through the Night.' "

I just stopped him and said, "What are you doing?! Those were *your* singles!"

"Oh, no, these people will sell a lot of records and you'll make all your money back."

"Yeah, but how could you do that to me? Me, in the bed sick."

He was so crushed because he thought he was doing me a favor. Roger cut the first record on "Me and Bobby McGee."

Lyle: I didn't realize that you produced Kris' stuff.

Fred: Yes. I also had Roy Orbison, and we had that long string of hits. Roger loved him. He said, "How in the hell can he do that?" and I said, "I don't know. I just don't know," because Roy said he couldn't at first. He'd hit any high note in falsetto. That worked okay until we got up to "Running Scared," and I had eight voices, twelve strings, four horns and a full rhythm section. It didn't have any repeats of any kind, no chorus, no nothing. It just started [down here] and went up, and the last note is a G above high C. Well, we only had two tracks to work with in those days, so there was no way to isolate the voice or do any punching in or overdubs. You couldn't do it. It was mixed as you went. When we got up to those high notes, particularly the last one, he just disappeared. The falsetto voice got lost in this cacophony of sound we had going. I went up to him and said, "Roy, you're going to have to hit that note, at least that last one, in full voice."

He said, "I can't do that, man."

"Then we're going to have to change the arrangement," and we'd spent three weeks working on the arrangement.

He said, "Oh, man, I love the arrangement."

"So do I, but it won't work."

"God, I can't do that, man, it's going to be awful."

"Why don't you try it once? If it's awful then we'll just do something else. Nobody will ever hear it but us."

He said, "Well, Okay."

I forgot to tell the musicians that we were going to go for that, and it was obvious sixteen bars into the song that this was a magic take. Everything was just breathing, it was alive! I thought, "Oh, God, please." He hit that last note right in the middle, dead center, it was like an explosion, musicians came up out of their chairs, but fortunately they kept playing. After that he never had a problem hitting any note he wanted to hit. There was no effort. Linda Ronstadt asked me one time, "What kind of tricks were you using on him to get those high notes?"

I said, "I'm not using any."

"Well, you don't have to tell me if you don't want to."

"But I've told you."

So then Roy and I were out in L.A. one time and ran into Emmylou Harris. She invited us up to her house that night for a party, and Linda came and saw Roy and just freaked. Linda said, "Now, I'm going to ask you because Fred wouldn't tell me: what kind of trick are you using audio-wise to get those high notes?"

Roy looked at her and said, "What trick do you mean?"

"Well, you know you're not hitting those notes."

He said, "Well, yeah."

"I don't believe you," she said. Emmylou just hands him that big Gibson guitar with the rose on it and says, "Roy, would you sing one?"

Roy said, "Well, okay."

Sitting on the sofa he sang "Crying," and he hit those high notes with no effort whatsoever. I thought Linda was going to die! She said, "That's the most amazing thing I've ever seen!"

Roger used to say, "I wish I knew how he did that," and I would say, "Well, a lot of people do, I think."

Lyle: Did Roy and Roger ever meet?

Fred: Yes. I was not around any time they were together, but I know they met, because Roy talked about him quite a bit. He just loved his work and he was a big fan. He loved Roger's writing.

Lyle: Roy always struck me as a laid-back kind of a guy.

Fred: He was. Roy had all these tragedies in his life. His wife was killed and two of his three children were burned to death in a fire. I asked him one time, I said, "I have no idea how you can bear up under all that." And he said, "Well, the trick is this: when you have great things happen to you, you don't get too high, and when bad things happen you don't get too low. You just sorta try to stay even if you can." And that's how he handled it.

Lyle: Did they rebuild the house after it burned down?

Fred: No. It was next door to Johnny Cash's house. John went to Roy—and I don't know the exact particulars of this, because Roy told me but it's cloudy because it's been so long, but it was something like—"What are you going to do with that property? Are you going to rebuild?"

Roy said, "No."

"Would you sell it to me then? Because it joins my property."

"On one condition: You plant an orchard on it and you give me the first fruit."

"You got a deal."

So John fenced it in with this beautiful log fence and he planted an orchard and gave Roy the first fruits.

Glenn: I was writing for Tree Publishing for about fifteen years and Roger was always around. He was the quickest person I ever knew with comebacks. Hank Cochran and I were out partying one night and got to kicking around ideas. We got this great idea we're going to start a fire department in Brentwood and you have to be a member to have this fire department protect your home. We would come and put your house out with Puree water. We need a little bit of money for investment, so we said, "Let's call Roger." We called Roger in the middle of the night and said, "Roger, we have this great idea, man. We're going to start a fire department and put your house out with Puree water." And he said, "Damn, that's a great idea, but I wish you would have called me yesterday. I just invested all my money in a pearl mine."

[I spent well over an hour with the guys and we got into chatting about the state of country music...]

Fred: You know, this is the only business I know of where they just throw away the experienced people. I don't understand it. It's the only business I know of that turns its back on the achievers. General George S. Patton said one time, "Give me an army of men forty years of age and up and I can conquer the world in six months. They won't make mistakes."

Lyle: I agree. I can't even listen to the radio any more.

Fred: You can't listen to that crap.

Glenn: You go back, you had an artist and their music. You got Willie and his music, Merle Haggard and his music. Now we just have artists and songs. Where are we going to be twenty years from now?

Fred: The local union office, the American Federation of Musicians, was one hundred years old in October, so we did this big show. Somebody asked Bergen White, who was an arranger and did the Orbison stuff, "I wonder what they're going to be playing a hundred years from now if they have another one of these." And Bergen said, "These same songs."

Roger was just a great buddy, I loved to hang out with him, I was really sad when he moved away, then Kris moved away, and I went "Waylon, everybody's leaving me." Then Roy died...shoot. So, Waylon and I used to hang out some, then he goes away... Harlan Howard and I used to hang out—then he was gone. Harlan, he really loved Roger. All in all, it's safe to say there will never be another Roger Miller, not even close.

Kris
Kristofferson

Gordy Collins

Kris Kristofferson is probably the most successful crossover musician-to-actor in history. He's as cool today as he ever was. Kris has played some amazing roles on screen (A Star is Born, Blade, Planet of the Apes) and has written unbelievable standards like, "For the Good Times", "Lovin' Her Was Easier", "Help Me Make It Through the Night" and "Me and Bobby McGee" (co-written with Fred Foster).

Kris: Roger was a guy that I was going to get to know. I had been singing his songs in the army over in Germany and I just felt like a kindred spirit. I first heard Roger when I was flying a helicopter. I thought, *'There's another one'*. If he can get away with that stuff like "Dang Me." "Dang Me" was so autobiographical for me at the time, I'm sure that it put it in my head to go to Nashville. I remember I went to the Pentagon to get out of the army 'cause I'd already done my time, but they wanted me to go to my next assignment and I was getting a lot of static from them. I didn't know anything about the big build-up that was coming in Vietnam. This was back in 1965. All of a sudden I saw the name of this colonel that I had known from years ago when I was in boot camp and he had been a captain there. I said, "Can I talk to Colonel Apt?"

And the guy that was giving me all the trouble said, "Yes. Talk to Colonel Apt."

Apt says, "Kristofferson, boy genius, what are you doing still in the army?"

I said, "I'm trying to get out. I want to go to Nashville and be a songwriter."

He said, "Good. You could be another Roger Williams."

He said Roger Williams, but he meant Roger Miller. I said, "That's exactly what I want to be." And it was.

Everybody in Nashville, when I got there, was trying to write like him. Most imitators pick up the worst stuff and beat it to death, so you had a lot of nonsense songs. Roger was responsible for making country music cool to the pop music world. It was a brand new thing to get that kind of respect.

The first time I ever actually met Roger was in an all-night café, where people that were on the Opry used to hang out. He had just won five Grammys. I was walking up there with Marijohn Wilkin and Roger Schutt, who they called "Captain Midnight". Captain Midnight just looked in there and said, "There's Roger sitting all by himself celebrating his five Grammys." And by God it was Roger Miller! They both knew him, I didn't know him then, and we sat down with him. He was all alone on the night he had won. At the time he was the hottest thing in music and I was a janitor at Columbia Recording Studios. He came in on a Saturday to record. They flew him in on a jet. I volunteered to work that day just so I could meet him. I remember when the engineer, or Buddy Killen, said, "This is Kris Kristofferson," Roger said, "What's he pissed off about?" I think I was the only guy there that realized he was referring to what my name sounded like. They all looked confused. He never did cut anything that day. He was pretty scattered at the time, calling his airplane on his cell phone.

One of the funniest things I remember before he was my friend... I was down at Printer's Alley one night when Mel Tillis was performing and Roger Miller was in the audience. He was in town for something. Some drunk guy in the audience kept yelling, "We want Roger Miller!" And Mel was trying to sing up there. Finally Roger goes over and says, "You want Roger Miller? You got him!" And he dove across the table at that guy, grabbed him around the shirt, around the neck, and the guy got up and he was huge! He never stopped getting up! I ran over there 'cause I thought the guy was going to kill him, and I'm holding them apart and I was saying to the big guy, "Listen, he didn't mean anything. This is Roger Miller, you know."

The guy looks down at me and says, "Well, what are you going to do about it little man?"

And I looked around and Roger was gone! He was already out the door and had split. I was sitting there holding the remains of this guy, this pissed-off fan. But I got away with my life.

Lyle: Did Roger ever bring up him taking off from that fight?

Kris: No, never. And it wasn't really a fight I was just sort of separating them and got stuck and it looked stupid when he left. I don't know if he even remembered it.

Roger was so much fun to be around. Actually, I think he was responsible for maybe half of the funny jokes that are told. They just bubbled out of his brain. I can remember him coming up to me and saying, "I guess it's true what they say about a man getting to look like his pets. My neighbor just chewed me out for shitting in his yard." He'd say things like he was so high he could go duck hunting with a rake. David Huddleston, the actor, told me that when he first met Roger he said, "Who makes your toupees and why does he make them so thin?" And David's bald!

Roger said a lot of really funny things and out of respect for his relatives I'm not gonna say them all. He was just such a bright spirit. I think he's right up there with Mark Twain and Steven Foster, real American originals. We got to be very close friends. As a matter of fact, he is a distant cousin of mine through some kind of marriage in Texas. Mary Miller was the one that told me about it. It pleases me to even think that we would be related. There was a time when I thought we looked alike, back when I was in the Army and he had short hair, and then later on again we looked alike again. He grew a beard after I did.

I remember back when Johnny Cash had his TV variety show and Roger was on it, I called up Mickey Newbury one day and he said, "How quick can you get down here? Roger wants to fly us back to L.A." Roger had to go back from Nashville to L.A. to be on some TV program, *Daniel Boone* or something. He wanted us to fly along and pitch him songs because he was going to record when he came back. I just about broke my neck getting to the hotel. We got into the car with Roger and had the craziest ride to the airport I've ever seen. He literally was riding on the sidewalks! We made it to the plane, but I don't know how we ever did. He flew us out there first class and we spent like three or four days, Mickey Newbury and I, and he never listened to a song! He would go do the work on the TV show and then go to bed.

I said, "Well, Mickey, this was a great trip, but what was it for?"

On the last day, right before we were going back on the plane to Nashville, Roger said, "Mickey tells me you got a great song called 'Bobby McGee.'" He made me sing it to him, and he cut it! And he cut two other ones as well. It was like having Bob Dylan do it, to have Roger cut it... I mean, you have to understand that he was huge. I was singing his songs over there in clubs in Germany in the army before I ever came to Nashville, and when I got there he was the guy that everyone wanted to be. To end up being his friend and very close to him was really something. I've been lucky that way. I've been able to meet some of my real heroes and be close friends with them, like Muhammad Ali, Willie Nelson and Johnny Cash.

Lyle: Did you ever talk to Roger about the art of songwriting?

Kris: Not really. I can remember one night him and Willie and I were trying to write a song together. Can you imagine three more fertile imaginations? All night we didn't come up with nothing! We ended up with one line! I can remember one time he had a great version of a song I wrote called "Loving Her Was Easier," and he wanted to put it out. As soon as he did—it was back when my first album was kicking up some dust—Fred Foster put it out for me. I called up Roger and said, "Jesus, man, I'm sorry." And he said, "Listen, you're just finding out what the record business is like." It was the absolute truth. Time moves along all by itself.

You couldn't help but learn from him about songwriting, about words, about alliteration and levels of meaning that he would pile on. He had so many different levels that you could appreciate his songs at. You can't learn that little spirit of humor he had. That's something he was just born with, like a songbird or something.

Lyle: It appeared that Roger wasn't all that lucky with some of his releases. He'd cut songs like "Honey" or "Me and Bobby McGee," and shortly after someone would have a huge hit on the same song. I believe Janis Joplin's version came out after his.

Kris: Oh yeah, that's where she learned it from.

Lyle: Did Janis and Roger ever hang out together?

Kris: No, his hair was too short.

Lyle: I know Roger was interested in getting into the movies. Did he ever talk to you about that at all?

Kris: Just the fact that's it's very difficult when it's not up to you whether you work or not.

Lyle: Did he ever ask you how you got your acting career going?

Kris: No, I just lucked into it. It either happens at that time or it doesn't. At the time when I started performing it happened to be at the Troubadour in

L.A., where all these movie people were, and it happened to go over very well. I think they were just hungry at that time. It was a little past the peak of Roger's popularity. He halfway got back into going around to some of those little clubs I was working, like the Troubadour, but he really didn't like it, I don't think. Then he got involved in writing the musical *Big River.*

Lyle: Did you hang out with Roger in Las Vegas at all?

Kris: He invited me there when "Bobby McGee" first came out. But again, this is when Roger was cleaning up his act and I didn't know anything about performing at the time, not realizing that it takes a lot of energy. So he would do his shows and then he'd go to bed and sleep until it's time to do the next one, which is exactly what I would do years later. But for me being there at the time, it was like, "Well, what the hell do I do now?"

Lyle: You're one of the first people I've heard mention that Roger slept.

Kris: This was when he was resting up after about a decade of furious burning.

Lyle: Did you hang with him at the King of the Road Hotel?

Kris: Yeah. I can remember back to when he was building it. He was walking around the foundations of it like it was Fountainhead or something. He was building this big building and I'm thinking, "Why the hell does Roger Miller, who is the greatest songwriter in the world, want to own a hotel?" Steven Brooden, my guitar player, said it was the best hotel ever because it was full of pickers. I can remember hearing Merle Haggard and Charlie Rich, everybody up there.

Lyle: Is there anything you could tell me about Roger that most people wouldn't know?

Kris: I know when he was living alone he had a television set on in every room with no sound on. Just to keep him company, I guess. That was when he was between families. The main thing about Roger that was different from everybody was that humor, and he had this funny little way of looking at everything. He would put together his songs with this great energy, almost with a Shakespearean love of the language, but with the wild original wacky humor that nobody else had.

The last time I saw him was very rough. I remember he was close to dying. His hair was all gone from chemotherapy. I walked in and he barely was awake. I said, "Geez, they told me you were sick, you know." He kind of laughed but he was really hard put to pay attention to anybody else.

Lyle: Did you ever cut any of his songs?

Kris: No. It would be like cutting Mickey Newbury songs. I don't want to hear me doing them, I want to hear them. There are songs that I've cut by other people, but not many—Billy Joe Shaver, John Prine. To me, having Roger Miller cut my songs was like the way I felt when Bob Dylan cut a song of mine. I probably wouldn't do one of their songs but I sure was thrilled when they cut mine. Talk about a guy that didn't get his flowers… Mickey is so respected among songwriters but never really was a big star. An absolutely great singer, songwriter, musician.

Lyle: Are you still writing songs?

Kris: Yeah, but much more slowly.

Lyle: Why is that?

Kris: I'm way out of the loop. I don't feel an urgency to record because the last couple of things that I've made haven't been marketed. I'm pretty happy with my family out here [in Hawaii] right now.

Lyle: Sheb Wooley wanted me to send his best to you.

Kris: I love Sheb Wooley. He's one of the first guys who ever cut a song of mine. It was a terrible song called "The Sun Also Rises." Cowboy Jack Clement recorded him on it. Sheb Wooley is a neat guy, really a good man.

Lyle: I've always loved the story about you getting a song to Johnny Cash in your helicopter.

Kris: That's true. I had already been his janitor for almost two years and I had pitched him every song that I ever wrote and he knew who I was. He was good to me in those days. I would never have done it before I knew him. I was lucky he didn't shoot me!

Lyle: I was wondering how you got that helicopter in his yard. It's not a big piece of land.

Kris: Back then the lawn went right up over the house, kind of stretched over the house. I don't think I actually landed on the house but I did land right up there above it. And I wasn't carrying a beer. He described it one time as me getting out of the helicopter with a beer in one hand and a tape in the other. He often saw me with a beer, but never in a helicopter.

Lyle: After Roger cut "Me and Bobby McGee," did you plug any more songs to him?

Kris: Yeah, and he cut some. He cut "Darby's Castle"—he did a great version of that—and also "Best of All Possible Worlds." He was perfect at it.

A lot of the times that we spent together we were higher than a kite. I will always be grateful though, for the times that I spent with him because they were always spent laughing.

Jimmy Snyder and
Gordy Collins

J immy Snyder is a singer/songwriter in Nashville who has been around
for many years. Everyone seems to know him and he seems to know
everyone. I'm told he is partially responsible for Tim McGraw's success.
Jimmy's roommate, Gordy Collins, is a former member of the sixties country
act Collins Coins and is currently a photographer in the Nashville music
scene.

Lyle: How did you first get to know Roger?

Jimmy: Mae Axton, she's the one that introduced me. I was playing the
Palomino Club and she brought him in there and introduced me. It had to
be between '66/'67. [Later] I was playing in Sacramento and Thumbs Carllile
called me and said, "Hey, me and Roger want to go fishing."

I said, "Cool, man. When you want to come down?"

"How about Sunday?"

"Fine."

He got down there about six in the morning and we started loading the
station wagon, and Roger said to Thumbs, "Thumbs, you're gonna be
pissed off."

"What now, Roger?"

"I've got an appointment with my business managers at one o'clock. I'm
not going to be able to go fishing. I forgot all about it."

Thumbs said, "Ah, man."

I said to Thumbs, "Why don't you just go fishing and I'll take Roger back to
San Francisco?" which was only 125 miles from Sacramento. Driving back
to Frisco I said, "I better pull over here and get some gas."

Roger said, "Can you buy me a Coke? Would you believe that I'm a
millionaire and I haven't even got a dollar on me? Look at this," and he
pulled his billfold out and about twenty or thirty credit cards folded out. He
said, "That's all I got, but I'll buy you some gas if you buy me a Coke."

So I bought him a Coke. Every ten or fifteen minutes on the way up there
he'd reach into his coat and get a couple of those pills. He had a flat-top

guitar in the back seat and he'd grab that every once in awhile and sing a few things, then he'd kind of pass out for a few minutes and close his eyes, and [then] get kind of awake and reach back there in his coat and get another couple of pills.

I hung with him all day and took a little nap when he had his meeting. That was on a Sunday and I stayed over 'til the next night. Thumbs caught a ride back. That was on a Monday night at the Fairmont Hotel in San Francisco. That particular night Roger was doing his show, and all these people were dressed in tuxes and the gals had gowns on and jewelry and diamonds and pearls and everything. Roger sang his songs, "Husbands and Wives" and "Chug-a-Lug." I think the public just went, "Who is this nut?" They had to go see who it was. He got a standing ovation on "Orange Blossom Special," and it pissed him off because "Orange Blossom Special" got a standing ovation and his songs didn't.

He didn't care too much for that high-class crowd in San Francisco, and San Francisco was not ready for Roger Miller, especially the Fairmont Hotel. But he had them packed in there like sardines. We went up to the room and he ordered a six-pack of bottled Coke. The maitre d' brought it up to the room and he told him, "Just hang on, I want you to witness something." He pulled all the caps off the Coca-Cola, took the bottles and shook 'em, and he just sprayed the room—the fireplace, the curtains, the couch, the bed and everything! This maitre d' is just going, "Oh my god…" As soon as he got all the Coke out of the bottles and sprayed everything in the room Roger said, "This is what I think of your goddamn San Francisco and I don't care if I ever play this mother again! You can go down there and bring your manager up and figure out what I owe you for this room and I'll pay you for it."

Thumbs Carllile was one of the greatest guitar players in the world, admired by Chet Atkins and people like that. Thumbs played with me for maybe a year, and then he left my group in '63 and went to work for Roger when "Dang Me" came out. They stopped through Billings [Montana] one night and I asked Thumbs, "Well, how's Roger to work for?" He said, "He's a beautiful dancer." Of course they were both nuts anyway, taking those pills. Those L.A. turnarounds is what they called that.

One time, at the Fairmont Hotel, the door was about a third cracked open and Thumbs walked in the room. Roger had the window open and he was standing out there [on the ledge]. Thumbs said, "Roger, what are you doing?"

Roger said, "Well, it's a nice day out here in San Francisco. I just thought I'd fly around and look at the city."

Thumbs grabbed him by the shirt and said, "Oh come on, Roger, you don't want to do that, come on," and pulled him in. I'm telling you what Thumbs told me. Thumbs don't lie about stuff like that.

Another story, in Hollywood there was a guy by the name of Sammy Jackson who was a disc jockey. Way back in the mid-sixties he had a TV series that got cancelled. One night Sammy Jackson, the star of the show, was in the Palomino and Roger made a joke out of it. He said, "Ha, ha! I heard your TV show got cancelled." Sammy knocked him right on his ass!

Gordy: Most of the time I was around Roger was long before he became famous. I wasn't around him a lot after that because he was always gone and we were gone too, doing our own thing. I was with Roger when he started to write "Dang Me." We were doing the Opry. It was the Saturday night after President Kennedy got killed and everybody was down, really down. In fact they had thought about canceling the Opry but back in those days people bought tickets a year in advance and they'd come from Europe and all over the world to see the show so they couldn't cancel. People would line up for three or four blocks to get in. My brother Denny and I were over at Tootsie's waiting for the next segment. Of course, Denny and I were too young to drink anyway so we were just drinking Cokes. Roger came back and he sat down with us and said, "Boys." Everybody was feeling kind of down. Roger was high but he was down. He was trying to bounce pills off of things into his mouth. Anyway, he said, "Boys, I'm sitting here high, ideas floating around. Ain't this a hell of a way to live?"

I said, "Roger, there's a song right there."

He said, "Hey you got that right, man." And that's when he started to write "Dang Me."

Of course I never heard it until we left here and went back to Billings, Montana, for a little bit. My brother Denny and I joined the Marine Corps. I was at the rifle range between San Diego and L.A. the first time I heard

"Dang Me." All of a sudden, boom! It was number one. I hadn't heard a radio or seen a newspaper or anything for weeks and weeks, so the very first thing I heard was "Dang Me." In the middle of the song he said, "One more time, motherfucker!" And it was on tape! It was released, so the first pressing of "Dang Me" had it on there. You could barely hear it but you could. When the song became number one they had to recall what they had out there and mix it out and re-release the singles. That was on the master: "One more time, motherfucker!"

Jimmy: I heard it too. Gordy pointed it out to me. I couldn't believe it. It was on the jukebox when I heard it.

Just like Buddy Killen said: He'd come up with a one-liner and you'd hear it on the radio a month later like, "Home is where I hang my head," instead of hat.

Gordy: Roger was a prolific writer. Ideas just came to him. One time he was on tour with somebody before he was a mega star himself, I think in a little hotel someplace like Wallace, Idaho. He wrote some song on a wall. He'd stand on the bed because he couldn't find no paper and ideas were hitting him, and he wrote the whole damn song on the wall of the hotel.

In later years Jimmy Day was ill and lost a lot of weight. Somebody asked Roger if he had seen him lately and Roger said "No, why?".

"He lost so much weight you'd hardly recognize him."

Roger said "Come to think of it, maybe I did".

Jimmy: Between '59 and '60 I was playing the Palomino Club. A few months after I was introduced to Roger, he came in one night. They had hamburgers and stuff like that and he said, "Snyder, you got a bar tab?"

"Yeah."

"Man, I'm a little low on cash. Andy Williams just recorded one of my songs and I'll have some residuals in a few days. Is it okay if I get a couple of hamburgers?"

I said, "Yeah, that's cool."

It was on like a Monday. Well, I noticed Roger in there about every other night. When I got paid that weekend I owed the bar $30, and I was making about $150 at that time. He drank and ate on my tab all week long! I never did ask him about it 'cause we were buddies. 'Til this day he hasn't paid me.

I got a call from Grant Boatwright—he was a friend of Roger's, a songwriter. At the Spence Manor on Music Row, Grant [got Roger's friends to do] a personal video to Roger while he was in the hospital there in Santa Monica. I brought that [old story] to Roger's attention that day. I said, "Hey man, what are you doing in the hospital? You better get out of that hospital and come back here and see me. And by the way, in 1959, when Andy Williams cut that song of yours, you drank and ate hamburgers on my bar tab and you still haven't paid me. I'm not really worried about that, just get well!"

When he died, I went down to the memorial service at the Opry house and said hi to Mary. I said, "I just wanted to ask you a simple little question."

She's crying and everything and she said, "What's that Jimmy?"

"Did Roger ever see my video?"

"Yeah, he did, and he just laughed." He thought it was a joke!

Lyle: Do you have any favorite one-liners that come to mind?

Gordy: There were so many of them it was incredible. Thumbs was the same way. Thumbs would walk up to you and put his nose right against yours and just stare you in the face and say, "Who's the fastest guitar player in the world and why am I?"

One thing Roger used to say that people now use in movies is: "No matter where you go, there you are."

Jimmy: Clint Black wrote a song with that title. That's probably where he got it, whether or not he'd admit it.

Jeannie Seely

J *eannie Seely is a Grand Ole Opry legend; an Opry member since 1967. Along with Jack Green, she was one of the first country acts to work the Rooftop Lounge at the King of the Road Hotel.*

Jeannie: There was always laughter around Roger, and he laughed at himself and would show you that it's okay to laugh at yourself. He was one of my heroes in this business and certainly an inspiration. I feel so fortunate to have known one of the most brilliant minds of our time, and I truly mean that. It often hits me that there's no telling what else Roger could have done if we'd been able to keep him longer.

Most of the time that I spent with Roger was early in our careers in the early sixties in California. I was living out there and Roger moved out there and rented Lee Hazlewood's guesthouse. Roger called me when he first moved into Lee's guesthouse, to help him get settled. So I went over there and was trying to get his linens fixed up, stock his refrigerator and get everything put away. As a joke I tried to play on him, I short-sheeted his bed. Little did I know how seldom Roger went to bed! It turned out to be a joke on me because it was weeks before he ever noticed it. After I got through fixing up his place, I made a couple of quick stops on the way back to my apartment, and when I got there he was sitting on the step and said, "It's lonesome over there. I didn't want to stay." He came inside and went to the refrigerator and asked me, "What's to eat?"

I said, "Nothing. I spent all my time getting your fridge stocked up!"

One time he called me because there was no heat at the guesthouse he was renting. He said, "I am freezing to death. I need to buy a heater and I don't know a thing about heaters. Will you come with me?" So we went to the Broadway Department Store and I took him up to the housewares department, where all the heaters were. I told him to check them out because there were all kinds of shapes and sizes and then I went over to the next department. All of a sudden I heard this sales clerk say with obvious distaste, "May I help you, Sir?!!" I thought, 'Oh God, what's he doing?' So I went over there and Roger was on his hands and knees with a guitar pick strumming the rungs on the front of the heater! He looked up at me and said, "I want to buy a heater in the key of D."

Bob Moore

Gordy Collins

If the total number of recordings a musician plays on could determine status, then Bob Moore would be arguably the most famous session bass player in country music history. He's played on thousands of sessions with everyone from Roy Orbison to Elvis Presley to Roger Miller. He's the one playing the famous bass intro on "King of the Road."

Bob: Roger had a song written called "When Two Worlds Collide." One time he was saying somebody else's song had sold a hundred thousand [and he said] "I know I'll never sell a hundred thousand."

I said, "Well, I'll bet you that song right there sells a hundred thousand."

"Well, I'll bet you a hundred dollars it don't."

"Ok, you're on."

He come to me a few months after and brought me a hundred dollar bill, "That just crossed over a hundred thousand. I'm happy to pay this bet."

He called me one day and said, "Hey, let's go get a moustache."

"A what?"

"A moustache. That guy on *Laugh-In*, he's got a moustache. Let's go get us one. I found this place down here yesterday, the guy's gonna make us one." We went down the street to the store he had found and the guy gave us a moustache and we wore them around for three or four days.

He used to tell the story about where he was so poor they couldn't afford any clothes, so his Daddy bought him a ball cap and sat him in the window to look out the window so people would think he had clothes.

Manuel

Manuel is a Nashville clothing designer who has contributed a lot to the image of the music industry by designing clothing for dozens of superstars. Everyone from Bob Dylan, Gram Parsons, Johnny Cash, The Beatles to Aerosmith have worn his one-of-a kind designs.

Manuel: I remember one occasion he called me on the phone and said I should get immediately to Little Rock, Arkansas, because his suit didn't fit. I said, "You're kidding me. They always fit so don't give me that baloney!"

He said, "No you better get your butt over here in the morning."

I didn't want to come but he said I should really service that account, so I did. The minute I got to Little Rock it was slushy and cold and miserable. I said, "Why did you call me over here? What is wrong with the suit?"

"Nothing, you needed a vacation."

"A vacation to this place? Forget it."

"You're working too much. Come to the show."

"I'm so sleepy. All this getting on the plane so early in the morning and coming here."

"Don't worry. What you need is something to keep you awake."

"You're not giving me drugs, are you?"

"Never. We're friends, I'd never do that to you. This is just to keep you up for awhile."

"Ok, I'll take this but I tell you, you better not give me drugs of any kind."

"I wouldn't do that to you."

"Let me have a glass of water so I can take it."

"No, no what you need is a coffee with it."

I took this pill he gave me. The only thing that I remember was the next day Roger said, "It's time for you to go to the airport, man."

"What happened?"

"Oh, we had lots of fun. We had all the tequila in the world. I called you on stage and you came up there. It was so much fun. Everybody was laughing."

I said, "I'll be damned, man, I don't remember anything!"

Lyle: How did you start hanging out with him?

Manuel: Well, it was actually the opposite. It was him hanging with me because I was the guy in the shop and they'd all come and play music. I'm talking about Dennis Hopper and Peter Fonda and other people like that. That was when Peter Fonda and Dennis Hopper wanted to be musicians. Of course, they ended up being actors. When he hung out with me it was the Californian group of people—Willie and Charlie Rich and Glen Campbell, people like that. They were all kids at the time. They were kids to me, anyway. I keep telling everyone that I've been around since 1810. I mean, come on, I remember Johnny Cash being young, and Roger, and Glen was like a little kid.

Lyle: I think you look younger than all of those guys you mentioned.

Manuel: I know. I just took care of myself all the time.

Lyle: Did Roger tell you what style of clothing he wanted you to make him?

Manuel: He trusted me. He would say what he wanted but I don't give too much room to my clients to tell me what they want. I feel that I could do it for them. I just let them write their songs and sing their songs and I make my clothes. They write on paper and I write on clothes.

Courtesy of the Country Music Hall of Fame

Roger with Molly Bee on *The Jimmy Dean Show.*
Courtesy of Jimmy Dean

The Golden Door Knob Award given to Jimmy Dean by Roger.
Courtesy of Jimmy Dean

With Gail Davies in 1975.
Courtesy of Gail Davies

Roger with Bobby Goldsboro.
Courtesy of Bobby Goldsboro

Roger with Thumbs Carllile and Randy Hart.
Courtesy of Randy Hart

At the White House – July 20, 1976. From left: Patrick Patterson, road manager; Craig Fall, guitarist; Marc Durham, bassist; Dan Moss, manager; President Gerald Ford; Betty Ford; Roger; Mary Arnold [later Mary Miller], background vocalist; Steve Turner, drummer; Darlene Gronsky Smotherman, background vocalist; and Micheal Smotherman, pianist.
Courtesy of Marc Durham

With Buck Owens at the
Academy of Country Music
Awards.
Courtesy of Buck Owens

Roger and Gary Mule Deer.
Courtesy of Gary Mule Deer

Roger and Mary ride in the Easter Parade, Atlantic City.
Courtesy of Gary Mule Deer

Performing at Farm Aid in 1986.
Courtesy of Lee Rollag

Las Vegas Hilton –
1978.
Courtesy of Randy Hart

Roger in concert.
Courtesy of Gary Mule Deer

Poster for the Roger Miller Show.
Courtesy of J. Kitsalano

Roger had a reputation for taking
spontaneous and wild Lear jet ventures.
Courtesy of Randy Hart

Roger in Brisbane, Australia in 1981.
Courtesy of Randy Hart

In Australia with Danny Gatton and Shannon Ford.
Courtesy of Randy Hart

Performing with Danny Gatton and Lee Rollag at the San Diego Wild Animal Park in 1983.
Courtesy of Lee Rollag

Another singer bounces back from health crisis

Roger Miller: I've beaten cancer

Country music's "King of the Road" Roger Miller says he's beaten deadly throat cancer that he feared would kill him — and the gutsy star vows he'll soon be back on the road singing again!

Miller had to undergo weeks of grueling radiation therapy to win his battle. But he credits the love of his wife and children for pulling him through, close friends of the star told The ENQUIRER.

His harrowing ordeal began last year when the 56-year-old singer, whose hits include "Dang Me," and "England Swings" suddenly became hoarse.

By October, when his voice hadn't improved, the worried star went to see Dr. Robert Ossoff of Nashville's Vanderbilt University Medical Center — and was stunned to learn he had throat cancer.

The devastating disease, is every singer's worst nightmare.

cords and it was cancerous, I went numb."

Dr. Ossoff told the singer the tumor had been caught early and he was hopeful it could be successfully treated with radiation.

But Miller was terrified his life was over.

"I could see my career ending right there on the spot — having the radiation and then chemo and then surgery and nothing working," Miller confided to a pal.

But strengthened by his

Love of my wife & kids pulled me through, he says

furnace," he told the friend. "From that point on it just gets worse."

In the next two months Miller became weak as a baby, his throat became blistered and raw and he lost nearly 25 pounds.

Miller, who stayed in Nashville during his therapy, told his friend:

"There were times I felt like quitting and going back to my home in New Mexico. And at those times it was the thought of my dear wife Mary and my two precious

GREAT NEWS! Roger Miller is the happiest man in the world now

National Enquirer article from February 1992.

Courtesy of Gordy Collins

ROGER

MILLER

January 2, 1936 - October 25, 1992
★ ★ ★ ★ ★

The program cover from
Roger's memorial service at the
Ryman Auditorium in Nashville
November 9, 1992.
Courtesy of J. Kitsalano

Merle Kilgore

Gordy Collins

Beginning his music career as an artist with the likes of Hank Williams, Patsy Cline and Johnny Horton, Merle Kilgore is respected as an accomplished songwriter. He is best known for his hits "Wolverton Mountain", "Johnny Reb" and "Ring of Fire," which he co-wrote with June Carter Cash. He was full of amazing stories to tell including a ghost story about how his friend Johnny Horton contacted him from the other side. Merle worked as Hank Williams Jr.'s manager from 1964 until Merle's passing of cancer in February 2005.

Merle: I first met Roger in 1962 when I came to Nashville and he was struggling. I think he had one hit with Ray Price ["Invitation to the Blues"]. I remember he took me to his apartment and he had one BMI award on the wall. We became friends. We all hung around together—Hank Cochran, myself, Roger Miller, Mel Tillis—back in the early sixties. That was about the gist of the songwriters that had credibility. Later on Roger finally got some hits, and my agent packaged me up with Roger as his opening act [on the road]. We worked a lot of dates together. One time, in Boise, Idaho, Roger and I shared a suite. We had bedrooms that opened up into a central living room. I told Roger, "Man, I have to write a song for Carl Smith." Carl Smith was a big artist back then on Columbia Records. "I already gave him the title and I told him I'd have the song when I come back."

Roger said, "Well, I'm working on something else."

Marvin Rainwater was on the show. He had some hits in the past—"Gonna Find Me a Blue Bird," and a lot of other hits on MGM—and said, "Well, let's me and you write that song."

So we were up there in the suite after the show writing that song. There was a disc jockey, Marty Martin, that just begged me [to let him] hang around. I said, "Hey, man, we're not gonna party, we're gonna work tonight."

He said, "Man, it's so boring in Boise and I never get to see anybody from Nashville."

I said, "Okay, come on up."

"I'll just stay in the corner I won't say a word."

So Marvin Rainwater and I were writing that song "Why Can't You Feel Sorry For Me," and Roger busted out of his room into the central living room and said, "Hey, man! Listen to this song that I've been working on."

I said, "Roger, excuse me, Marv and I are writing a smash here for Carl Smith and we got to finish it. Do you mind?"

He said, "Oh, I'm sorry," and went back in there and worked some more on his song.

We had just barely finished the song and said, "Man, this is a country smash." It was a great song and Carl Smith did record the song, but Roger kept coming out, "Listen to this. I put a few more lines to it…"

I said, "I don't like train songs, and man, cigars stink. But hell I like the tune, it's a good melody."

Roger said, "Okay, well, I'm gonna finish working on it."

I said, "Hell yeah, you got something there."

Then we sang him our song and he said, "Man, that's a damn good country song."

"Yeah, we wrote a smash hit."

Well, he wrote a standard! When he opened the King of the Road Hotel, he made damn sure he flew me in to make sure I was there for the opening so he could tell everybody that story. And that disc jockey, Marty Martin, became Boxcar Willie!

Lyle: Did you guys ever talk about songwriting?

Merle: Constantly. He was prolific at writing ballads and little novelty stuff. I worked with Hank Williams when I was a kid and he is the king and god of all country music, so I always shared what Hank Williams told me: "You gotta have a title first and go from that. If somebody says something funny, write it down in a little notebook."

Roger said, "God, I've been doing that for years."

"Well, that's what I've been doing because the great songcrafter Hank Williams told me, and I asked him a million questions about writing songs."

Just about everything I told Roger he said, "That's the way I've been doing it and nobody told me to." Hank Sr. was just like triple Elvis in country music.

He died when he was 29 and that helped make him a legend. Right now, Hank Sr. still has a new album on the charts and he has four major television commercials…fifty years after his death!

[At the time of] my second million-seller, Roger said he had to take back a trailer full of stuff from his first wife and had to drive to Oklahoma to get rid of the stuff. He had this old car—this was '62—and he said, "Look, I need somebody to drive me to Little Rock."

I said, "Man, I'm waiting for my new song to come out called 'Wolverton Mountain.' "

"'Wolverton Mountain'? How do you spell that?"

"W-O-L-V-E-R-T-O-N. I'll ride with you."

"Hey, man, I'll buy your ticket back to Nashville," which was about $25 back then.

I rode with him and we heard "Wolverton Mountain" for the first time being played on the radio. Roger turned it up and we listened, and he said, "I don't like the way he says 'hon-ey,' damn it."

I said, "I was at that session and I thought he ruined the song when he said 'hon-ey.' "

"I think he did."

Well, the song sold about five or six million! It was number one country and top ten pop and Nat King Cole, Bing Crosby, Dean Martin—everybody recorded it. [Later] Roger said, "How could I have been so wrong?"

I said, "God, we both agreed about 'hon-ey,' but that's what sold the record."

I ran into him on the plane and he said that he'd take me home from the airport. Those planes had rubber tubing [old-fashioned earphones] when you'd listen to the stereo, and Roger took his with him off the plane. He had an old-time Mercedes convertible, the top was ripped. It was so loud and noisy, the engine and the wind blowing through the old top, that we couldn't carry on a conversation. Roger said, "Stick this in your ear," and we talked to each other in that rubber tubing going down the freeway!

I was playing with Johnny Cash in '63 and we were in Las Vegas, playing at the Mint. Johnny had lost his voice, so we called Roger to get him to come in and help fill out the show because Johnny had laryngitis so bad. Roger had started going with Anita Carter. When he got there, he had a big lump right between the eyes. I think it was Anita's ex-husband had come over there and gave him a shot. He got punched in the head! Roger said, "I can't go on."

Johnny said, "Yeah, you gotta go on, man. I can't talk."

"What about this egg?"

"Well, make a joke out of it."

One of the most tragic moments [I can remember with Roger] was when Luther Perkins, who played guitar for Johnny Cash all those years, went to sleep with a cigarette and got burned up. Roger and I went to the hospital and Johnny came out and said, "God, I don't think you guys want to see him. He's all burned up."

Roger said, "I do."

I said, "I don't. I don't want to see him burned up."

Roger went back there and he came back out and he had tears [in his eyes]. I had never seen him cry before. He said, "Man, I'm so glad you didn't go back there and see that. I'll never get that off my mind."

Roger never drank much because he always took pills, but he said, "Hey, Merle, let's go to your apartment. Do you got anything to drink?"

We went back and had a little drink, and he said, "Man, I really needed this and I don't even drink."

Lyle: Did Luther die shortly after that?

Merle: Yeah, he did.

Lyle: I know Roger was one of the first people to arrive at the site of the Patsy Cline plane crash. Did he ever talk to you about that experience?

Merle: No, not to me but I remember that he went down there. He said everything was in pieces. It hit him real hard.

Lyle: One of the few songs that my friends and I play full-blast whenever we hear it is "Ring of Fire."

Merle: Bless your heart, thank you. That's on an Applebee's commercial right now. Roger used to sing it as a parody. It was hilarious—something about Preparation H. He said he did it on stage a couple of times, just ad-libbed it. I don't think he ever wrote down most of his stuff.

The last time I saw him I won the first CMA Manager of the Year award. Roger was the emcee of the event. When he opened the envelope he screamed out, "Well, the old racehorse wins the race! *Finally*, he wins the race!" and announced my name. He was so excited.

Roger was just so full of spontaneity, so clever, that you felt good being around him… He had this suite at a hotel and a lot of entertainers stayed out there. We were having an eat and I had a lady friend with me. Roger kept saying, "I got a kidney problem," and kept going to the bathroom. "Let's go back to the suite and I'll sing some new stuff for you."

We went into the suite and he said, "Man, I gotta use the bathroom."

We could here him peeing and he peed for five minutes! We were saying to each other, "My God, what a bladder!"

Roger came out and said, "Did y'all hear me peeing in there?"

"Yeah, man, you got one hell of a bladder. It was about five minutes."

He went and showed us that he got the trashcan and filled it full of water before we went to eat. He had set us up! He was always doing things like that. If he'd get in a serious mood then he'd jump out of it because he didn't like to be like that. I never gave him an opportunity to have a pity party because I never got into the negatives.

Roger said, "I always like to be around you because you're always positive."

I said, "Yeah, man, fuck being negative." No matter what, you gotta think of the positive side.

Bobby Bare

Gordy Collins

In May of 2000, I got a chance to see legendary recording artist Bobby Bare in concert in Grand Forks, North Dakota. It was the most expensive concert I've ever been to in my life! A buddy and I drove from Winnipeg to North Dakota and just as we pulled into town, the motor on the used vehicle I had just bought privately blew up! We took a taxi and checked into a hotel right next to the auditorium. It turned out to be the hotel where Bobby was staying. I hunted Bobby down and he came over to the room to chat for a while. I'll never forget him walking into the room, slowly pulling out the chair, sitting down and putting his feet up on the table as he sipped a glass of water. He was the most laid-back guy I ever met. I don't even remember his facial expression changing at all. Bobby told me it would take a day to share his memories of Roger, so two years later I was in Nashville (with a new car) and visited the Bare's house on the lake in Hendersonville.

Bobby: I lived in California. I went out there in '52 or '53 and ran into a songwriter [who] used to work with Bob Wills, his name was Lee Ross. Lee said that he'd met a very talented young teenager from Oklahoma named Roger Miller. He said, "Look out for him." Then me and Harlan Howard, Buck Owens, Hank Cochran and all those guys, had a little fleet going out in California. Hank, Harlan and his wife, Jan, moved back here to Nashville. Harlan had a couple of hits like, "Heartaches by the Number." I'm just bumming around the country, and when I'd come around to Nashville I'd stay at their house. When they first moved here they just had a little house in Madison. The first time I ever saw Roger he was standing out in their front yard all by himself. He looked real lonely.

Roger always hit me as being kind of a sad person. So am I, so we immediately became friends. There was such a small clique at the time. There were only five great writers in town at the time who were having success, so everybody knew everybody and the only place they hung out was Tootsie's. A lot of times there wouldn't be anybody there but us.

I remember I was in town one day. I was living in California and I came to town, and we were up there at Tootsie's in the back. I was going to stay at

Roger's house. Him and Byron Binkley, 'Bink,' who was a TV producer, had a little condo or apartment somewhere out in West End, so I was going to stay at their house. Bink was gone somewhere. We were down at Tootsie's for two or three hours talking and I said, "I'm getting tired. I want to go to bed." I remember it was the first time I met Merle Kilgore. And Kilgore, the way he talks so loud, so abrasive and everything… I was tired and he was getting on my nerves. I said, "I gotta get away from that son of a bitch." Of course, I [grew to] love Kilgore after I got to know him and realized that's how he is. We went to Roger's house and I went to bed and Roger stayed up. I guess he loaded up on pills and he had to drive to Albuquerque. I remember he had glue and that fuzzy stuff and he was putting it on the doorknobs. I don't know why, but I guess just for something to do. Then he took off to Albuquerque, driving his nice Rambler.

Another time I had come to town, Roger was still married to his first wife. They had kids and lived across the Cumberland or somewhere. By then I was having hits and I was staying at the Downtowner, which was the only hotel in town. Songwriters and publishers would keep coming bringing songs, because I was in town recording. Anyway, I decided to go by Roger's house and rest. We got there and his wife was pissed at him because he'd been gone two or three days. I didn't get a whole lotta rest.

Lyle: I heard when you were around Roger you couldn't rest at all.

Bobby: No, you had to stay on your toes, be alert, and stay up forever. But I learnt early on to never say, "Well, I gotta go," or anything. You just kinda eased out. I'd always have a separate room when we were at a motel. I'd just kinda slowly go out the door and go to bed. I wouldn't say good night or none of that stuff, because you would get pulled back in.

Lyle: When you were having hits before Roger did, was he trying to plug songs to you at all?

Bobby: No, I don't think Roger ever plugged songs. I never caught him doing that. People would just hear them and say, "I want that." All he had to do was sit around and sing them. Actually, Roger had hits before anybody. He had that "In The Summertime." It was a medium hit but it was enough for him to book out. It was a great record. I think Chet cut that on him. Then he came to California when I was living out there. He'd come out there and book out and we'd hang out, go to the Palomino Club, because it was the only place to go.

I remember one night Willie was in town. Roger was working the Red Barrel, about a forty-minute drive up the freeway. Willie and I were supposed to meet him at the corner of the Hollywood Freeway and Sunset, so we went up there and Roger picked us up and we went to the Red Barrel. We're sitting around there and Roger would get up and sing. Some old boy just came up and pushed himself into a chair and sat down and wouldn't leave. I told the guy he was in somebody's seat but he wouldn't get up. Roger got up and got an arm lock on him and threw him out! Willie hopped up to watch Roger's back. This is all new to me, because this is Texas style. Oklahoma and Texas, that's what they did there. Roger threw him out. Roger was strong. Willie was right with him in case somebody wanted to jump in and help the guy, and I just sat there and watched. It was just like watching a show.

Lyle: Did you ever record any of his songs?

Bobby: I don't think I did. It was almost immediate in early '62 that I started having hits. Then Roger started having hits and he recorded everything he wrote. Up 'til then he had songs available, but once he started recording he was using them all. He had his hands full writing enough for himself. He was running like a dog everywhere.

Lyle: When I met up with you a few years ago, you mentioned you had a picture of Roger that would be great for this book.

Bobby: I wish [my wife] Jeannie could find that picture. It's of Roger with the black eye. He took the picture! Right after the Palomino Club we went over to my apartment over on Lexington. It wasn't very big, but we'd all wind up over there. This particular night it was me, Roger, Willie, Joe Allison, and Roger had a doozy. It was about two days old, so it was *there*. I think Sammy Jackson had popped him one.

I remember this one time we were working Madison, Wisconsin. It was me, Buck Owens and Roger, and Roger had just put his first band together, which was Thumbs on guitar, Bobby Dyson on bass and a drummer—I can't remember his name. This drummer didn't last very long and I'll tell you why. We had two shows to do and Buck had come in from New York and his band wasn't there, so Buck was using my band.

Buck wanted to go on first so he could make a flight to California. So Buck was on and Roger and I were standing by the curtain watching Buck and I asked Roger, "How do you like your new band?"

He said, "They're great. Thumbs is great, Bobby Dyson is a great bass man. But that fucking drummer can't play a lick. He drags, then he rushes…"

What we didn't realize was that the drummer was standing right behind us listening. It just devastated the drummer. He went next door and got drunk, and that was probably his last gig.

I said, "I think he heard that, Roger."

And Roger said, "Oh, shit," because he liked him as a person, he just couldn't play.

When he kicked those pills, his wife at the time had a big party for him at the King of the Road Hotel. We went to that. I think he'd been off them for nine months or something.

[At this point Mrs. Bare sat down and joined us.]

Jeannie: That was a giant party. Everyone showed up and the hotel really was beautiful. We're standing on the roof of the King of the Road, the most beautiful hotel at the time in Nashville, looking out over the city. And because they all go back as far as to who had fifty cents for the gas tank Roger said, "One song can build a hotel like this." So we went, "Yeah, wow. We have to put this in perspective, don't we?"

Lyle: I saw some press releases stating that he quit taking pills and I thought that was a little strange. But I didn't realize they actually had a celebration for him quitting pills.

Jeannie: Yes, it was his wife's idea. There was a specific party and everybody showed up.

Bobby: I remember Bobby Russell was there and he got real drunk. His wife [Vicki Lawrence] was the star of *The Carol Burnett Show* and she took him and laid him down on Roger's swinging bed.

Lyle: Did you guys ever chat about the music business at all?

Bobby: Yes, we used to earlier on. We used to come back here for what they called the DJ Convention, probably in '60, when nobody had a deal. We were all more or less broke. I remember me and Roger and Jerry Reed at the old Andrew Jackson Hotel. They had a balcony that ran all the way around the side, and me, Roger and Jerry were standing there watching all these country music fans and the stars come in and I distinctly remember, "Here comes Webb Pierce!" and the fans scream. And "Here comes Carl Smith!" or somebody, and they would scream. And we said, "Oh, one day that will be us." And so it was, it came to pass.

Lyle: I've seen your name for songwriting credits on some of your earlier albums.

Bobby: I used to write. I'd write and I'd write, then I would come to town and I'd call Roger, Willie and Waylon and everybody, and we'd meet at the old Andrew Jackson and get a room up there. Somehow we'd come up with a washtub and put ice in it and beer. We'd just sit there and have a guitar pull. I'd listen to Roger's songs and Willie's songs. Every time they'd sing one of their songs I'd eliminate one or two of mine in my mind. I wound up with one song I actually would sing out of that whole bunch. Shit, I was out-classed and I knew it.

Once you have a hit record, you're hard pressed to write, because you have to think positive to write songs and you have to be mostly alone to write, or at least I did. It's not possible if you were on the road 'cause you're never alone, you're never without pressure. You're just not in the frame of mind to write. And Roger, he could take a couple of pills on a long plane flight and write three songs.

Lyle: Did he ever pull any practical jokes on you?

Bobby: No, but I got him once. Roger was in real pain so I took him to the hospital. It was his gallstones. I had a couple of friends in from Michigan and they could do anything. One of them was an older guy and the other one was a disc jockey and also on TV up in Grand Rapids. So we went up to see Roger and I had one dress up like a preacher. We went in and he started giving Roger last rites and that freaked him out. He didn't know what to do about that. He thought he was dying! I knew he wasn't going to die.

If you want to see something real interesting, get Roger and Roy Clark on a roll and just sit back and watch that, because Clark, he is very quick, and with Roger it's just like a damn duel. It's kinda like a rap-off. Very talented. That was a real treat, him and Roger on a roll in some motel room. I mean everybody would sit back and watch that happen.

I was doing a movie once in Flagstaff in the summer of '64, and Roger was interested in movies so he hopped on a plane and flew out there for a couple of days to hang out with me. Roger showed up with the words to "Dang Me." He'd been hanging around with Dorsey Burnette and had written on this piece of cardboard, the stuff that's left in your shirt by the dry cleaners so your shirt won't crease. We were sitting around the room and he was singing this thing. It sounded to me like talking blues, but it was clever. Somehow he left in the middle of the night. He was gone 'cause that's the way he did it. I'd call his room and they'd say, "He's gone." But I had that cardboard with those lyrics on there until our house burnt down. The smoke gutted it out. The house over in Madison, not this one.

Lyle: I know you love to fish. Did you guys ever go fishing together?

Bobby: No, he was too nervous to fish. I took Waylon fishing. It was a joke! We had a lot of laughs, but Waylon didn't want to touch the fishing bait. It takes a certain type of person to go fishing. Roger probably would have been on speed, and speed and fishing don't mix.

Lyle: Is there anything about Roger that you could tell me that most people wouldn't know?

Bobby: Roger was very sad. You could see it in his eyes. I could. I could relate to it because I am too. And I can understand why because our backgrounds are kinda the same. We were bounced around a lot when we were kids, and there's a certain amount of sadness because you don't trust many people.

Lyle: Did you hang out with Shel Silverstein?

Bobby: Yes, more than you could imagine.

Lyle: Waylon was saying that Shel lived at the Playboy Mansion.

Bobby: Hefner got him an apartment there. I've gone myself to the one in Chicago to see Shel, and then when he moved up to the one out there in L.A. He had his own little apartment. Shel even took his son out there for New Year's. They'd go out there and hang out. Shel was a good friend. I miss him.

Lyle: I always saw a connection between Shel and Roger in their style of writing.

Bobby: I'm sure the connection you saw was the imagination, the creativity, the brilliance. It wasn't that they wrote alike, it's just that they saw things so differently from the normal person. If a normal person would see it like this, they would be watching it from over there somewhere. They were both so creative and there was no lines for them to cross over 'cause they didn't give a shit. Somebody would say, "You can't do that. They won't play it on the radio." It didn't make a difference, they would go ahead and write it anyway. That's what they had the same... I want to call it bravery or balls, but it was just unlimited creativity. They didn't put limits on themselves.

[At this point Bobby got up from the table and got himself some chewing tobacco]

Lyle: I was reading somewhere that chewing tobacco isn't good for you.

Bobby: Probably isn't. Nothing is good for you.

Lyle: Obviously Shel and Roger knew you were close friends with both of them. Did they ever comment on each other's work?

Bobby: There was a lot of respect there. I had them both on my TV show [*Bobby Bare and Friends* on TNN] separately. Roger had just finished the Broadway play. I asked him how he got it started and he said, "I just wrapped a rope around my bellybutton and pulled it." He sang a bunch of songs like, "Hand for the Hog." It was before it ever came out and we were talking about the soundtrack for the play. Whoever marketed that dropped the ball because that could have been a huge soundtrack. It could have been really big. Whoever they worked the distribution deal out with, they should have shot 'em.

Lyle: I'm a little surprised that more people don't know about *Big River.* Everyone knows *Cats* or *Rent.* But musically *Big River* blows them away.

Bobby: I went and saw it in New York. I couldn't imagine how it could hold my attention because I'm not a big fan of musicals, but it did. It was the songs that did it and the deliveries. It held up, and I wasn't prepared for it to hold up. I knew Roger was brilliant and I knew the songs that were in it. I would have much rather heard Roger standing up there singing 'em, until I got to see the play and I realized what they had done.

Lyle: How did Roger affect your life?

Bobby: He raised the bar. I mean, I thought I was pretty good then I realized that I was mediocre and had to kick it up a notch. I had to kick it up two notches. And that's what's important about being around really talented people. When you're growing, you have to know what you gotta do. He raised that bar way the hell up there. I mean, just spitting it out like a computer. He was one of the best love-song writers. A lot of love-song writers knew G, D and C. Harlan knew G, D and C. You get in a guitar pull with Roger, especially with Roger and Willie back at the Andrew Jackson… I got the full dose. They know which line is strong, they know dynamics, when to come down and all of those tricks. And they're both great guitar players. Roger was a really great musician, he could play anything. You hang out with people like that, you better get off your ass and do something. I knew real quick what great songs were, and what great songs were not. And I saw the delivery.

Lyle: I am just blown away by all the great songs that you have recorded. How did you get Shel Silverstein's songs first pitched to you?

Bobby: In '69 or '70 I covered Dr. Hook's "Sylvia's Mother." It charted and was a fairly good record. But I left RCA and went to Mercury for two years, and after the two years Chet wanted me to come back to RCA. I said, "You have too many producers over there and they confuse the shit out of me." At that time Chet had stopped producing. All that Elvis stuff would keep you up all night, and they had gone to sixteen-track recorders. Where normally Chet could do a whole album in one day, it was now taking months to record an album. He just quit producing. So he said, "Why don't you just produce your own records?"

I said, "OK, I'll do it."

So I went back and I did, and the first album I did had a hit single in it with a song that Billy Joe Shaver wrote called "Ride Me Down Easy." I immediately wanted to do an album of songs all written by a great Nashville writer. I figured it would be impossible for Harlan Howard or Hank Cochran or Roger or any great writer to write ten or twelve songs and not have less than a couple of big hits in it, so I went to all them. But back then singles were the thing. They all had what they considered to be a couple of hits, but the album freaked them out. You say, "I need twelve sides," and nobody responded. They were all geared for single records. Well, Shel called me Monday morning and says, "I got you an album."

I said, "Great! When can I hear it?"

He said, "Well, how about today?"

"How are we going to do that?"

"I'll hop on a plane and be there at three o'clock."

So he did. He was in Chicago and here he came. He came in the office and grabbed his guitar and he had this song "Lullabies, Legends and Lies." Well, in my mind that didn't sound like much of a hit song. Then he got down into it and got to singing "The Winner" and I got caught up in it, and it got so funny and outrageous. Shel was relentless with the way he writes. I got to laughing so hard that I had to make him quit once. Then he went through "The Soup Stone." I said, "I'll go in the studio and try it, a couple of sessions, and see how it goes."

So I did. I got Red Lane to play some acoustic guitar, and Larry Lennon on drums—good musicians over in Studio B—and I just sat down, because I figured it was like doing a demo or something. We did about four sides and goddamn it sounded good, so I said, "Yeah, let's do this." We did the whole album. That's how I got started with Shel. That was so much fun, and it was a big success. The first thing out was "Daddy What If" with Bobby Jr. Jerry Bradley said if he had known what I was doing, he would have stopped the album, because it was such a departure. Record companies want you to do the same thing over and over until your nose bleeds, then they kick you out, because you stopped selling because people already got that shit. But this was a total departure.

Lyle: It is an amazing album, somewhat of a concept album.

Bobby: It was a concept album. It turned out to be a double album. We didn't have anything pressed up. I had an acetate that I gave to a promotion guy in Atlanta. I said, "Listen to this and see if you hear any hit singles on it." Well, he listened to it and immediately took that cut with me and Bobby Jr. to WSB in Atlanta, which was the biggest station in the south at the time. And they played it and the damn phones lit up and all hell broke loose. They rushed the record out and then everybody was happy. If it wasn't for that song hitting in Atlanta they probably wouldn't have released it, because it wasn't what they were wanting from me.

Lyle: One of the songs you do that I think is just awesome is "Big Dupree."

Bobby: Yeah. Before Atlantic Records folded here in Nashville, we were in the middle of doing a Shel tribute album and I cut Jerry Reed on that. It was great.

Lyle: Was it released?

Bobby: No, they folded. But it was Reed singing "Big Dupree."

Lyle: Could you give any advice on trying to make it in the music industry?

Bobby: You know, you gotta take chances. The only success I ever had was taking chances, getting away from mainstream. It's the only way. You got to figure out what everybody else is doing and do the opposite. It's a gamble. If you got something going, it's a gamble. If you don't have anything going, then you got nothing to lose. Whatever the mainstream is, go the opposite way, because by the time it will go mainstream, there's a whole lot of people who will be sick of it.

Lyle: You are the best singing storyteller I've ever heard. You have such a unique warmth in your voice.

Bobby: Well, I think that's what I do best. You know it's funny because I don't notice it. But I must have a distinctive voice, because people recognize it immediately. We were going to New Zealand once, me and Tom T. Hall, and we got off in Hawaii to change planes. We had a couple of hours and we were going to get a pack of cigarettes. We walked up to this counter and the woman was down underneath the counter doing something. You couldn't even see her. We were standing there talking, waiting on her to come up, and we heard her say, "It's gotta be Tom T. Hall and Bobby Bare." She recognized our voices! Tom has a distinct voice too. A lot of times I'll be on an airplane or something and people will come up and say, "I thought that was you, and when I heard your voice I knew it was you."

Lyle: That's one thing you don't hear on country music radio today, the distinction between the voices. I find most of the artists today sound the same. You can't tell the difference between who's who. But when you listen to you or Johnny Cash, Waylon or Willie—you guys are so distinctive.

Bobby: And today's music sounds great technically: the drums sound wonderful, the guitar sounds so good, the voices are great. It's sad, because it's so good and so bad at the same time. It's boring, and that's the worst thing you can say about music. I did an interview in the late seventies when everything was disco and disco was in the burn-out phase. Somebody at The *New York Times* was calling about a story on country music and I told them the same thing, "Well, it's gotten boring. I'm at the point where I can't stand to hear disco. [But] that's good, because what that means is there is a demand for something new and fresh and somebody will come along and fill that need. Right on the horizon there's a lot of talent that's ready to make their move, and it's going to happen." They didn't print none of that. All they said was I said that it was boring. It wasn't six months 'til Randy Travis was just blasting. It's that same old opposite thing. Disco and Randy Travis, it's just the opposite. I'm sure he didn't figure it out, he just stuck to his guns. This is what I do. Faith Hill has just gone totally pop. She gave in, I guess, to the pressure of the powers that be at the record label, because they want to sell ten million and you can't do that in straight country.

When Roger hit he was so big. He went straight up into the stratosphere and that took him completely away from all of Nashville. I mean, here was Nashville and way up here somewhere was Roger. So that put him in a different atmosphere.

We still stay in touch with Mary. She lives here. Fact is, a year ago I had vertigo and my whole world started spinning. That's what vertigo is. Your inner ear gets fucked up. I went to the doctor and he gave me stuff, but it still wasn't going away. Jeannie had lunch with Mary and she said she had that for a long time, two or three months, and it scared her to death. They had MRIs and CAT scans and a whole bunch of stuff. Finally, she's on the board of directors at Vanderbilt Hospital and she got the top ear, nose and throat guy there. She saw him and within five minutes she was cured. It's a procedure where you lay over this way for awhile, then you raise up and go this way for a while, and you stay with it. Then it quits and that's it. So she did that to me and it worked just like that.

Lyle: Was that Dr. Ossoff?

Bobby: No, this was Doctor Miller! I don't know who she saw at Vanderbilt, but it worked like a charm. She was telling me that I had to take these immune factor pills, the Andrew Lessman immune factor pill, and I said, "Mary, if you told me to eat shit I'd do it at this point." So I got me some and took them. I usually had two or three colds a year that would go into laryngitis and bronchitis, and I started taking those pills and I haven't had a cold since.

Lyle: Are you involved with the Country Music Awards next week?

Bobby: No, they want new faces, they don't want old people. I'm going fishing next week.

[Author's note] Just then the phone rang and it was Bobby's close friend and fishing buddy, Jerry Reed, another huge talent. Passing time looking around the room, I noticed Bobby's cigar collection and we chatted about it when he got off the phone. He pulled out a Davidoff Grand Cru and said, "Enjoy." I took it, thanked him, and then told him that I could never smoke it. To me Bobby Bare is like Elvis, and you don't smoke anything the King gives you. You frame it.

Curly Putnam

urly is a very talented songwriter with a ton of hit songs, including "Green, Green Grass of Home," "He Stopped Loving Her Today," and "My Elusive Dreams". Curly is one of the few people who co-wrote with Roger.

Curly: I would say Roger is one of my favorite all-time writers, plus person. I met him before he became known as "Roger Miller." He was playing for Ray Price at the time I met him in Huntsville, Alabama. He was singing harmony and playing rhythm. After the show was over, Ed Hamilton, who used to be a disc jockey in Nashville, gathered [with us] over at the hotel where Roger was staying and we tried to write a song together. After that Roger told me to come to Nashville and I moved there later on in '64. In the meantime, Roger told me if I was ever in Nashville to come by Tree Publishing.

After I came to Nashville I'd see him pretty often. The first time I ever put down some songs myself at Tree, that was on Seventh Avenue then, Roger happened to come by and help me. He even sang harmony on a couple of them. I got to know him and after that we just become real close friends. I loved him. I used to go to his shows back in Reno. In Las Vegas he would invite me to come out and be with him and even get up on the stage as if he was as proud of me as I was of him.

Whenever he had friends come over to his shows, he'd introduce them to the audience. They say in Vegas you just don't call anybody up on stage to sing or perform. I've heard Jimmy Dean say that there are some places that you just don't do that. But it seemed very natural for Roger to call me out on stage to sing with his band. I did "My Elusive Dreams"—I had the first record out on that song—and "Green, Green Grass of Home."

He's one of the best songwriters I've ever heard. He's the quickest and can write with quality, plus his comedy songs, his "Chug-a-Lugs," "Dang Me's." When you get down to the real nitty gritty of things, like "Husbands and Wives," "When Two Worlds Collide," he just had feelings from one spectrum to another. Of course it shows in a lot of his writing. Roger could write in his head in five minutes what takes people weeks and weeks to write. I wrote a couple of tunes with him but they were the kind of things we don't want the whole world to know about. After he wrote "Dang Me," I had an idea. "Dad Blame Anything A Man Can't Quit" was the name of it. So we sat down and wrote it.

Lyle: "Dad Blame Anything A Man Can't Quit" is kind of a strange saying.

Curly: I'm pretty much a commercial title thinker. I was thinking mainly that he had just had "Dang Me" earlier, which was one of those country sayings. "Dad blame" is something people used to stay instead of "damn."

Lyle: When was "Green, Green Grass of Home" written?

Curly: I moved to Nashville in January of '64 and wrote the song possibly towards the later part of that year. I didn't even know what I was doing. Sometimes you do better when you don't know what you're doing. I had my first album [as a recording artist] with ABC Records. Roger wrote the liner notes for me. I had about three albums, but I was kind of disgusted with not writing as good as I was before.

Roger was good to me in a lot of ways. He recorded some of my songs. "What I'd Give To Be The Wind" was one thing he recorded of mine. He used to do "Green Grass" but he would also do a parody on it "It's good to smoke the green green grass…"

Lyle: Roger also recorded "Elusive Dreams", could you tell me a little about what inspired that track?

Curly: A little bit of it was based on what I was going through, trying to get to Nashville, to find myself. All the places I used—starting out in Alabama… I was working for a Tom McCann shoe store and they moved me around a bit, and I went to Memphis and we had our first child, then we came back to Nashville. Part of that was like the whole beginning of our marriage. I don't think I was ever up in Alaska. Roger told me on several occasions, "'My Elusive Dreams' is one of the greatest love stories that I have heard. You're following somebody no matter how bad the times are." And I never thought of it as a love song.

Lyle: You are one of the very few people that Roger ever co-wrote with.

Curly: He wasn't typically the co-writer type. I think it was because I approached him with something simple and easy and he knew it would be something very simple for us to sit down and do. It wasn't something that we had planned or set aside to do. That's something I don't like to do that people do nowadays. They set appointments to write. People like Roger and myself and a lot of the older writers, they kind of let it hit them at the time and not…paint yourself into a little place where you had to write.

I believe he let a lot of little things in his life, like awards, sneak by him. When he was playing up in the charts and playing the Vegas shows, he let a lot of that simple stuff slide by. It was not as important as it was later on in his life when he started realizing that he won all those Grammys. I think when you're doing that, living it, it's something that you take for granted. You don't think about it much until you start reflecting back when you get older.

Robert Oermann

Gordy Collins

Journalist Robert Oermann is a country music historian. There are few Life and Times Biography or other documentaries filmed in Nashville that Robert doesn't appear in. I met him at a Roger Miller tribute fundraiser in October of 2002, and he invited me to a party he was having at his place with a bunch of local editors and writers. He went out of his way to make me feel welcome.

Lyle: So what were your first impressions of Roger Miller when you came to Nashville?

Robert: Well, I was a huge fan before I came, but he was gone by the time I got here in the 1970's. When the opportunity came to spend the day with him I said, "Absolutely!" It was at the old Spence Manor with a guitar-shaped swimming pool across from BMI on Music Row. He was camped out there. Mary was with him. We reminisced about his career and his relationship to Nashville and talked a lot about his past. As the afternoon wore on he wanted to have a guitar pull, so I called up some friends and we broke out the beer and a bunch of unknown songwriters that he didn't know came. He treated them like they were Hank Cochran or Willie Nelson. He didn't want to sing himself. He just wanted to enjoy their youth and their songs and it was great. And oh, my God was he quick, funny, completely off the wall and a complete delight to be around. You could see why he was so popular with everyone, he was just amazing. He would say things that would be song titles. Any lesser person would have stopped and written a song, but for him they just tumbled out so quickly it was just like spewing words.

Then he came back again for a television special and we did an interview then. At that time he was very wistful and nostalgic about Nashville, wondering if it was still the same and was Tootsie's still there. The third time we spent together was right when *Big River* was exploding on Broadway. That was a great thing for him, it was a huge comeback. I rode with him through that whole period, the *Big River* era. I went to New York to see the show, then there was a TV special made on the riverboat. There was a whole lot of activity here surrounding *Big River*.

When he got sick we did a phone interview from New Mexico. He said that he was better and he had licked the cancer. It was in January of '92 when we talked. He said that he was doing well with his radiation treatments, saying it wasn't the end of his singing career, it might be the beginning. That obviously turned out not to be the case. The interview was set up specifically to talk about his health. Stan Moress, his manager at the time, lined it up, "Roger wants to talk to you about his health." And that was to be the substance of the discussion, for him to put that spin that he was having a successful cancer treatment. I'm still puzzled about why he decided to do that. Rumors continued to fly. Then people started making pilgrimages out there to say their good byes, not right away but I think that summer.

It all started with Brenda Lee. She was out on the road with Roger and she had some throat problems. He mentioned that he was having difficulty and she recommended that he go to Dr. Ossoff, who's the throat specialist who had treated Brenda. That's how they found the diagnosis of cancer. It must have been like '91.

Lyle: How was he different to interview than most other celebrities?

Robert: In my experience, the bigger they are, the nicer they are, but Roger, he was too goofy to act like a star. He was incapable of it. He just enjoyed being around people. If it was an interview, fine. If it was a songwriter talking to him, fine. If it was a relative, fine. He just liked to have company. He was always very media friendly and not at all "starish."

Lyle: I understand that Roger loved to talk about the history of country music. With you being a country music historian, was he questioning you quite a bit?

Robert: No, he was not a scholar, that did not concern him at all. He was very much in the moment…not one for details. He probably couldn't tell you when he had his hits. He was just not like that. He wasn't at all interested in his legacy. If you asked him about Ray Price he would talk about him. If you asked him about being a bellhop he would talk about that. He didn't dwell. He wasn't like some of them who tell their same old stories over and over again. It was more like the magic of songwriting. His attitude was like, "It's in the air here. It's Nashville." He always felt that way about this town. Every time he came back it would plunge him into this misty-eyed "songwriting is so great" mood. "There's something magical in this valley," I think he said to me once. And this was in the 1990's, long past the magic era!

Lyle: So he didn't have a bitterness towards how country music evolved?

Robert: No, it was more like, "We had our fun, now they're having their fun now. Let them roll around on the buses and pop their pills and tell their stories and do their thing. Right now I'm not at Tootsie's... But somebody else is."

[Author's Note] Robert was a huge help in gathering information for this book. He made copies of many articles he wrote on Roger including his last interview about Roger's health appeared on the front page of the Tennessean. *He mentioned to me that at the time he felt like this was just a put-on article to ease people's minds. Ironically a few months later, in the exact same spot on the front page of the paper, was the news of Roger's passing.*

Ray Walker and Gordon Stoker

Ray Walker and Gordon Stoker are two original members of The Jordanaires. They are the most recorded voices in the world. They've sung with practically everyone who is anyone in rock-and-roll and country music, from Elvis to Ricky Nelson to Patsy Cline to Roger Miller. They've also sung with some people who are nobodies in the business, including myself. In May of '95 I had a chance to sing with The Jordanaires. I'll share a funny story: I had a photo taken with the guys, all except Neal Matthews (one of the original members), who was ill for that performance and had a replacement. The next time I saw the guys I brought that photo to be autographed, and this time Neal Matthews was with them. I asked him if he would sign the photo and he said, "That's not me." I said, "I know, but I'd love to have your autograph." So he signed it. Except instead of signing his name he signed the name of the guy who had taken his place!

Ray: RCA was trying to get Roger to sing like a country singer and he had this unusually uncanny way of getting all the words in. He was country's original:

> "…poet from Iran
>
> Whose verse one scarce could scan,
>
> He said, 'I'm no poet, my verse will show it,
>
> Because I'll always try to get as many words in the last line
> as I possibly can.'"

They were trying to get him to sing in meter for regular country songs, but if he got to a place were he couldn't get the whole message in, he just kept singing. And they didn't realize the jewel that they had. He just recorded it like he felt it and I think that was the secret. When they finally let him alone and he started doing things like he wanted to do, he came right to the top because it was so unusual. I was really glad they didn't kill in him the thing that made him Roger Miller.

We were on *The Steve and Edie Show* with him. Ray Charles was there. I can't tell you that story. It's clean but with the lack of perception the nation has today they would figure it racist, and Roger certainly wasn't racist. Ray

Charles was sitting at his piano and he said, "When my boy Roger gets here let me know, let me know." Well, Roger got there and sneaked up behind him and says something to him while he was on the piano bench that made him laugh so hard he rolled out on the floor and put his hands and legs up in the air. Ray Charles loved Roger Miller and Roger loved him. He thought that he was the king of soul.

Gordon: One of the funniest things I ever heard was when he told Ray Charles, "How do you know you're black? You've been blind all your life?" It would have made another blind person mad, but Roger Miller saying that to Ray, Ray thought that was funny and laughed his butt off. Ray Charles absolutely fell out and everybody else did too. We thought Ray Charles would have killed him.

Lyle: I think Roger was the only one who could get away with saying those sorta things.

Gordon: You're exactly right.

Roger was out of it so much on pills when he was here in Nashville around all of us, it just wasn't anything too pleasant to remember. He'd say and do funny things but we knew he was out of it on pills. Like Grandpa Jones would say, "He'd take a button if you gave him a glass of water." But you know what was really funny about Roger is that he acted about the same when he was on pills as when he wasn't on pills, so you really didn't know when he was on them. He'd drive a long trip to go play a date somewhere, and when he got back to Nashville he was so high on those pills he was mad because he didn't have any other place to drive.

Lyle: Was Roger prepared for the sessions you recorded with him?

Gordon: Most of the time he wasn't prepared. Some people were not. Elvis was never prepared. He never knew what he was going to do when he got to the studio. Sometimes we'd kill the whole night on one song. Money-wise he didn't care and neither did we, because we were working by the hour not by the session and all the musicians were too. Roger was pretty much the same way. Roger was an easy-go-lucky type of guy who took whatever came along, never got upset, and wasn't prepared for what he was going to do most of the time. Sometimes he had it written down, sometimes he didn't.

Bobby Goldsboro

Gordy Collins

I've mentioned the King of the Road videotape a number of times. Well, one of the best clips on there is Roger singing "Whistle Stop" on The Bobby Goldsboro Show, television's highest-rated variety show in syndication in the seventies. Bobby, a great singer/songwriter, began his career as a guitarist for Roy Orbison in the sixties. After he launched his solo career in 1964, he had the distinction of opening some dates for the Rolling Stones on their first tour of America. Bobby's recording hits include "Watching Scotty Grow", "Honey" and "Little Green Apples," and his songwriting hits include "With Pen in Hand."

Bobby: We were like a couple of kids every time we got together… just constantly coming up with crazy stuff and crazy noises and sounds. He's one of the wittiest, quickest, funniest guys I ever knew in my life. We met in Nashville down at Printer's Alley one night. He knew so many people that I did, we were like old friends when we met. We just kind of hit it off. Usually if there was a lot of people around it was constant joking, and if nobody could keep up with him with the jokes he would just move on to somebody else.

He loved gadgets and so did I. Everything that came along that was brand new he was the first to get it. He had this one thing that evolved into the Clapper. It was a thing where any noise that you made twice in a row would turn the lights on and off. And it wasn't just clapping your hands—it was any noise. He was showing it to me and we started making noises and sounds for over an hour, just rolling on the floor and laughing and making crazy noises like my frog noise to turn the light on and then he would do something to turn it off. If somebody was standing outside that room they would have thought there was a circus going on in there or something. He had one of the first portable telephones. It was a big thing in a briefcase. He told me that the thing cost him $2,500 or something. He got right outside the city limits and he couldn't get anybody [on it]. It was brand new so naturally they didn't have all the kinks worked out of it.

[One time] he had a Lear jet he chartered and he flew me up to Lake Tahoe. It was supposed to be just for the evening but we ended up staying three days. I didn't even take a toothbrush. He sent a limo by and picked me up. I stayed up with him for two days and finally I just said, "Roger, I gotta lay down just for a minute," and I was gone. When I woke up I think Roger felt bad that we had been there for two days and I didn't bring a change of clothes. It was a Sunday morning and the only thing that was open was a men's store in one of the casinos. He had bought this little…something a guy wears on a yacht…the jacket and the hat. That's all he could find that would fit me. So I woke up and over across on his bed was this outfit. I'm thinking there's no way in the world I can ever put that thing on! He said, "Bob, I got you something so you got a change of clothes before we head back." I said, "Man, that is gorgeous but that is too nice to wear right now. I'm going to save that." I don't think I ever wore it. That was the way he was. He couldn't do enough for you.

That was the period where Roger, unbeknownst to me, was taking uppers. I didn't know that, and I would stay up with him! I was the most naïve guy ever when it came to that. I just thought boy, it's amazing he can stay up for two or three days and then just disappear for a couple of days and then be right back to normal. He'd go to sleep for two days and stay up for three.

Lyle: And you kept up with him?

Bobby: I tried to until I realized he wasn't doing it naturally. I just loved being with him. We just had such a good time all the time…always coming up with crazy things to do.

Lyle: Whose TV show came first?

Bobby: Roger's did. Gosh, he was about the hottest thing out there and I was just pretty much getting started with my solo career. I'd been with Roy Orbison for three years, playing guitar for him on the road. I finally had a hit record and started going out on the road, and then I had my second record out. I think it was about '66 when I got with Roger and started seeing him when I'd go to California. He was already established by then with his own television show. I didn't get my show until the mid-seventies. I did my show in '73, '74 and '75. Roger did it every year, he'd come on and do the show. He was about one of my favorite guests because you never knew what he was going to say… It was constant laughing. I was always hoarse by the time Roger would leave.

Lyle: Did he give you any advice on having your own TV show?

Bobby: We didn't talk about it very much because it was several years after he had his. But I remember when his show was about to go off the air, one of the reasons, he felt, [was] that the network was wanting to put people on there that had shows on the network. They were trying to promote these other shows and they weren't the right guests for him. Not that they weren't nice people and things like that, but they just didn't fit with him and he wasn't that comfortable with some of the guests. I think that happens all the time. You see shows go down the tubes like that, because all of a sudden what got a person to a certain point in his career…people wanting to watch him… All of a sudden they want to start changing everything around him. With Roger, when he was up there singing and performing he was great. But when they put somebody on there that was an actor that decided he wanted to sing and had a show on the network, it just didn't seem to fit. I know that bugged Roger.

From '65 to '75 I would see him less and less because he was traveling and I was traveling. That's the hardest thing once you're in this business. A lot of your close friends… You say they're your close friends but you rarely see them because everybody's always gone.

Lyle: Did you ever witness any of Roger's eccentric behavior?

Bobby: There was a time when Roger would get paranoid. I don't know if it was from the "medication" he was taking or what. Supposedly one night in Vegas he came out and they started hollering, "Sing 'King of the Road!' Sing 'King of the Road!' " Finally he said, "If that's all you want to hear…" And he sang "King of the Road" and left. That wasn't the normal Roger Miller. Like the old saying, "He had some demons," I guess.

I know that one time that he thought the pills that he was taking [were] writing the songs for him and I told him one night I said, "It ain't the pills. There's other people out there taking pills and they ain't writing hits like you are. So it's not that."

Lyle: Did Roger have an influence on your songwriting?

Bobby: I hope he did because he was such a great writer. People like Roger and Orbison, I like to think they influenced me because they were unique in the way that they wrote. Roy Orbison, if he wanted to say something and it didn't quite fit in the number of beats in a measure, he would just add a couple. Usually you have to use 'x' amount of syllables for it to fit, but Roy would just say it the way he wanted to and add a couple of bars to it. That was unique. Roger was the same way. He could put a lot more words in a measure than most songwriters because of his delivery. With his talk-singing style, if it didn't phrase good singing, he would say it, say a lot more syllables. He did have a unique way of turning a phrase.

Lyle: I love the song that you wrote called "With Pen in Hand." I love Roger's version of it and I think it's one of the best songs Conway Twitty ever sang.

Bobby: I have to tell you something because it's odd that you bring up that song. I wrote that song about Roger. I was with Roger when he and his wife were having problems. I knew them both and I really didn't think either one of them really wanted to get divorced. I felt they were both stubborn and hard-headed and they ended up getting divorced. I was thinking about it when I was driving in Alabama on my way to Nashville in a rainstorm. I said, "Boy, it's amazing that two people who really neither one of them wanted to get divorced end up getting divorced because they're both too stubborn to just say "I'm sorry." I'm sure it happens all the time. So I got the idea for the song and by the time I got to Decatur, Alabama, I had this whole song done in my head. I stopped the car in the middle of the storm on the highway, pulled over on the side of the road, and got in the back seat with my guitar and started playing "With Pen in Hand" to make sure I wouldn't forget it. And it was about Roger.

Lyle: Did Roger know that it was about him?

Bobby: No, I never told him.

Lyle: Who recorded the song first?

Bobby: I did. It was on the *Honey* album and was going to be my next single. Bob Montgomery, who was my co-producer, was producing Johnny Darrell and Johnny had just cut that song for his album. They called me and begged me to let him come out with that as their single, but I said, "That's gonna be my next single. What do you mean?" They said, "But you got so many good things in the album." I think they were going to drop him from the label if he didn't have a good record so I let him release it. So Johnny Darrell actually had the first single on it. Many other people cut it. Vikki Carr had a big pop hit with it, Jerry Vale had a number one easy listening hit with it, and Billy Vera cut it as kind of a rhythm and blues song. Everybody started cutting it left and right and putting it on albums so I never came out with it until several years later.

Lyle: Do you recall any of Roger's one-liners?

Bobby: You could fill a book with them. Some lady walked in with a leopard coat one night and he turned around and said, "I spotted her the minute she walked in." That was the way his mind was working, it was always churning.

One of the best things he did for me… I would go out and stay with him in Las Vegas when he was playing there. Watching Roger on stage and seeing how he would work with the audience and how he would prepare for his show and how he would go over stuff with the band afterwards… Things like that helped me a great deal. Even though I'd been with Orbison for years, this was different. Las Vegas is totally different than any place else. At least it used to be. I was always pretty much terrified of playing Las Vegas. I said, "That's where Sinatra and all these people play. That's not what I do." But Roger went out there and Roger was one of the first performers that had a guitar and sat there and was funny and did stuff like that instead of the finger snapping big band stuff. He was one of the first to ever play out there like that. I'd stay out there for three or four days with him and just sit backstage and watch him. In '68, after I had "Honey", they were wanting me to play out there and I kept turning it down. I finally said, "Well, heck, I'll give it a shot," and I ended up playing there regularly for the next ten or twelve years. I think Roger helped me get over the fact of me thinking I wasn't right for Las Vegas.

Lyle: Did you notice if he did any sort of rituals or anything before he hit the stage?

Bobby: Just making crazy noises. I think he would loosen himself up. I know that Roger would get nervous before a show, but Roger was also very confident. He was insecure in a lot of ways but he was still confident in his talent, in his ability to do a good show. I think there was a combination of nervousness and insecurity and also the fact that he just knew that he could go out there. Sometimes a heckler would actually be good for Roger because he was so quick and he could come back and shut him up and be funny with it. But other nights when he was not in the right mood a heckler could throw him off. It showed me that you gotta try to keep an even keel because you never know what's going to happen out there. That's one of the most fortunate things from my whole career I rarely had any hecklers or anything. The kind of songs and things that I did never brought that kind of people out I guess.

Lyle: Was Elvis playing Vegas the same time you were hanging out there with Roger?

Bobby: He wasn't out there when we were there [together], but when I played he was there. I went to see him. Some friends of mine called and said they had a table to go see Elvis. They had seen him two nights in a row. This was the night that Elvis obviously was under the influence or something, because the night before they said it was the greatest show they'd ever seen, and then when we went people got up walked out because he never finished singing a song. He would turn around and throw a glass of water on the bandleader and whisper to guys on stage with his back to the audience and laugh and make up words to songs. It was really strange!

From what I understand he would never acknowledge people in the audience, but all of a sudden he mentioned I was in the audience and had me stand up. They put a spotlight on me and I was slumped down in my chair because of the way the night was going. It was nice to be recognized but I think I'd rather have been there the night before when they said it was the greatest show they'd ever seen.

Lyle: Did you meet Elvis after that show?

Bobby: No. I met him though. We flew on a plane together. I left Nashville to fly to L.A. and he got on a plane in Memphis with his guys, and then he came up and sat with me and we talked all the way out to L.A. He was a big Orbison fan. We talked about Roy a lot because he knew I had been with Orbison.

Lyle: Do any other memories of times you spent with Roger come to mind?

Bobby: Gosh, I'm trying to remember all the times, 'cause we were together quite a bit out there when I would go to L.A. He was such a good friend and very gracious. I was really just getting started. Even though I had been on the road with Orbison, I was just a sideman with Roy and I didn't even have a band at the time. I was out doing every TV show that came along, from *American Bandstand* to *Where the Action Is,* and shows like that. I would stay with Roger and it saved me from having to get hotels. He'd get a limo and he'd drive and I'm just thinking, "Boy, this is the life!"

I'll never forget… He bought Clint Walker's house. He picked me up in a limo and we were driving up and the gates opened and we're going up to this big huge house, and here I am straight out of northern Alabama at the time, and I said, "Golly, you must be a millionaire!" And without pause he said, "Multi." He said it as if it was a matter of fact. Now I use that all the time. If someone brings up being a millionaire, I always say, "Multi." That was Roger. He was proud of what he had done, but not cocky like, "I'm better than somebody."

I was out doing the music for *Evening Shade,* the TV show with Burt Reynolds, and we were living out in L.A. at the time. I had the studio outside a little ways from the house, and my wife called over and said, "Did something happen to Roger Miller?"

I said, "Well, no, why?"

She said, "Well, they're doing kind of a tribute to Roger on one of the shows out of Nashville but they keep saying 'He was, he was.'"

I said, "Well, no, they're just doing a tribute to him." I knew nothing. Nobody had called me or told me or anything, and this was probably two or three days afterwards. In fact it might have been almost a week before I knew about it.

Dr. Robert Ossoff

W alking into Dr. Robert Ossoff's office is like walking into a major label office on Music Row. Wall to wall gold albums and thank-you letters from the biggest names in the music industry line the hallways and offices. He is the Executive Medical Director of the Vanderbilt Voice Center at the Vanderbilt University Medical Center in Nashville.

Robert: I remember a phone call from Roger one day when he was in Santa Fe, telling me he just had this sense that one of his vocal cords wasn't working, that one of them had gone on strike. I told him that he needed to come out and see me as soon as he could. Indeed, one of the vocal cords wasn't working. It's kind of a unique story about Roger and just how in touch, how intuitive, he was not only with the world around him in terms of his creativity as a writer, but also how intuitive he was with his own body and his own soul in terms of having a real sense of one part of his performance mechanism, vocal cords, not working. I truly believe that Roger was the first to have made his diagnosis, not me.

Roger came to see me in the office one day after we had done some work to try and strengthen his voice while he was under treatment. He said he had been out at the Opry over the weekend and had bumped into Whispering Bill Anderson, who had immediately come over to Roger and said, "Hey, I gotta real beef with you. What are you trying to do, steal my act?" Roger thought that was kind of cute, because Roger's voice was bordering on sounding like Whispering Bill's.

One thrill that will stay with me until I pass on will be that I was part of the *Roger Miller Remembered* TV special. The opening number had multiple people in it who had in one way or another touched his life or been a part of his life, singing as a chorus to "King of the Road." The people to my left and right said the only way that I could do that was if I lip-synched and didn't sing. That was sort of the ultimate thrill, to be on stage in the Grand Ole Opry as a participant as opposed to a frequent observer going in through the backstage. It was something that I, as a laryngologist, a non-singing laryngologist, would never have dreamed to participate in.

Randy Hart

R andy Hart was Roger's keyboard player and band leader from 1978 to 1984.

Randy: I moved to L.A. and had a friend who had a friend who was Roger's guitar player. Actually, Roger's band had been kind of stolen by Glen Campbell. This fellow, Craig Fall, called and asked if I could come down and audition because the first [show] date was January of '78. This was in the winter of '77. So I went down to Roger's home in Beverly Hills, where he and Mary lived at the time, and played a couple of things. I had been a fan, although Roger didn't necessarily enjoy me telling the story of when I was twelve and my mom took me to see him. I was very familiar with who he was. I was twenty-two or twenty-three. I tell people he kind of took me through my twenties, which is kind of an impressionable, vulnerable time. It was a kick.

Roger hated to rehearse. He liked to perform, he didn't rehearse. My first night with Roger was in Las Vegas, January '78, and there was the house orchestra, a phenomenal house orchestra, strings and brass, and I think we were only doing thirty minutes. We were opening for John Davidson. Roger was on stage at the soundcheck. In rehearsals, we came to "King of the Road" and Roger chose not to want to go through that one. "Everybody knows this, played that a thousand times, don't need to do that." I had nothing to compare it to. It was my first time, I'm in awe, I've got this incredible orchestra, and there's Roger and I'm in my early twenties. Well, come the performance, the opening show, "King of the Road" has a modulation in it, a half step modulation. We start in B and modulate to C. The band modulated and the orchestra didn't and it was as much of a musical train wreck as you could imagine, with the song being played not only in two different keys but two different keys that are just the biggest rub that they can be. I remember lifting my hands up off the keys and my eyes must have looked like moons. It was kind of a forerunner of things to come as far as Roger and rehearsals and stage.

Lyle: I've heard many wild stories about Roger from the sixties to mid-seventies. While you were working with him, was he starting to mellow?

Randy: He definitely had started to mellow. I heard stories, and Roger shared some with me himself, but he had met Mary sometime before I met him. They then got married. We had a date in Reno or Tahoe in February '78 and he and Mary got married Valentine's Day '78. He was just head over heels for Mary, always was. Very committed to her.

I gotta boatload—eight years' worth—of memories. Some fond, some now funny, but at the time they were kind of tough. Roger at times would be tough on the band on stage, which I've got some tapes of. As time's gone on memories have kind of distilled down to people really just acknowledging primarily the genius and how special and unique he was. When he was around and we'd be doing dates, we'd run into concert promoters that said they had horror stories about working with Roger in an earlier part of his life, when he was a little crazier. But you don't hear those anymore, you just hear the really good stuff, which is kind of cool.

Lyle: When you guys went on tour, was it by bus or plane?

Randy: Ninety-nine percent of the time it was by airplane. We were doing some fairs, mainly showroom dates. We'd get booked for one or two weeks at showrooms primarily. We had musicians coming in from all parts of the country and we'd co-ordinate flights...all meet at the job. It was a very special group of musicians during that period and we just had an absolute blast. Danny Gatton has passed away, but we all still keep in touch and reminisce.

Lyle: Were you on the *Austin City Limits* performance?

Randy: Yeah, and in fact we did two shows back to back. One was for a fundraiser for PBS, and then we changed clothes and did the real *Austin City Limits*. I can't remember which one it is that they will continue to re-air, but they put a graphic up at the end of it now "In the memory of Danny Gatton."

Lyle: In that performance, Willie Nelson sings "Old Friends" with you guys and he looks very emotional about it. Do you recall if there was anything going on behind the scenes at that time?

Randy: No. Roger and Willie I think communicated, if not saw each other, with pretty good regularity. That was really at Willie's peak, or a peak for Willie, with his kind of resurgence, so the crowd went absolutely nuts. We did "Milk Cow Blues" and we did "Old Friends." I remember going back to the hotel and of course they hung together until all hours. I went and got ribs for everybody and there was a mountain of rib bones everywhere you looked.

Lyle: I wasn't sure if that might have been the time when Willie found out Roger was sick.

Randy: No, that was taped long before. Roger had a throat episode when we were in Las Vegas. It wasn't unusual for people to get throat problems, but I remember we were at the Golden Nugget downtown in Vegas and Roger had to cancel shows. This was way early. To this day I don't know if that was kind of a precursor of cancer or not.

Lyle: You mentioned Roger was actually the opening act for people like John Davidson. I find that hard to believe with all the hits he had. I notice that there wasn't as much focus on him media-wise during the seventies and eighties compared to his peak in the sixties. Did that bother him?

Randy: I don't know if it bothered him, but I think maybe it did on some level. I made the comment during probably that first week that I was with him—you know, I was a kid—something along the lines of, "You need another 'King of the Road.'" And he kind of looked at me and said, "Well, that's what they tell me."

Lyle: When Roger would jam with the band, would he do mostly his own music, covers, or would he make up stuff at the spur of the moment?

Randy: Sometimes we'd do some Bob Wills, who was a main influence on him. He wouldn't make up songs. You asked about covers. We did "Little Green Apples," we'd usually open the show with "Bobby McGee." I don't know that Roger would ever make great pains to say that he did not write "Bobby McGee." A lot of times there was an assumption, because people would come up and ask me afterwards, "I didn't know he wrote 'Bobby McGee,'" or "I didn't know he wrote 'Little Green Apples,'" and he did not. But he did incorporate those in the shows.

Lyle: Did it bother Roger that there was an expectation for the songs that made him famous?

Randy: I think maybe on some level for a while it may have bothered him. This is just an educated guess on my part, but when *Big River* came along, it gave him the opportunity to showcase and have a reason for some new material. There were a few reasons that was really special to him. One, he could finish something, and two, he could get on Broadway. Roger always wanted to make it very clear that he was not just a hillbilly country singer. Believe it or not, he thought a lot of people lived here in Nashville were like that. Anytime he could get in front of... We did a special Smithsonian artists series one time... Or certainly *Big River*... He really appreciated the opportunity to be known as something a cut above. John Hendricks, a legendary jazz singer had befriended Roger, and said to me one time, "Did you know that Roger is an amazing jazz singer?" And it never really dawned on me to have somebody who was obviously a legendary jazz guy say that to me. It was very profound. In some circles people saw him for what he really was, and [in] other circles they thought, "Oh yeah, Roger sings those country songs."

Lyle: Do you know if there is a Roger/Elvis Presley connection?

Randy: Roger told me that he had seen Elvis at the Las Vegas Hilton, which was my first stage with Roger. He made a comment that it was pretty much unlike anything he had ever seen and that [it] was a real moment for him as far as seeing somebody that just had an undeniable, incredible, indefinable quality. One time we were in Vegas and Colonel Tom, who was living at the Hilton, came to a show and met with Roger. I remember Colonel Tom saying to me that he thought Roger should do a live album from Vegas.

Lyle: Can you tell me anything about Roger's hobbies, like his clock rebuilding?

Randy: You've done your homework. I'll tell you a clock story. I went down to San Bernardino and got Roger an old clock that was not working because he loved to work on them. I was so happy that I found this clock. It was a cool looking old clock and it wasn't working, so I knew he could kind of lose himself in it, which he said he liked to do. As I gave it to Roger and he took it out of the packaging, the thing started! Just as I handed it to him!

Lyle: I know many performers have specific rituals before they go on stage, be it doing vocal warm-ups or meditation or saying a prayer with the band. Did Roger have any rituals before he went on stage?

Randy: That is a loaded question. No, he didn't have anything regular that he did. When Roger hit the stage he was really *on*. Hand in hand with the fact that he didn't like rehearsing, he loved the spontaneity. Anything that wasn't spontaneous, be it rehearsal or preparation or anything like that, he just gritted his teeth and got through it, if even that. A lot of nights after we were finished, Roger and Mary would invite the band up to the room and have food brought in and we'd just all hang out. Roger loved that. He would still want to perform. We'd always call it being 'summoned by the King.' Some of us would already be in bed and Roger would call and say, "Hey, you guys wanna come up?" We didn't want to say no, so we'd call each other and say, "Well, we're being summoned by the King." And he'd continue to perform. Sometimes he'd play something he'd be working on, but a lot of times it was just pretty wacky, zany stories and one-liners.

Lyle: Were there any songs that Roger sang for you that were never released?

Randy: Yeah, there was some, because again I would tape a lot of live shows. There were things that we'd work up and nothing ever happened to them. Did Buddy Killen tell you about giving Roger his publishing back?

Lyle: No, I don't believe he mentioned anything like that to me.

Randy: I had lunch with Buddy one day and he made some references [to] some songs. He gave Roger his publishing back.

Lyle: I got the impression that Buddy was very proud of his accomplishments with Roger, but that he was a little disappointed in Roger's lack of discipline.

Randy: But that was all a part of him. I remember there were times when my mom and my stepdad would come to the shows, or friends or something, and Roger sometimes would not necessarily have the greatest social graces if he just wasn't in that frame of mind. As time went on that was just all part of the guy. If you didn't have those elements you might not have the other incredible things.

To be in his presence…through the years I've come to appreciate it. The band was an extraordinary group of musicians… Listening to old tapes now the musicianship didn't really matter that much to the presentation, because the charm was the lyrics and the melody and Roger doing his thing. But he had Danny Gatton and Thumbs Carllile, and other musicians that we had put together, and it was just a very powerful thing. When Roger would let the band do "Orange Blossom Special" or something it was a freight train behind him. A lot of the times we were frustrated musically because that job didn't have the opportunity for us to let go.

Lyle: Can you tell me anything about Roger's appearance on *The Muppet Show?*

Randy: *The Muppet Show…* We were at Lake Arrowhead. Roger and Mary were up [visiting] with her aunt and I was over there visiting. We were downstairs having a beer and I said to Roger that I thought he would be great to host *The Muppet Show*. And on cue the phone rings and it was an offer for Roger to host *The Muppet Show*. I remember Roger getting the call and hanging up and looking at me thinking I had an inside track or something. Yeah, he loved doing that. I remember them going over to London and he just came back and raved about it.

Lyle: Was Roger's home in Santa Fe a ranch?

Randy: Roger's home was actually in a town called Tesuque. As I recall he had about five acres. I do not remember it being a ranch, per se, but much of the acreage was not landscaped. I do believe he had at least a horse.

Lyle: Do you recall the last time you saw Roger?

Randy: I don't know if this is the last time but there was the 50th anniversary of the BMI awards. I had at the time moved here and was working with Steve Wariner and had written a song with Steve and had received an award that evening. I saw Roger. As I was walking to the bathroom he was talking with a group of people, and we kind of passed each other and spoke very briefly. I closed it by saying, "I love you, man." He looked at me and said, "I love you too, Randy." If that was the last time, what a beautiful thing…

Steve Bess

Steve Bess is a musician whose stepmother was the legendary Tootsie from Tootsie's Orchid Lounge.

Steve: What I know is more about how Roger got started in Nashville, actually through my mom and dad. My dad was big in the music business a long time ago, on live radio. His name was Big Jeff, and my mom was Tootsie from Tootsie's Orchid Lounge. Actually she was my stepmother, but I mean she was the only mom I ever knew. She raised me, she was my mom.

Roger came into town when they owned a club. This would have been in the fifties, about '57, give or take a year, and this was when he was working as the bellhop down at the Sam Davis. My dad's club was the first place he ever sang in Nashville. All the people on the Grand Ole Opry used to come to Dad's club. It was the only place then for country music in Nashville, if you can believe that! With Dad being real big in live radio, he started about half of the musicians on the Grand Ole Opry. He was kind of a proving ground. If they could get through Dad's boot camp then they were ready for Grand Ole Opry. When live radio went under because of TV coming in so big, Dad got into clubs and bought nightclubs and restaurants. Since all those people knew him at the Opry, they would all come out there after the Friday Night Frolics, as they were called instead of the Opry. Then after the Opry on Saturday they would all come out, and some of them would also come out during the week simply because they knew the place and they knew Dad and felt comfortable there. It was like a watering hole, kind of like Tootsie's turned into when they got that place.

Lyle: What was the name of the club?

Steve: It was called Tootsie's as well. Before Roger ever came to town, they owned another one on this side of Brentwood called Big Jeff's Country Club. They moved and it was called Tootsie's on Clarksville Highway. A lot of the entertainers came to both of those places. Roger showed up about the time they got the place on Clarksville Highway. He kinda let it be known that he was a player and a singer. Dad would just bring everyone up, it was just open mic all the time there. Once he got to know someone and knew that they were serious, then he would let them go on stage. That's when I got to know Roger. He was very young then. That was when he first got to Nashville and didn't know that many people. Dad and my mom were nice to everybody, they tried to be, and Roger truly loved them. He and I became very good friends through that.

You know, in his very young days at Dad's club he just had that laid-back attitude about him. That's what struck me, because it was so different. Everyone else would get all excited and all hyper, but Roger never did. Even when he was a bellhop, he was laid-back. If he got excited it was all inside.

I think he was probably the first person to make me realize that it all starts with a song. Roger was always saying in one way or another, "Just remember, man, you got to have a song first." He was definitely a songwriter first and everything else second. He was trying to get more out of being a songwriter than just words and melody. Roger was very into the dynamics of a song. He was more into the production end of it than people realized. The few demo sessions that I did with him—back then you ran through demos, you did a song every five minutes practically—Roger would take as much time as he could to get the production down, because he would hear some of that in his head. A lot of songwriters don't worry about that.

The thing that still comes to mind about Roger is that he was so grateful to Dad and my mom. He would always come up and hug her "bye" before he left the club, and he didn't have to do that. He was a very caring, loving person and I don't know if a lot of people saw that in him. Then years later Roger really got caught up in the fast lane for a while and we kind of went our separate ways. Roger moved out of Nashville and I didn't see him for a few years, and that's when he had the hit television show. He had all these monster records. He had changed just a little. I heard this from very close friends that I knew I could trust that were very close friends of his also. I guess the last time I saw him, I was at Opryland Hotel and I went to this suite and Roger was in there and everyone was wrapped around him. He looked up and saw me and just screamed out my name and ran over and hugged me. We talked for a while and got in the corner of a room, and I guess he sensed that I was kind of shocked as to how he was and all. He looked at me and said something to the effect of, "You're remembering that I was pretty much an asshole for a while." And I just said, "Well, that's what I had heard. It sure is good to see you back." He just kind of got misty-eyed and I did too.

It was so good to see that he came full circle, and I guess that's the point to my story. Practically every person that gets that big has to go through something and he had to go through something. But he came back to being the good old Roger that I first met when I was twelve years old and he wasn't much older.

Lyle: I was told that you used to perform at the King of the Road Hotel.

Steve: Yes, I forgot about that. I followed Eddy Raven in there in '73, '74, and I was there for a year and a half until they sold it. It was called The Rooftop Lounge and at that time it was very popular. All of the country artists would come up there because it was *the* place to go. I would call people up on the stage—that was the way of doing things back then. One night Barbie Benton, the girl that was in *Playboy* and was big at the time, and Waylon Jennings, Johnny Cash, Charley Pride… There were about seven or eight huge stars singing at the same time and we just had a ball up there. Charley Pride used to come up a lot when he would be in town, because he liked to sing blues stuff and he just couldn't do it on his road shows, he had to sing country. A lot of the artists that had just gotten contracts… As a matter of fact I got my major contract while I was up there. It was the premier hotel in Nashville when it opened. The weird thing is the entire time I was there I never saw Roger. I was working Roger Miller's King of the Road and I never saw Roger.

Lyle: Do you know why that place went under?

Steve: I do. I guess it's okay to tell it now, everything is long ago by the wayside. There were too many fingers getting in the cash register, and it wasn't The Rooftop Lounge. The Rooftop Lounge was packed every day until the day they closed the place. It was the hotel itself, which was very high maintenance and had high overheads. There were problems too with the infrastructure of that whole thing. That was supposed to be a huge chain of hotels and it should have been. It should have been like the Holiday Inn, as far as my thoughts go, because the concept was there.

Billy Burnette

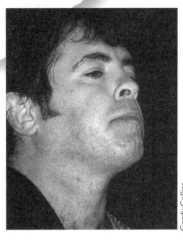

Gordy Collins

Ever wonder where the term 'rock-a-billy' comes from? Well, Billy Burnette, the son of singer/songwriter/ music pioneer Dorsey Burnette, is the 'billy' in rock-a-billy. An excellent guitar player, for three years he played in Roger Miller's touring band, then later with Fleetwood Mac and most recently with Bob Dylan.

Billy: Roger was our neighbor from the old days. My dad knew him, they go way back. My dad was the only songwriter that had an outside song on the "King of the Road" album—"Ain't That Fine." Both the families lived in Woodland Hills [California]. Roger would usually come over about one or two in the morning. They'd get together that time of night because they were both all-nighters. My bedroom was right by the door there so I'd hear all the stuff going on when I was a kid. Roger would call my dad and say, "What are you doing? Well, I'll be right over." There would be a knock on the door and there he'd be with one of those big briefcase phones. This had to be in the late sixties. I guess I go back with him as far as I can remember. He was always around.

We'd play a place out there called the Palomino, where all the country guys in L.A. would hang out. Everybody played there, from Merle Haggard to Waylon to Willie. Everybody that came from Nashville would go through the Palomino. I played with my dad's band and Roger would get up and play with us. I introduced him to a couple of guys, Micheal Smotherman and Marc Durham from Erick, Oklahoma. Roger got to liking them and hired them in his band.

I've been an artist my whole life, since I've been out of school. All I've ever done is records. In the mid-seventies I needed something to do during one of those times where there was not much going on in my career. Roger's guitar player couldn't make a gig in Denver so I went to fill in for him. We did the show and Roger was real happy about the show and asked me to come aboard for the rest of that year and some of the next, so I was with him for a couple of years playing guitar. That must have been '77. He loved my playing. In fact he even let me do an original song during the show. He loved his band at that time too. We had a great band, it was like a family.

When I went to work for Roger it was in the days when there was a lot of cocaine around. There would be a big pile on the table. All the comedians would be there after the show, everybody from John Byner to Red Foxx. We were doing shows with Flip Wilson and after the shows we'd go over and play all night with Campbell and Roger and all of us passing around the guitar. It was just unbelievable. I think he kind of ran at night because he was so popular at the time, he was such a big star. He couldn't roam around anywhere freely so they hung at night when nobody was around. And the pills… That's what killed my old man. He took eighty or ninety a day.

I'm basically a rhythm guitar player. Roger showed me a lot of cool country rhythms, swing rhythms. He'd kick me and say, "No, no, no, no. Come here and do it like this. It's this type of stroke." I learned a lot from him that he learned from the real guys. He taught me to take an arena or a club in Vegas or a showroom and turn it into a living room. I took it all with me when I joined Fleetwood Mac. I was with them for eight or nine years and none of them did too much talking, so I kind of took over the thing of emcee and used what I learned from being on stage with Roger. He was a philosopher. Stuff would just come off the top off his head. He'd say things like, "I tried to commit suicide one time. I tied a rock around my foot and jumped in the lake and on my way down I met a fish with a balloon tied around its neck." He told the drummer one night who was rushing a little bit, "You can play as fast as you want to but we still gotta go to 12:30."

When I left the band it was a tough decision. Chips Moman had called me from Nashville and said, "Come on, let's do a record on you. You need to get back here." Somehow he talked me into it. The next day Glen Campbell called me and said him and Roger had plans to do a record with me. It was a really tough decision, really hard for me. I chose just to go back to Nashville and make a record with Chips, 'cause I'd made a couple of records with Chips already. Chips is the guy that did the "Suspicious Minds" Presley stuff and cut so many hits—"Hooked On a Feeling," BJ Thomas, Aretha Franklin, and just on and on. He cut the Waylon and Willie records. I said, "Chips is hot right now, he's got it going so I'll go back and do a record with him."

Roger found out I was leaving before I could tell him. It was at the Hilton in Vegas. I think we were working there with John Davidson. Roger said, "I can't hear the guitar tonight," and I thought, 'He knows.' I didn't get a chance to talk to him about me leaving. It was tough at the time also because most of the band with Roger was the band that I had that backed up my dad. My dad knew these guys needed the work and he wasn't working that much at the time so they went with Roger.

Roger was like an electric bolt of lightening sometimes. It was just, *Wow!* He was something to watch. He really had a major impact on my life and my dad's. Everybody would always be quoting what Roger just said: 'Did you hear his latest one?' People talked about him. Glen Campbell would get on stage and do all of Roger's jokes. We'd go and see Campbell's show and Roger would sit there and go, "Okay?!"

Lyle: Did that upset Roger, hearing Glen using his jokes?

Billy: No, not at all. Roger was really confident about who he was. He was kind of a private guy too, and he really was funny about who he hung out with. If somebody was a little weird it would throw him off.

Lyle: I understand you guys had some wild times in Vegas.

Billy: We'd do the Nugget, the Hilton, MGM Grand, so we were just there for three months at a time, all summer. We'd drive over in Roger's Rolls. One time his bumper had fallen off and he tied it back on there with two coat hangers. He loved McDonald's. We'd drive into Vegas and hit the first McDonald's.

He showed up late one night at the Golden Nugget for a show and somebody yelled out, "Roger! Where you been?"

He said, "I've been watching TV. Where have you been?" He was about twenty minutes late.

The big boys came in. We got off stage and there were these guys in suits around and it was kind of a scary deal. They said, "Mr. Miller can we talk to you a minute?" and got him off to the side. Whatever they worked out, Roger had to work the next week for free. We're talking about a hundred thousand dollars, or whatever he was making a week there, you know. He had to bite that and pay the band and work a week for free to get back with them. Back in those days you didn't mess with them guys.

Every show was different. The songs might be the same, but then he'd throw something else in. Sometimes he would tear them up! He played the fiddle and sang and he was so witty. He didn't go with the same stuff. Every night it was fresh stuff. It was just unbelievable where it came from. Sometimes he'd get like Merle Haggard to get up with us and Merle would turn around to the band and say, "You boys know any country music?" And we'd go, "Yeah, yes we do."

It was great. So many people came… Cash, when he was in town… Willie sat in with us one night in Denver with a broken leg. He broke his leg when he got busted for pot down in Jamaica or somewhere and jumped off the porch at the courthouse.

Right before I joined Roger's band Steve Martin was opening for him. Out of all the people we worked with, Roger had a little edge on the comedians, because he was so natural. I think those guys sat there and wrote their stuff out, but Roger's just came so natural 'cause he was just himself. It was just amazing to watch him. He was so rhythmical, just as natural as you can be. People know whether you're real or not. Roger had that gift of turning the place into his living room. I've never met or seen anything like Roger. He was really relaxed on stage, always entertaining, and such a great songwriter. There's so many songs that people need to dive into his catalogue and get.

Lyle: Was there a Roger Miller/Elvis Presley connection?

Billy: I believe they'd hang out sometimes. He talked about Elvis. We worked the Hilton the day that Elvis died and I went and stood right on Elvis' mark, a little 'x' there on the stage. I said to Roger, "Man, look. This is where he stood."

Roger got in a car wreck on the way to the rehearsal the day that Elvis died. I said, "Are you all right?"

He said, "Yeah. There was a big wreck right in the middle of the intersection. I didn't know what to do, so I just pulled out my razor and started shaving."

Lyle: Could you tell me a little about your dad?

Billy: He had a lot of hits himself like, "Hey Little One," "Tall Oak Tree," "Big Rock Candy Mountain." He wrote the Rick Nelson hits "It's Late,"

"Believe What You Say," and "Waiting in School." Before that, him and my uncle Johnny Burnette had pioneered rock-a-billy music in Memphis, pre-Elvis. My dad used to run Elvis off from the projects in Memphis where they would rehearse down in the laundromat. My cousin, Rocky, is Johnny's son. The name rock-a-billy came out of Memphis when [my dad and Johnny] wrote the song "Rock-A-Billy Boogie" and dedicated it to their sons, Rocky and Billy. That was in '53 when they wrote the song. They were the pioneers...incredible. The Beatles had done their stuff, Led Zeppelin, Aerosmith, the original hard rock guys.

I can remember Roger and my dad. Roger'd come over and they'd just sit by the fireplace in the den and talk all night, listening to music, passing the guitar back and forth. Their love for music... They lived for that.

Jan Howard

Gordy Collins

Jan Howard is a recording artist and the ex-wife of the great songwriter Harlan Howard. She has been a member of the Grand Ole Opry since 1971. She recorded a song Roger Miller wrote called "A World I Can't Live In." She was part of the Johnny Cash Show from 1975-1979. Jan has lived a life of triumph and tragedy as shared in her best-selling autobiography Sunshine and Shadow.

Jan: I met Roger when we first came to Nashville. Of course Harlan and I were married. Roger, Bill Anderson and Harlan had a mutual admiration society going with writers and we became friends. He'd show up at the house at all hours. He just became kinda like a fixture, a favorite friend.

One time I was in Los Angeles recording and I had to be out there for two weeks. I had lived in L.A. before, but I was depressed and wanting to get out of there, and I was staying in an apartment instead of a hotel. While I was on the phone with Harlan there was a knock on the door and it was Roger. He was out there doing something, so I told Harlan, "Roger's here. Do you want to talk to him?"

I handed the phone to Roger and he talked with him for a minute. Roger came back and said, "I got to work in a town outside the city." This is before Roger had much of anything going on. In fact, it was the only time I ever saw Bob Wills. Bob Wills was performing and Roger was supposed to open for Wills. Willie Nelson and Tommy Alsup owned the club. This is before Willie was famous. Roger said, "Why don't you come with me? It's about sixty miles outside of L.A."

I said, "Okay. I don't have anything to do this evening."

"Well, John's working in Vegas." Johnny Cash, he's talking about. He and June are in Vegas. This is before he and June are married, I believe. "He wants me to come over there. He's hoarse and he wants me to fill in for one night. So what we can do is just drive up there and just drive on to Vegas."

I said, "Well, I have to be back here in a couple of days."

"That's all right, we'll just go over there and you can fill in also. We'll just fill in."

"I'll think about it on the way up there."

So we went to this club and Roger worked and did a little bit of his funny things and then Bob Wills came on. We watched a little bit of Bob Wills, then we were going to leave and drive on to Las Vegas. But Roger still had to get paid, so he went upstairs to the office to get paid. He said, "I don't know if I'm gonna get all my money or not." I said, "I'm gonna wait down here while you do that." He went up to the office, came back down, and said he didn't get all of his money. But there was a mixing panel there that had all the lighting, outside and stage lights, and it had tape under each knob saying which turned on what light. So we took all the tape and re-arranged it so you didn't know what was going to come on when they switched the lights! And then we split. We left there and headed to Vegas. We got halfway to Vegas and both of us were so tired—this is like three in the morning—and I said, "Roger, I don't think I can make it all the way to Vegas."

He said, "I can't either."

So we stopped and got a cup of coffee and I said, "I don't think I can do this."

"I can't either. But we sure can't check into a motel. I don't care if our rooms are two miles apart. It would be back to Nashville before we even got in the room."

"You're right."

"Wait a minute, I'll be right back." He went and made a phone call, came back and said, "There's a flight from L.A. to Vegas at seven in the morning. We can drive back to L.A. and catch that seven o'clock plane."

We weren't even thinking we could have been in Vegas by the time we got back to L.A. But we did—we turned back around and went back to L.A., turned in the rental car, and flew to Las Vegas. I don't know if Roger went to bed or not, but I did. We worked that night and Roger had to drive on to Tucson, Arizona. We played blackjack all that night with Luther Perkins and Margie, his wife, until about seven in the morning. I didn't see Roger any more that trip but I assume he did somehow go on to Tucson and work.

That was one of the craziest trips I've had in my life! I've never laughed so much in my life.

When we first moved to Nashville from L.A., we lived in a rented house until we found a house we wanted to buy. When we moved from the rented house to the one that we had bought, Roger rented the house. We left up the deposit for the house and the telephone because Roger didn't have the money for the deposit. Everybody said it was because of Roger that everybody started having to put up a hundred dollar deposit to get a telephone!

Then he moved from here. He had to move from Nashville to be discovered really, because nobody did take him seriously. Just like Willie Nelson, he had to move from here to really come into his own.

Paul English

Courtesy of Electric Recordings

I've always loved the Willie Nelson song "Me and Paul," and I've always wanted to have a photo of me and Paul. Now I have one. I met up with Paul English, long-time drummer in Willie's Family, after a concert they played in Fargo, North Dakota. Paul shared a bunch of stories of his adventures, and some Willie Nelson stories, too. One of my favorites is when a lady went up to Willie and said, "I know you don't remember me..." And Willie said, "No, but I sure appreciate you remembering me."

Paul: There was a time in California when Roger wasn't working too much and I guess he was at home watching a lot of TV. One of his favorite shows was *The Price is Right*. We were in town during a time when Willie was having trouble with his third wife and they were in the process of getting a divorce, a friendly divorce. Anyway, Roger came off of Willie's bus and said, "What we need to do with Willie is to have him spayed and neutered."

I heard that him and Willie were writing songs together but they were with different publishing companies, so what they did with the songs was they laid them down on the table upside down and dealt them out to each other. Only one of them got credit for each of the ones they wrote together, so we don't know who wrote what. I don't know if it's true, but it's a pretty good story. You might want to ask Willie about that.

One time Roger was in a restaurant and went to the restroom. When he came back out he asked the waitress, "Who did I come in here with? Would you point them out to me?"

Willie Nelson

Richard D. Moore

Just a few days before I did this interview, my goddaughter saw Willie Nelson on TV singing and said to her mom, "Look, Mom, it's God singing." Willie Nelson is the only artist I know of whose music is immediately recognizable not only by his unique voice, but also by the distinctive way he plays guitar. Because of what happened behind the scenes, this interview definitely stands out in my mind. Willie's publicist set me up with backstage passes and amazing seats to a concert in Fargo, North Dakota. A friend flew from Calgary to meet me in Winnipeg and then we drove over two hundred miles to Fargo. I didn't know what time the interview was going to take place, so we arrived in the late morning. A few hours passed and it was time for soundcheck. One of Willie's guys came in and chased us out, telling us he didn't care who told us we could watch it. I told him I was there to do an interview and he said, "After the show." After the concert we waited at the back door until almost everyone, including the local crew, was gone. At this point I was starting to worry. Then the same guy who had kicked us out of soundcheck came by and said, "Come to Willie's bus in forty-five minutes and he'll meet with you." Next thing we know, we see Willie's bus drive away! I asked one of the crew if he was coming back and he said, "Hell no. He's off to the next show." I could have died. We stood there for a good ten minutes wondering what to do. Just as we were about to leave, I looked in the distance. Willie's bus was coming back. The bus stopped and someone inside waved us over. We walked over, the door opened, and next thing I knew a guy yells, "GET ON!!!" I said, "My buddy's going to come in with me if that's..." Next thing I know he grabs me by the jacket and yells, "Here's your fucking chance! Close the door! Close the door!!!" It was as though Osama bin Laden were behind me or something. I flew on to the bus on my knees, looked up to my left and there sat an Indian chief in full traditional Indian dress. Then I looked straight in front of me and there was Willie sitting at his table looking at me. His facial expression didn't change one bit. I was in shock. Not only was one of my heroes in front of me, but I felt like I had just been physically assaulted.

Nonetheless, I tried to regain my composure and conduct an intelligent interview.

Lyle: What is the first memory that comes to mind of the times you and Roger spent together?

Willie: His sense of humor was the greatest. He was probably one of the funniest guys that I ever knew.

Lyle: How did you meet each other?

Willie: I was playing a club in Fort Worth and he was traveling around. Him and Bill Anderson came through town. They had both been working with Ray Price and they had written a song that Ray had recorded. I forget the name of it, "City Lights" or something. They came to the club where I was working.

Lyle: How did you guys start performing with Ray Price?

Willie: Well, he played with Ray Price before I did. He had already left Ray before I went to play with him.

Lyle: What brought on your album with Roger?

Willie: Well, the title song of the album is "Old Friends," and that's exactly the reason that I did the album with him, because he was one of my closest friends. I loved his writing. He's one of the best writers that we ever had and I wanted to do a tribute to him.

Lyle: You initiated the project?

Willie: Yep.

Lyle: What was the song selection like?

Willie: Wasn't hard. We just sat down and started singing Roger Miller songs. We did ten, but we could have done twenty more.

Lyle: Did you do any shows together to promote it?

Willie: No, but in the past we've done some shows together. I used to be a promoter and I used to hire Roger to come play on my shows.

Lyle: Do you have any memories from being on stage together?

Willie: Well, we weren't on stage together that much. He would do his show and I would do my show and when we sang together it was normally in the studio. When "Old Friends" came out, we did that a few times in different places.

Lyle: Were you ever around him when he was writing?

Willie: He wrote a song about me one time called "Sorry Willie." It was a song that he wrote about me and my ex-wife. I was right there. I was in the hotel room with him when he was writing it.

Lyle: So it was a true story?

Willie: I don't know, could have been.

Lyle: Did you talk about your songwriting techniques?

Willie: No. We didn't have any. We didn't have techniques, we just wrote.

Lyle: I was talking to Paul and he said that there was a rumor that you had written songs together but you were on different publishing companies.

Willie: I don't think we ever wrote a song together. Me and Roger and Kris Kristofferson were in a hotel room one night and we all were sitting around drunk and were gonna write a song. We stayed there all night long and the only thing we wrote was, "I've got AIDS. If you fuck with me I'll kill you." That's it, that's the whole thing. We sang it in three-part harmony for about four hours.

Lyle: Do you think Roger got the recognition as an entertainer that he deserved?

Willie: Well, probably not. He was a superstar, but I really think a lot of people didn't really know Roger, didn't know how good he really was. I don't think he really did get the recognition that he deserved. Roger was mostly known for his novelty songs, but he was probably one of the best ballad writers there ever was. He never did really get the recognition for being the writer that he really was.

Lyle: Why do you think that was?

Willie: It was just the times. You have to have a lot of things going for you at the same time. You have to be hot on the road, have a hot record, have a hot TV show and all that. He had all those things but at separate times. If he could have just gotten it all going at once... He had a Broadway show and everything, but... He just never did get everything going at once in order to get the recognition that he really deserved.

Lyle: Did you hang out with Roger during his dry spell in the early seventies?

Willie: Never knew him then. Never knew that he had a dry spell.

Lyle: He went through a period of a few years where he was doing mostly cover songs, then he released the album *Dear Folks, Sorry I Haven't Written Lately.*

Willie: I don't call those dry spells. He was still creative, he was still doing it, he was still doing something. I used to worry about when I would go for a long time and not write anything. Roger would say, "Sometimes the well goes dry and you have to wait until it fills up again." During that time you do other things, you do other people's songs. That's when I did *Startdust*, that's when I did all those albums. So Roger did the same thing. You can't just lay down and die because you're not writing. So I don't call those dry spells.

Lyle: Can you tell me anything about the last time you saw Roger?

Willie: The last time I saw Roger, he came to see me. I was working in the Universal Amphitheatre. It was maybe three, four months before he died. I could tell he was real sick. He was trying to get his sense of humor back but it just wasn't there.

Rick Marcelli

Bill Rich

Rick has been in showbiz his whole life, working in the film, music and television industries. He's responsible for the successful careers of many entertainers, including Jenny Jones and David Copperfield. Rick is now partners with management guru and best-selling author Ken Kragen, whose clients include Lionel Ritchie, Olivia Newton John, Burt Reynolds, Travis Tritt and Kenny Rogers.

Rick: Roger was bigger than life to me. Big. Roger gravitated toward the unusual, Roger wasn't normal. I don't mean that in a bad way. He was an artist. He was extremely extravagant in his way of thinking. I am very pleased to know that someone is writing a book on Roger Miller. It's unfortunate, but a lot of people are forgotten in this world. I'm happy to see that someone will bring him to life, because he was really unique to country music.

I've been involved in show business probably since I was about eight years old. Got involved in the record industry when I was about fifteen…wanted to be in a rock band and that led me to work for Capital Records. So now I'm about seventeen or eighteen, nineteen years old, the record industry was huge because of The Beatles influence, and I'm a teenager loving music and digging the guitar and all that stuff, trying to actively stay involved in the industry. My memory is not always correct, but I recall I read an ad in the trades that they were looking for someone to be involved with a music publishing company. I had a meeting with a guy by the name of Charles M. Allred, known as Marty Allred, who was Roger's drummer and was with Roger for, I'd have to guess again, at least fourteen or fifteen years. I'd say that Marty Allred was funnier than Roger and quicker than Roger and that probably half the material Roger got—I don't mean written material, but the funny lines—came from sparring with Marty Allred. June Allred is still alive and lives in England somewhere. Marty died, as they all did.

Thumbs Carllile… I really got involved with Thumbs Carllile because I'd never in my life seen someone play the guitar like him, physically, and he played it beautifully. I think Tommy Mottola was either going to sign George Benson or Thumbs Carllile. They put Thumbs up at the Sheraton Hotel. I sort of put the deal together. I remember they told Thumbs that he didn't have the deal, and they didn't pick up his room service bill. It was really kind of sad.

Do you know about Thumbs Carllile? I mean, the guy was unbelievable. I try and describe to people how he played, but it always sounds like I am talking about a steel guitar and I'm not. [Thumbs played sitting down with the guitar flat across his lap.] He played it like a piano. He always told me that the guitar was never meant to be played the way it is, that it was meant to be played laying down, that somebody just accidentally picked it up. The way he played it, you kind of believed it.

Roger had these kinds of characters around him.

So I went up to the head offices at the Max Factor Building, which was on Hollywood Boulevard across the street, literally across the street, from Grauman's Chinese Theatre. If my memory serves me well, we were on the fourth floor and that office overlooked the Hollywood High School football field. Around two or three in the afternoon sometimes, Roger would come and visit and lock the door and they'd just light up, smoke a joint and look at the football game. I remember on one occasion Roger showing up with his motorcycle. He drove the bike into the building, into the elevator, up to the fourth floor, and came into the office. It was a small office. Literally, it was one office with a storage room, reception area and a secretary's desk. That was it.

Lyle: Did you guys represent anyone else besides Roger?

Rick: We had Larry Cansler, Michael Murphey, who wrote "Wildfire." They were all writers that we had music from. I remember taking Michael Murphey literally by the hand and shopping him to every record company in town. I remember taking him to ABC Dunhill, where the head of A&R proceeded to tell me after Michael played his heart out, "Okay, now play me something good." I just thought it was really uncalled for. I'm like twenty-two years old. People were such asses.

Roger would call me Dusty. He would introduce me to Mel Tillis as Dusty. They considered me a city boy and I was a city boy, I am a city boy, born and raised in Hollywood. So I was this new kid, the city outsider that was sort of being accepted, and also I was a good fifteen, twenty years younger than everybody.

Roger was getting high, extremely so. He opened the MGM Grand and I remember sitting backstage with him. I think he was the first act ever to open the MGM Grand in Las Vegas. I remember that a cocaine delivery had been made—twenty-eight grams for the entire orchestra, or twenty-nine, and one for Roger. And I remember sitting in the light booth and you could hear the band sort of sniffing and Roger turned around and said, "It's amazing how the cold is going around in the orchestra."

In those days we didn't know about drugs like we know now. We thought you couldn't be addicted. We thought you couldn't be too thin, too rich and that cocaine was okay. Obviously it's not. There's nothing good about it. Roger and Marty both were addicted to pills, but they were addicted since they were kids. Marty played in military bands and bands since he was twelve years old. He was from Alabama. They were country kids that got involved in pills. Crazy shit would happen when you took that amount of pills.

I remember one story where Roger was driving in Las Vegas with Marty, and saw a brand new Cadillac and said, "I want one of those."

So Marty got on the phone and called dealerships and they found a dealership, I'm gonna say in Downey or Torrance. It was Sunday night and Roger wanted a Cadillac. Marty said, "Well, they're going to be closed in two hours."

He wants it now and they were two hours or so away by car. So Roger hires a helicopter. They've been up for forty-eight hours and they look like they've been up for two weeks. A lot of bad road there. So Roger had Marty call and get the dealership to blink their car lights on the parking lot so the helicopter would know where to land. When they landed the helicopter, little to Roger's knowledge the entire press corps was waiting for his arrival. The guy had called all the press and the media. So there are some pictures out there somewhere of them getting off this helicopter looking like a hundred miles of bad road.

I also know another story from when Roger had his television show. I wasn't part of his television show. Roger decided to go to Las Vegas and took Thumbs Carllile with him. They had a full network rehearsal and taping the next day, at like eleven o'clock. Roger and Thumbs proceeded to party all night long, and somewhere around two or three in the afternoon Thumbs came knocking on Roger's door and said, "You know, we're late." So they got back to L.A. and Roger told Thumbs to go in and see if they still liked him, "You go in and check it out, you go in."

I said to Roger, "How did it go down?"

He said, "You know, Rick, it was a whole lot of fun until I had to write a $40,000 check for keeping a network crew on stand-by." In those days, you are probably talking about '66, that's a lot of money.

Glen Campbell and him were unbelievable friends. Glen wanted to be Roger, wanted to be as funny as Roger. Learned every joke that ever came out of Roger's mouth. Emulated him. I cannot tell you how much he wanted to be like him. It was pretty unbelievable at the time, but he really looked up to Roger—in a good healthy way, not in some weird wacko way. I mean, he really loved Roger. I don't know what he would think or say about Roger now, but they were higher than a kite. I was there with Glen when he got so screwed up from the same doctor that Elvis had that they told everybody to get out of the dressing room. Glen had been up for a couple of days. That's what these guys were doing. Mel Tillis, Johnny Rodriguez, Roger Miller—they were higher than a kite. What really floored me is I came from a rock and roll world thinking that rock and roll stars got high and that country boys were good all-American straight-shooters. I found out that the country guys got a lot higher than anybody I'd ever met in rock-and-roll. They just hid it well.

I remember one time I sat in a bedroom with Glen Campbell and Roger and somebody came and delivered an ounce of cocaine. They both argued over how much money they'd pay for it. I don't remember the numbers, but let's say it started off at five: Roger, "I'll pay you five."

Glen, "I'll give you six."

Roger, "I'll give you seven."

Glen, "Well, I'll give you nine."

Roger, "I'll give you twelve."

Talking about *hundreds*. But whatever was the price—I don't recall what drugs were going for those days—they were outbidding each other to pay more. It was very funny, I mean sadly funny. When you look at it really, it's very sad, but it was funny. Roger once told me that he liked cocaine because he could hide it in a saltshaker and his wife wouldn't find it. I was with Roger when he stayed in John Barrymore's aviary in Bel-Air. This is where he was living, it was a beautiful place. I remember he dropped a bunch of cocaine on the second floor and he had a shoebox over it. He would let the housemaid vacuum all around the shoebox. He would run up the stairs and take a big sniff off the rug and come downstairs and start writing or whatever he was going to do.

It was very much a drug time. You gotta understand we had *Laugh-In*, we had people singing about drugs. It was almost incredibly acceptable. A lot of peer pressure, because everyone was doing it. I had an act called Shields & Yarnell, a mime act on CBS. They were quite big and headlined in Las Vegas. Roger Miller and Robert Shields became very good friends. They got completely whacked out all the time. Robert and I are still friends. He's in Sedona, Arizona, and he's a very successful artist. Roger was very close to Robert because Roger related to Robert. Robert was an odd man out. He was a mime act in this world of ours. Everything I've done, with David Copperfield or whoever it is, I've always dealt with odd characters. Roger was as odd to country music and music as Shields & Yarnell was to being a mime act on TV, as David Copperfield was to the world of magic. They're all off-centered kinds of guys.

Roger got totally involved in Beverly Hills, he almost turned his back on country. I feel it's because he felt he was uneducated and felt that he wanted to sophisticate himself and he wanted to be above all that. He didn't embrace his roots at that time. I remember he was on *The Tonight Show* and he made the biggest blunder by saying how he got a flat tire on his Bentley. And I went, "No, Roger, a jeep, a truck, not a Bentley. Don't say that." He used to wear these alpaca sweaters, which was very non-country. I think if he would have been more country and less Beverly Hills it would have been better. At that time he kind of turned his back on Nashville and that whole thing and became kind of Hollywood. And you know what? It didn't serve him well. He should have never turned his back on Nashville. I think that's why he's not recognized to a large extent, because I think he alienated himself with some people. People were a lot tighter then and a lot less Hollywood, and here's Roger living in Bel Air. Roger had a Cartier watch. Roger's about sophistication, he was about a Rolls Royce. He wasn't about a pick-up truck and living on the farm. Uh-uh. He was uptown now.

We both had the same dentist. I still go to this dentist, Jerry Albus. How I met him is Roger was in the hospital and I went up to see Roger. Well, he didn't want to see me. Why? Because he had every tooth in his mouth taken out except for one. He looked like a country hick. He sort of covered his mouth and we kind of laughed. Jerry was bolting every tooth in his mouth to his jaw. This is back in '71, doing cosmetic surgery so that Roger would have good teeth.

Lyle: What drew him to L.A?

Rick: I don't know… Roger didn't have the publishing on "King of The Road." Tree Publishing pissed him off. He never had the dollars that were generated from his publishing. He made a lot of money, he spent a lot of money, he threw a lot of money away… I know that Tree Publishing had his work and when we started Roger Miller Music he was starting his own publishing company. That's what I was a part of.

Lyle: How long did the publishing company last?

Rick: I don't recall. Certainly two or three years, maybe three or four years… when I was twenty or twenty-one. I'm gonna say '72, '73, '74.

He used to scare the hell out of me. He'd scare me to the point where I could not talk. He'd get mad at me and say, "Talk to me! Why aren't you talking to me? What's wrong with your tongue?" Now I'm a very glib guy, I don't know if you can tell, I cannot stop talking. I couldn't talk in front of him. I admired him so much, he scared the living crap out of me… You had to be really quick with these guys 'cause you'd be stepped on, right to the point where Roger would say, "What's wrong with your tongue?" The more you didn't talk, the more you couldn't come back with something fast, you got eaten up alive… A lot of times I thought he had ice running through his veins because he could be cold. He could be very, very cold, very cutting. He'd get on stage and sing two songs and turn to Marty and say, "Let's go gamble." Then he'd walk right off stage. If he did it once he did it a hundred times. He had the worst reputation for just walking off stage.

Lyle: That's the first I ever heard of that.

Rick: Are you kidding? It happened all over, all the time. It happened at The Nugget, it happened everywhere. He'd just turn to Marty, turn around to

Thumbs, and go, "Let's go to the pool. Let's get out of here. Let's go gambling."

Lyle: Was he a major draw at the casinos?

Rick: He was huge. He had, I guess, more Grammys than The Beatles had. For the longest time he held the record. Way into the eighties he held the record.

One night he had come over to my apartment in West Hollywood, he and Marty. It was the night before Easter Sunday. I have a Gibson guitar, I still have it, and he would just start playing the guitar. Marty fell asleep on the couch and Roger proceeded to tell me that Marty was a bad guy and that I should stay away from him, that he was a hustler and that I should watch myself. And you know he wasn't wrong. He was absolutely saying the truth. He was actually being very honest with me. He was very suspect of Marty taking him to the cleaners, stealing money from him…and he wanted to protect me, which is really nice. Marty was also very nice and generous to me. He's the guy that really gave me the job under Roger. Marty fell asleep and we stayed up all night straight through Easter Sunday just talking.

Lyle: With you working for his publishing company, did he ever discuss songwriting with you at all?

Rick: I'd overhear him, but I don't have enough to give you. I was always in the room when he'd be picking up his guitar and playing something. I can't give you anything that you could put your arms around.

Lyle: I've found it pretty surprising that a lot of guys, like Waylon Jennings or Willie Nelson, never talked about songwriting. I thought that would be something they would have talked about a lot.

Rick: Well, I could tell you one thing about Willie Nelson. I heard Willie Nelson sing and I rushed into Roger's office with Marty and I said, "Willie Nelson! I just heard this guy with this voice that I never heard anybody have in my life. This guy's going to be a huge star."

And they both laughed at me and went, "That's Willie."

I said, "Willie nothing. Let's go after this guy. This guy's going to be huge!"

"Ah, it'll never happen."

I used to tell them all the time, "I guess it did happen." Because it was an odd voice for the time, different, they never suspected that Willie would ever make it. They would have taken a bet that he would have never made it.

Lyle: What can you tell me about The King of the Road Hotel? I've been told that the Mob owned that place.

Rick: At that time the Mob was involved with everything. You gotta understand, the guy who owns the MGM, his father was a hit man for the Mafia. The whole Vegas scene was mob related. Roger wouldn't have known it [beforehand, but] he might have found out about it. In other words, I don't think he would consciously go in on something that had the Mob involved. That wasn't Roger's style.

The real stories about Roger are incredible. It's just whether or not people will let them loose, 'cause everybody wants to paint everybody into such a saintly corner that you take all the character out of that person. My problem is, I wish I could remember the sentences that he would form because he was brilliant. It was a natural brilliance, not something that you go to school and study. This guy just thought different than anybody else. Look at the songs that he wrote. You don't write songs like that, nobody has. Nobody has, nobody's doing it, nobody will. He just was an odd character. I'm not saying that you should write dirt. I'm saying that in my opinion you should write the color that Roger was. I'm not interested in talking about the drugs, that's not my issue. The issue is this was a guy that was bigger than life and he lived life to the highest. Roger didn't know how to be straight. I'm not saying that's where his genius came from.

These guys would be up for four and five days, and I mean up. I don't mean like he took a nap and got up. I mean *up*. I don't even know how you do that. These guys would take a Black Beauty… I don't know if you know what those are. It's just a big black pill filled with speed, and they popped the whole thing, maybe take two of them. This would give probably ten people a major heart attack and these guys would pop them like candy and stay up. It would be like they had four cups of coffee the first thing in the morning. That's how they'd be two days later, talking and carrying on and doing whatever. And about by the third or fourth day they'd start to twitch and smell bad. They'd start to rot and they'd have to lie down. It really was that pathetic. At the very end, when I saw Marty out in front of my place where I was living, I had to call up his wife June to come pick him up, and it just was really bad. It got really dark, really, really bad.

Some of the things that went on were insane. I'll tell you one example: I was up at The Nugget with David Copperfield. The stars would be treated differently than the opening act. The stars had a house that they would give them with a butler and maid. I know that Marty and Roger and everybody stayed in this house. Now I'm up there with David Copperfield four or five, six years later, and I'm going around to the different cupboards and the armoires or whatever and everything is bolted down. The vase is bolted down, everything's bolted. So I land up in this conversation with the owner of The Nugget, John Ascuaga. I said, "How comes everything's bolted down?"

"Well, we had some country guy up here and the band took the entire furniture out of the house."

Well, I knew who that was. It was Roger's band. I saw stuff from The Nugget all over everyone's houses. It was kind of funny, tragically funny.

We were at the Troubadour on Santa Monica Boulevard in West Hollywood. Roger was working there that week. Lo and behold Dylan was in the audience. I go up to Roger, "Roger, Bob Dylan's here. He wants to know if he can come up and sing a song with you." Roger was like, "Oh, wow, cool." He's up on stage and Roger's in an alpaca sweater—you know, he's not rock and roll. Roger Miller is Roger Miller, kind of a conservative guy. In this country way, Roger said with that kind of way he kind of talked, "Ladies and gentlemen, I'd like to bring up a friend of mine… here's Bob Dylan." And Bob Dylan comes on stage, looks at Roger, looks away from Roger and never makes eye contact with Roger again. His entire band comes on stage, Roger's band walks off stage. Roger is standing next to him like they're going to sing a song together, and Bob Dylan goes into what apparently was the set that he was going to do when he was going on tour the next day. They were just rehearsing and proceeded to do his entire set. Now Roger is standing three feet away from Bob Dylan like he's going to chime in on the chorus, and he realized that Dylan is not acknowledging him at all. Roger is kind of like bopping with the band and turning around like, "Okay, I'll just come in at the next chorus." There is no look at Roger at all from Dylan. Finally Roger inches a little farther back and finally walks off the stage. And it was Dylan the rest of the night. It just pissed Roger off.

Roger had a big impact on me. I've never been intimidated by a star ever again in my life except for Roger Miller, because I was young and naïve and I really thought that he walked on water. But I have since learned that all they are are just children. If I knew then what I know now I probably could have helped Roger stay alive, 'cause I would have grabbed him by the back of the neck and told him to grow up. But nobody could stand up to Roger. I certainly couldn't, I was just a kid. He taught me a lot about just being nice to people. I saw him be really rude to people and hurt people and I decided I didn't really want to be that way. I also saw a guy that was in a lot of pain. You could just see emotional pain. I don't think you could get as high as he got without being in emotional pain. You're hiding something.

He had some big issues but they were clouded with major drugs. You gotta understand, we didn't know alcohol was a disease, we didn't know cocaine was addictive. We've come a long way in terms of understanding. We didn't know drugs could make you depressed or that if you got high on a Monday your nerve system would be shattered on a Wednesday. We just thought it was time to get high again. It's sad because Roger basically died young. So did Marty. There's no reason Roger should be dead right now, or Marty. But they took more drugs than any pharmacy has in stock over a course of twenty, twenty-five years. They beat themselves up.

Robert Shields

Courtesy of Robert Shields

When I was a kid Robert Shields kind of freaked me out with his mime act on TV. But as an adult I really admire his talents as a performer, artist, restaurateur and successful business man.

Lyle: How did you strike up a friendship with Roger Miller?

Robert: I became his opening act and we got along. I've worked with a lot of acts but there was something about him. He was beyond just another singer/songwriter. There was some great depth. He started doing these different variations on a theme...almost like a Mozart of country in a way. I think if he didn't do so much drugs he would have gone beyond, but back then people were hung up in that shit. Most of them were. As you know he was one of them. But he was a true genius, Roger Miller. He was like almost a country Dylan in a way. Something in his voice... He had a wonderful mystery in his voice. When he sang, when I saw his show live, I was just amazed at his stuff. All I knew from him was "Dang Me" and "King of the Road". But something about him live really hit me and we started hanging out. Of course he liked my act. We were very innovative at the time, Shields & Yarnell, doing physical comedy and stuff. I'm a physical comic. Roger does what I do with his words. I was fascinated with that. The way he would place words, the way he would talk and the way he would verbalize was just like magic. Sometimes he would go on stage and because of the drugs he'd blow it, and then sometimes it would be brilliant. Sometimes it'd be beyond genius, sometimes it would be just nothing. I remember one night Roger kicked the speakers in ['cause] he couldn't get his sound right. He kicked 'em in pretty hard, broke 'em. This was in Denver, like 1979.

Lyle: Did you tour quite a bit with him or was that just a one-time thing?

Robert: Just a one-time thing. But after that we started hanging out, went to his house, went out to dinner. The guy became someone I hung with, became a very good friend of mine, in fact. He had a lot of my art. I'm a painter and a sculptor and an illustrator. I have four stores in Sedona and I wholesale to four hundred stores across the country. I gave him a lot of my art.

I liked just listening to him talk. He used to take clocks apart and put them back together again. He used to take these clocks apart and he'd say, "You know, these clocks are like life. Each piece, each part is something, and when you put it back together it's like the human body. It just all works."

Lyle: Did you hang out with him in Vegas at all?

Robert: Yeah, he'd come to see me, I'd come to see him. Roger had a terrific sense of humor and he loved to imitate Gabby Hayes. I'm a clown. I was a director of clowns for Ringling Brothers. My whole thing is comedy, voices. (*imitates Jack Nicholson's voice*) "How the hell are you? This is Jack. If Barbie's so popular why do you have to buy all her friends?" I do jokes, things like that. That's why Roger and I got along. I used to sit there and imitate him. He loved Chaplin and Keaton. He really appreciated good stuff. Roger was good. Some of these cats are just ok. Like you take someone…like even what's his face? Spiders and snakes? Jim Stafford, he's okay. Roger was fine wine. He really was. It's unfortunate that… If you listen to all his music, all of a sudden there'll be some songs that pop out that are just amazing. When you're with him personally though, you really see his genius more than any other time.

Lyle: Did he ever talk to you about the music industry?

Robert: Yeah, he did. He felt that at one point they just kind of passed him by. He probably did it to himself, don't you think? I don't know. I know he used to tell me that Willie Nelson was just this kind of guy who was struggling and would always try and go see Roger like, "Can you help me?". And all of a sudden Willie Nelson is a gigantic star and Roger is like second banana. I remember that kind of hurt him. What happened with Roger was, when Roger was in style Roger was wearing tuxedos, and all of a sudden country started getting 'countrified' and Roger was still wearing tuxedos. Don't you think that's what happened? He was bigger than any of those guys before they even hit. He was kind of as big as Hank Williams for a while. He had a variety show. This was before country was fashionable, because he crossed over so well. He was fine-lined. Roger really was great. If it wasn't for the cocaine, he would have been even greater.

Lyle: Do you recall any of his one-liners?

Robert: "Rebel without applause." That one really sticks to me. One time Roger told me a story that I'll never forget. I always tell people this who are in show businesses. It's about ego and business. He's playing the Cow Palace, and the Cow Palace is a big stadium. Everybody's screaming "King of the Road! King of the Road! King of the Road!" They wouldn't let him play. So he plays "King of the Road," then after "King of the Road" he says, "Well, that's how I close my act, so good night!" and got into a helicopter and flew out! Can you imagine? How's that for a story?

When I was hanging out with him, he was kind of like trying to come back. I saw him when he was doing B acts and B places. When I worked with him in Denver it wasn't like a stadium, it was a nightclub. Fame can destroy you, you know. Fame and drugs and alcohol and too much attention… You start feeling like you're a god.

Lyle: Was he upset about going from the A stages to B stages?

Robert: No, because he still was treated well. The limos still came and he put up a good front, still had the parties afterwards, still did a great show, people were still pumping up his ego. And I as one of them. I was just, God, I just couldn't believe it, I was just a young kid. I just thought he was *great*. "This guy is great. Jesus, he's so good!" He's just got this wonderful style and way about him. I wish you could have seen him live, man. He was way better than Glen Campbell or some shiny little rhinestone like that. Roger had some depth going. I can't explain it. He would just talk to the audiences and he would tell them strange things and little stories.

Lyle: Did hanging out with him influence your life at all?

Robert: Yeah, it influenced my life a lot. I started using that white stuff and it was hard on me. It took a lot to get out of there. I was twenty-eight years old, I think, when I first started, and it lasted about five or six years.

Lyle: You picked up that habit from spending time with Roger?

Robert: Yeah. He was doing it and I wasn't so I thought, "Okay, I'll do some." And you know how that works. It was the seventies and that's what happened. That's how he influenced my life, because he loved that stuff and if he didn't have any he didn't want to see you. One time I came over and he said, "I got no dope." And that's it, bottom line, no fun.

Let me tell you something that's really going to be unusual to you. I'm not going to drop names on you but I headlined all those hotels, I had my fame in the sun and all that shit. We were a very big act for a long time and just about everybody did coke. From the people that I could mention you'd just go, *What?* Everybody in the late seventies. That's when I did it, in the late seventies early eighties, on and off. I only could do it on weekends because I'm an athlete. I was the first street mime. We took physical comedy and were the first ones to have a TV series out of it. We were a household name. We still are. Anybody over thirty-four watched the Shields & Yarnell Show on CBS. And everybody was doing coke. It was part of the culture, it was just a common thing. It was country, western, classical, contemporary, pop, rock-and-roll, agents, managers, doctors, dentists. It was a major thing. It was a terrible thing to go through. It's a horrible, horrible drug. I hope you never try it. It's like making a pact with the devil. I'm not Christian or anything, but it's the closest thing you can do to going into Satanism. It's just so weird. It makes you feel so good and then makes you feel so bad that you gotta pay for your high. And then you do more and you can never get off of it. And it is psychologically addicting, so it really messes with your head. Roger was a big user. I was a weekend user, social user. He was a very, very big user. He'd buy tons of it.

Lyle: Did he ever give you any advice on show business at all?

Robert: Yeah, because I wanted to go into a rock-and-roll band. I was doing a lot of music and he says, "Man, you're the greatest mime in the world. You're like Chaplin. Just stick to that. Just do what you do well. Just keep what you're doing. Don't be anything you're not." 'cause I was really young. I wanted to be in a rock-and-roll band because I had the energy, and I saw videos were coming out real strong. I'm the one who got Michael Jackson to do the robot and shit. Oh yeah, I created the robot. Michael Jackson would watch my show every week.

Lyle: Do you remember the last time that you saw Roger?

Robert: Yeah, it was an interesting day. Two of my really good friends in show business… Now I only have two—Roger Miller and Jackie Mason. Both came to see me in L.A. at the Hermitage Hotel. I got them both in my hotel room. Can you imagine Roger Miller and Jackie Mason, both of them together? Isn't that wild? That was the last time I saw Roger. He was doing great. He looked liked he was clean, he wasn't doing any drugs or anything.

Lyle: Did you ever hear anything about a briefcase full of herbal remedies that he'd carry around when he was trying to get over his pill addiction?

Robert: Yeah. He had all those herbs in a briefcase, all these things he was kind of getting better on. And all these things like echinacea and things he was taking. And I thought he was just nuts. I was still pretty young. I was living in Sedona doing spiritual stuff at the time and I just thought well, that's great, Rog. I didn't think he was strange, I thought he was healing. I was so proud of him because I used to be so sad for him. It was just so great to see him clean. He was clean as a bell. In fact, he was kind of overweight.

Lyle: Was he sick then?

Robert: I don't know because Mary never told me when he was sick. I just kind of found out when it was too late.

Roger was like a little kid, you know. He really appreciated friends. I guess what I miss most about Roger is when you first see him he just lights up. He just gives you a big hug and you could feel the love… He was a really, really neat person in my life. I had the chance to meet every celebrity in the world. If I wanted to be friends with them I could if I pursued it, but I didn't want to be. He was the only one I'd want to hang out with. He wasn't just this… You know, one thing about celebrities is they're really not that interesting. Because they get so much attention and shit they don't really have to put out much. Especially people in the music business. They're some of the most boring people I've ever met in my life. *Damn.* They're so used to getting all this attention they just don't have much to say and they're not that interesting. Roger had a lot to say and was really interesting. I really miss the guy.

Chuck Blore

Chuck Blore is a radio/television commercial writer and producer. He was a close friend of Roger's.

Chuck: I had a very big career in radio before I got into doing commercials, and I had all these people who were friends of mine, so I wrote new lyrics to their songs. Mac Davis, Glen Campbell, Roger... Years ago when my commercial company first started, I used to have Glen Campbell as the guitar player on all my spots. One day I wrote a commercial and I asked Glen to compose the music for it and to round up a group of people to record it. The next morning we went to the studio and there was Glen with this other guy. I said, "Where are the musicians?"

"We're it."

"Just you two guys?"

"Oh yeah, that's all you need. We're going to overdub and overdub and overdub."

And so he introduced me to Roger. He was the other guy. That was fine, they did the music and the singing. I had written the spot to be kind of country and I had written it to read it myself. So I started reading a copy. They'd hung around just to hear the rest of the spot and Roger says, "Hey, Chuck, how'd you like that done authentic?"

I said, "Oh great, okay, good, go ahead."

So he read it. And then as he was leaving that day he said, "Hey, Chuck, how much money you think I made today?"

"Well, we did three spots, Roger." The scale then, believe it or not, was $32 per spot. I said, "Heck, you made damn near $100 today."

He said, "You think I could get it quick?"

Roger was out here staying at Glen's house sleeping on his couch. He was out here [in California] trying to sell songs. He was trying to make a living. He didn't stay here very long. Right after that is when everything happened for him. When he asked me how much money [he made] and I said, "$100," he said, "Boy, you ever want me to do 'em again you just call me and I'll come running." I told that to the advertising agency. Well, in the meantime they knew they had a personality on their hands. Suddenly he was a big star and they had this commercial running. They just kept running it over and over and over again. Pretty soon it got a little tired and they called me and said do another one. I said, "Come on, he's a superstar, I just can't call him."

They said, "Didn't you say that he said to you he'd come running?"

So I called Roger and I reminded him of that. He said, "Yeah, I said I'd come running and I will—on one condition."

"What's that?"

"You don't pay me any more than the first time." Now he was a superstar and I paid him $100 the second time too. Hell of a guy!

One time Roger was sitting on the floor in my office and I got a call from the NAB, the National Association of Broadcasters. This was the time when, for whatever reason I don't even recall, patriotism was somehow at an all-time low. So the NAB called me and said, "I need you to do some spot to tell people about how great radio keeps the economy running, blah, blah, blah. It's gotta be in a real patriotic tone."

So I looked at Roger, "Okay, Roger, here's an assignment."

We wrote a song called "Freedom". We were going to write the song that night and I said, "Okay, I'll see you about ten o'clock."

On the way to his house I wrote the first little stanza, and you know I'm not going to come in there and tell Roger Miller how to write a song. That wasn't going to work, I knew that! I said, "Roger, I have what may be a pretty good start here. See what you think."

I told him the first four lines of the song and he said, "Well shit, Chuck, there ain't no reason to change that," so we started writing it.

Lyle: Can you tell me anything about the recording session of "Freedom"?

Chuck: The producer of the album slowed it down, took the tempo and did it about in half. And Roger secretly never liked the way it was done. But this guy, this producer of the album at that time was so hot, *who the hell are we?*—you know. But we liked it better in a little more up tempo.

Roger invented a whole new kind of music. When you start going through some of Roger's songs, eight bars didn't mean shit. Nor do thirty-two. Before Roger, the way to write a song was you wrote it in eight bar phrases, and when you got to thirty-two the song was over. That wasn't Roger. He just did what he wanted, and he had no education in that at all. He didn't read music. When they wanted to publish one of his songs he'd just sing it into a recorder and somebody else would write it down.

Lyle: Did Roger ever talk about his songwriting techniques to you at all?

Chuck: He didn't have any techniques. He was just always doing it. Did you know "King of the Road" was written, maybe a couple of years before it was called "King of the Road"? He had written all the parts to it except the actual words King of the Road. He was on his bus one night and they passed this guy, this hobo, this tramp, on the way and someone said, "There he is, the king of the road." And Roger said, "Oh shit!" He went back and stuck it into the lyrics he had already written years before. He had to make a few adjustments he told me, but basically that was how "King of the Road" happened, how he got the title.

Lyle: It's funny that you mention "King of the Road" because a lot of people have mentioned that song and how it came to be written, and every story has been different!

Chuck: Really? It wouldn't surprise me if Roger told somebody else something else. Wouldn't surprise me.

Here's a funny story: [One time] Roger said, "You gotta call information and ask them a question they don't know the answer to."

I said, "Like what?"

"Here, watch." And so he dials 411, or whatever the hell number was back then, and he said, "How do you spell mariachis?"

411 replied, "What?"

"You know, the Mexican shoes? How do you spell it?"

"This is information."

"Yeah, well, that's what I want, information. I want information about how you spell mariachis." And he kept that guy on the phone, honest to God, for at least ten minutes. The guy never did know who he was.

I think that after Roger had his five years of superstardom—it could have been longer, I don't know how long it was—he wasn't ready for it to end. He just kept coming back and trying and trying and trying, mostly through writing songs, releasing songs, and so forth, but it just didn't happen. And then someone... What's his name? Shoot, the guy who eventually produced *Big River*?

Lyle: Rocco Landesman.

Chuck: No, no, no, Rocco was the Broadway guy. This was when it was in LaJolla. Do you know about it being in LaJolla?

Lyle: No.

Chuck: Well, when Roger first got this thing, somebody came to him and said, "We want you to write a musical."

Roger said, "I don't know how to do that."

He said, "Well, yes you do. It's so easy, blah, blah, blah."

So they made arrangements that Roger would write this musical which was going to open in LaJolla. Roger worked on it for, oh, I don't know, a couple of months, and did a couple of songs and so on. And then he lost interest in it totally. But they were out there spending money, buying sets and doing all sorts of things. They came to Roger and said, "We're about ready to start putting it up," or whatever the phrase it is they use. "Is it finished yet?"

And Roger said, "It's as finished as it gonna get it."

They said, "Oh, you can't do this."

Mary gave Roger hell. "Roger, you can't do that! These people have a lot of money invested. They are depending on you."

Roger said, "Alright, alright, alright."

So Roger went into... He told me later, "I went into my trunk, got out a lot of songs that I had thrown away, and I gave 'em to them."

That was the beginning of that musical. And of course we had to come down to LaJolla to see the opening night, and I tell you it was a piece of crap. There was one thing in there where the whole cast mooned the audience. It was just really...dreadful. Of course, you never tell Roger it's dreadful. Not that he wouldn't take the criticism, but when you told him that he would go into such a fit of depression it just wasn't worth it. Everyone said, "Ah, it's fine, Roger. It's fine, it's fine."

Later on it still had the same title *Big River* and it's still supposed to be somewhat about Huckleberry Finn. Well, we get a call from Mary, "Hey, we want you guys to come to the preview," which is the night before it opened on Broadway.

It's one of those things you don't say no to. We got on a plane and all the way [to New York] we said, "Oh God, I hope they took the mooning thing out."

My wife said, "I hope it isn't at all like that other one. God, how could it get to Broadway? Well, somebody's nuts."

We went down there and we saw this unbelievably delightful show. Roger had said, "Oh shit, this is New York. This is going to count," and he got up and he worked his ass off. My wife and I really were afraid to go to that preview. We were afraid it was going to be a rewrite, and if it had been only a little rewrite of what we'd seen, Roger was going to hang himself. But boy, it was really good.

You know, Roger was like most ego-maniacs—they just don't trust themselves. He, like every great artist way down deep, would say, "Why is this happening to me?" Then on the other hand, when it didn't, "Why ain't it happening?" He was really frustrated all that time in New Mexico before *Big River*. And then of course when he won the Tony for *Big River,* he got up and gave his little speech about how he wrote the wonderful thing and how wonderful Mark Twain was. But those of us that knew the truth were like, "Ah shit, Roger..." The only thing was he didn't even mention his wife. In fact, my wife was so pissed she wouldn't speak to him. She said, "How could you leave her out? If it wasn't for her you wouldn't have had the goddamn thing. She's the one that kept you going."

Lyle: Well, I think it was pretty obvious that he loved her.

Chuck: Oh no question about that, no question about that. He couldn't have lived without her. I'm not kidding, because he was damn near helpless. I know there was a long time where he was so hooked on pills... I don't know how he got over it, but the fact of the matter is he did. But he never got over—and he didn't want to—marijuana and coke. Those were things that he loved to do that didn't get in his way. But the other shit that he was into, he knew that was poison for him eventually.

When Roger got sick and the doctors couldn't cure him, he came out here to L.A. because of some faith healers. He said, "If the doctors can't do it, maybe God can." So he came out here to meet with these faith healers. I wanted to go see him. Mary and [my wife] Judy are and have been, literally, best friends, so Judy went down on the day they got here. She came back and said, "Chuck, Mary doesn't want you to come down there."

I said "Why?"

She said, "Because Roger has been taking chemo and his hair is gone and he's fat. She doesn't want you to remember him that way."

So I did not go down there. Instead I talked to him on the phone every single day. I said, "You know, Roger, they won't let me come down there."

He said, "You know, Chuck, that's a good idea."

"What? Not to let me come down?"

"Yep, you don't want to see me like this. I got all the mirrors taken out of this room because I don't want to see me like this."

They had a place on the ocean and the night before he died he came out on the balcony to see Judy and Mary and said, "Mary, say hello to Nancy."

Mary said, "Say hello to who?"

"My angel, Nancy. Say hello to my angel."

"Roger, nobody's there."

"Mary, don't be rude. Say hello to Nancy."

Lyle: Was Roger a religious man?

Chuck: I don't know. That's a very good question. I know that he had an angel named Nancy, so he must have had something going on.

Rocco Landesman

R occo was co-producer of Big River *in 1985 and of the smash hit* The Producers *in 2001.* Big River *won seven Tonys, including "Best Musical," "Best Score" and "Best Book," as well as many Drama Desk and Outer Critics' Circle Awards.* The Producers *won an unprecedented twelve Tonys. Before heading to Broadway, Rocco taught dramatic literature and criticism at the Yale School of Drama. He has been the president of Jujamcyn Theatres since 1987.*

Rocco: I've always been a Roger Miller fan. I was really fanatical about his music. I first heard it when I was in high school in 1964, '65, when those big hits started coming out. I was a fan of his all through college, and I would buy anything that he put out.

One day my wife Heidi and I were going down to the Lone Star Café to one of his concerts. It was a very rare New York appearance for him. We had the idea that maybe he could write the score for a Broadway show. We heard his concert at the Lone Star and went up to him afterwards and brought the idea to him. I don't think he really knew what we were talking about, but Mary really focused in on this and encouraged me to write a letter to him. So I wrote a letter, and wrote another letter, and another one, and kept trying to reach him but never heard anything. One day I got a call from Stan Moress, one of his managers, and he said, "Well, if you're really serious about this and want to meet Roger, you could meet him in Reno where he's going to be playing a concert." So I went out to Reno, saw Roger after one of his gigs, and we had this whole conversation. It was a great thrill for me because he played me a lot of his songs, which I knew of course by heart. He just gave me like a personal concert—one of the great thrills I've had in my life, actually.

I said, "I'm interested in you writing the music for a musical based on *Huckleberry Finn.*"

He said, "Well, let me know if there's a book written." 'If there's a script,' as he put it.

I said, "Fine, I will."

Finally, I did commission a book by a friend of mine at the Yale Drama School, where I'd been a student and a teacher. I asked a playwright I knew to write an adaptation of *Huckleberry Finn* as a musical, sent it to Roger, and he eventually signed on.

Lyle: When you gave him the script, did he come up with the ideas of what kind of songs to write?

Rocco: The script suggested places where there would be songs, so he started to respond to the different places in the script. There'd be a title of a song or an idea for a song, the song idea would be sketched in by the writer Bill Hauptman, and Roger would go from there. Often he wrote something that had nothing to do with the script just 'cause something struck him or something inspired him, and of course then we'd find ways to get it into the show. "Worlds Apart," "You Gotta Be Here With Me," "Leavin's Not The Only Way To Go" were songs that just occurred to him around this time or songs that he had been working on for a while. Other songs he wrote directly for the show—"River In The Rain," of course, "Muddy Water," a lot of those songs. "The Boys" was one of the first ones that he wrote. "Hand For the Hog" he wrote later in the process as kind of a character song for Tom Sawyer. There's an example of another song that's kind of more Roger than Mark Twain, perhaps, but we found a way to use it.

Lyle: Since you were essentially getting Roger to write songs for you, did he ever discuss his songwriting process with you?

Rocco: He didn't really discuss the process. It was always something of a mystery. He would tend to work very fast, by inspiration. He'd do things in a spurt, in a rush, very quickly. Most of what he was gonna get he would get in that rush of inspiration and then spend some time working things out, working out the music and the bridges and melodies. He wouldn't sustain concentration for all that long, [that's] probably one of the reasons that the songs aren't that long. He was a sprinter, not a marathon runner. He would have a flash for a lyric or a turn of phrase or a line, and that would be a song more or less. It was very hard for him to write to order. I remember we needed a song at a certain point in the show and we locked him in his room and told him "You can't come out until you've finished the song." He really got pissed off. He said, "If you want Rembrandt, Rembrandt takes time. If you want Earl Scheib, I can do that for you in an hour." Earl Scheib was a chain that painted cars. He would resist our attempts to get him to write to order for us, but he did. Actually, that song which we sort of locked him up in the room to write, ended up being "Guv'ment," which is one of the great songs from *Big River*. Johnny Goodman sang it in that show.

Lyle: I liked one of the interviews I saw where you said Roger had attention deficit disorder.

Rocco: Right. He certainly did. Roger was asked about how the project came to be and he answered, "Rocco made me an offer I couldn't understand."

Lyle: Were you already involved with the Broadway scene before you met Roger?

Rocco: No, this was really my first Broadway show. And to this day I don't understand how he trusted me to believe that I was actually going to get this thing on Broadway. I never really produced a Broadway show.

I'd been a professor at Yale in the Yale Drama School, so I had some credibility, I guess, as a result of that, though I don't know how much. Roger just took a leap of faith. This was on spec that I was even going to get this thing up and raise all the money for it. It cost two and a half million dollars to put up. He just took a chance that I'd be able to do what I said I'd be able to do. Mary Miller to this day says that he always believed everything I said. And I would always manage to deliver, to do exactly what I said I was going to do. The first production of it was done up at Harvard up at the American Repertory Theatre in Cambridge, in 1984.

Lyle: I heard that there was a big rewrite from the original one.

Rocco: Yeah, the original show had only seven songs. It was really a play with music. We had to do a lot of work between that production and the production that was done out in LaJolla later in the year. A lot more music had to be written, a lot of the show worked on and reworked. By the time we got to Broadway I think there were sixteen songs.

There were three different productions. The first one was up in Cambridge, Massachusetts, at the American Repertory Theatre, I think in February of '84. And then at the end of the year in '84 it was done at LaJolla Playhouse in LaJolla, and then it was done on Broadway in April of '85. Three different productions. A lot of music was added and it was recast, so a lot of changes were made.

Lyle: Did any songs not make it?

Rocco: Yes, there were some that went by the wayside, but none of those songs were ever released anywhere else. I'm trying to remember the names of the songs. There's a song, "How Much Does It Cost To New Orleans?".

There were lots of times when we didn't know if we'd be successful, if we'd make it. There were a lot of leaps of faith along the way. I remember one time before the New York show opened we were all sitting around in Roger's apartment that he sublet from Patty LuPone. She's a Broadway actress. I remember as I was standing up to leave—and everybody's nervous and on edge—and as I was about to open up the door to leave he looked at me dead in the eye and said, "How can we fail? We're so sincere." If it were only that easy! What if all you needed was good intentions? But we didn't know if the show was going to be successful or not.

Lyle: I understand in one of the original versions of *Big River* the crowd was mooned.

Rocco: There was a song called "When the Sun Goes Down in the South," and there was actually mooning in it. That was changed, it was taken out.

Lyle: John Goodman was the first person to play Pap, right?

Rocco: John Goodman joined the cast in LaJolla and moved with it to New York. He was the only guy that we brought.

Lyle: I heard that Roger took the part for a couple of weeks after he left.

Rocco: He did. Roger came in and played it for a number of weeks in New York. That was fun. We got Willie Nelson backstage visiting and everybody would come back and visit him in his dressing room. It was great—quite a scene. Roger really enjoyed it. Of course he adlibbed. He couldn't remember the lyrics, couldn't remember the lines half the time, so he adlibbed things, but it always worked out. He was quite charming in the role, actually. I have a picture of him on my wall, in fact, from his dressing room. Roger and Willie Nelson backstage when Roger was playing Pap.

Lyle: Is there anything that you could tell me about him that most people wouldn't know?

Rocco: He wrote in longhand, just on a piece of paper. I have the original manuscript of "River in the Rain" in my apartment.

Lyle: What was your relationship with Roger later on in his career?

Rocco: Well, it was very good. Once we did *Big River* we became good friends. I was hoping to have him do another show, in fact, but of course he couldn't do it, he died.

I saw Roger in Malibu just before he died. He looked terrible. He was all puffed up on steroids and stuff. Mary had gotten him a Malibu apartment overlooking the ocean, a condo. I saw him and he didn't look like himself. My wife, Heidi, and I were very depressed afterwards because we thought that would be the last time we'd see him and he just didn't look like himself. He was still making jokes. There were a couple of times that I'd say something just to Mary and thought he wouldn't hear me and he'd say, "I heard that!" He'd be attuned, alert. He was rational, but he was obviously very sick.

Lyle: What did you learn from Roger Miller that helped you in your career or perspective in life?

Rocco: I think one of the things you can learn is that not taking things too seriously can actually be a serious strategy for living and an effective one. Roger saw everything on a slant. Everything was off center with Roger Miller. I think it was great to be around him because he would upset the conventional and traditional points of view all the time. We tend to get locked into our groove and locked into our way of thinking, of looking at the world, and Roger always looked at the world differently. The world looked different to Roger Miller than it did to normal people, to us. I was always up after seeing Roger because I would see things in a new way. That's what I think a great artist does. He was a serious artist, but he didn't take the world too seriously.

Mason Williams

Mason Williams has an impressive history of accomplishments under his belt. An excellent writer and musician, he's written for tons of television shows, including The Smothers Brothers Comedy Hour and Saturday Night Live. He is perhaps best known musically for his composition, "Classical Gas." Mason's first job writing for television was for The Roger Miller Show in 1966.

Mason: I spent quite a lot of time with him. Roger was quite a mysterious person, real friendly in one sense but sorta distant in another. He was on guard, you might say. He extended his entertainer persona a lot off stage.

Lyle: I understand that Roger picked up your book of lyrics and poems *Bicyclists Dismount* and hired you to write for his show.

Mason: That's what I heard. It was on someone's coffee table and he picked it up and read through it, liked it and said, "Hey, let's hire his guy to write my show."

Lyle: It's interesting that he would choose you, because television and poetry are two very different mediums.

Mason: Yes, it was off the wall. In order to get to know Roger, I went on the road with him for sixteen weeks. We weren't on the road that whole time, but it covered three months or so before the television show started.

Lyle: In that period of traveling with him, was he talking about what he wanted out of the television show?

Mason: No, I think he didn't really have an idea. He was just being Roger. I did get to hear a lot of his humor and see him deal with people and get an idea of what his humor was. I got the impression that he was most impressed with Bobby Darin as a performer, and of course Frank Sinatra, but especially Bobby Darin. If there was anyone he would have liked to have been like as a performer it would have been Bobby Darin. The way Bobby handled himself on stage… He was relaxed and kind of cocky in a fun way. It was a personality that Roger could get behind. Roger used to kid around and twirl the microphone like Bobby Darin, and some of those things, but he always had his own weird little twist on things. He certainly commanded big stars. Bill Cosby was the first guest and he had all kinds of people on the show.

The reason I went on the road was to understand what Roger's personality was and what an extension of Roger would be. I wish I had written television before I got involved with Roger. It was my first show, so I was a little bit of a greenhorn and didn't really know how to stand up for what I thought Roger was all about. Because they had Gary Smith and Dwight Hemion and they were really top in their field as director and producer. They where regarded as "as good as it gets", because they did Barbara Streisand, they did all these other stars. But they had a couple of writers, Bernie Kukoff and Jeff Harris, and I like Bernie and Jeff but I kept saying to them, "Roger is country and he's not Jewish humor necessarily." It was a type of humor that would have been funny with Robert Klein or somebody, but I didn't think it suited Roger's country persona. So I didn't really know how to get across what I thought Roger was all about. Later on, when Roger came to *The Smothers Brothers Show,* I knew exactly how to handle him being on the show. I knew how to set it up for him so he came off well and so he felt comfortable, because I knew who Roger was very well. I just wish I had some of the experience I gained later. I would have had a better idea of how to mount a show around him. Writing for variety was a great education. I got to write for Jack Benny and George Burns. What a treat. Variety was quite the art form. It's too bad it's not on anymore. The stars don't need variety anymore. I mean, Madonna doesn't need to be on a variety show.

You know, Roger was just having trouble fitting in. I don't know if this was because of too much pills or an unhappy personal life. I don't know why. I just knew that he was struggling and he just wasn't happy with the way it was going. Not that he didn't try. I'm just not sure what all was going on in his life. He was starting to have trouble writing songs, I believe. He was running out of gas, so to speak. It happens to everybody, and nobody really knows why that happens. I think I know why it happens. Your craft is made out of two things: your chops—in other words, your ability to sing and play and write—and also the vision you have of what music is all about. You don't tend to think songs have a vision, but they do. When you get to Hollywood you trade your vision for what the industry is all about, as opposed to hanging on to your own. If you look at his early songs, they were in his vision. Later on he lost that vision and I think that's what happened to him.

I saw it happen to Jim Stafford, Jimmy Webb, Roger, and it happened to me. You would think going to Hollywood, a marketplace to be successful, would encourage you to be more creative, but it's not. That's why I think I was able to answer the question for myself. You desert your own vision by virtue of taking it to Hollywood.

You know, I always thought of Roger as a prime example. I used to say this all the time: "Television wants the artist to fit what they're all about, not the other way around." They don't want to adapt to the artist, they want the artist to fit their idea. It's a factory. Here's an analogy: If you were to make a movie, the special effects guy and the car chase choreographer, they already got it figured out and usually are repeating to a certain degree something that they have already done in the past. They've got a hit car chase or a hit whatever, and that's what television is. The variety [show] was already an established format, so it was very hard to be creative in what I thought was kind of a tired form. When I went on to *The Smothers Brothers Show*, we dumped that. Variety tended to be about the past and the Smothers Brothers was about now. That was the thing that I learnt later that would have been great for Roger.

Lyle: Was Roger involved with the writing of the scripts for the show?

Mason: No, Roger was busy with other things. I have to say, Roger was better at just improvising and thinking of things off the top of his head than doing the material. Not that the material wasn't good sometimes, but usually he had a pretty good knack for making things work and a lot of it he would just pull out of thin air. He used to end the show sometimes with, "Well, we're out of time, gotta go, so good night and God." It was like he didn't have time to say "bless."

Lyle: Was that show filmed in front of a live audience?

Mason: Yes, portions of it would be. It depends on production. In other words, you might do the opening number and closer and leave out something that required a set change or a lot of rehearsing. But typically, variety liked the presence of the audience. That's the way we did *The Smothers Brothers Show*. It was all done in front of a live audience because Tommy said, "I don't want canned laugher. I want real reactions because that's where you get off. If you're not getting a real reaction from the audience then the material probably sucks." They're your real barometer and I think Roger liked that, too.

Lyle: I understand that out of fifteen or sixteen shows that were supposed to have been filmed, only thirteen were done. Why was that?

Mason: I don't know, but it might have been ratings. I really have no idea. The first show was kind of a nightmare. It went on for thirteen hours in the studio. That's not that big a deal, a first show always has problems that no one anticipated. But people were asked to be around for a long time. I remember Bill Cosby was around for a long time. A lot of set problems, lighting problems, sound problems.

Lyle: Was that a one-hour show?

Mason: Half hour. It was possible that he was overworked, because that was the weirdest thing about television: they were constantly playing Las Vegas and trying to do a TV show. I ran into this with lots of stars we worked with on *The Smothers Brothers Show*. I remember Mickey Rooney was on a show and he was flying in every day to do his part and flying back for a show that night in Las Vegas. Roger might have just been worn out. And if he was doing pills and things, that really just made it worse. Then if you added the pressure of being Roger Miller and you were trying to escape being Roger Miller, then that would just make it worse. You would just get more and more depressed and have less and less energy.

One of the weirdest things that happened to me when I found out I was going to write for Roger Miller was, I was in San Diego visiting a friend and I went to a supermarket and, on a whim, bought a box of Cracker Jacks. When I opened it up—they have those little fortune cookies inside—it said, "Someone with the initials RM is going to cause you a lot of trouble." I wish I would have paid attention to it. I saved that. I just couldn't believe it.

Lyle: Did he cause you a lot of trouble?

Mason: No. What I mean is being a celebrity. That's just my philosophical take on it. I think the concept of celebrity is creepy, personally. I think being important is a huge mistake. I've done a pretty good job of avoiding both of them. I would have made a lot more money and I would have had a great career, but I think real life is superior to all that. The weird thing about celebrity is… I have many friends like Steve Martin and other celebrities.

What your career oddly enough is, is you're busting your ass to get to a point where you're well-known and rich and famous—a celebrity. And then you spend the rest of your career avoiding it. So there must be about a week in there where the balance is about right.

It's a philosophical decision that I made. I would rather have a real creative life than be known as someone who's creative as a celebrity. I just thought the opportunity intrudes on your creative life, which is sort of creepy, even though it's a chance to express yourself. It's kinda like being in the military. I'm glad I did my part, but I don't think I'd want to sign up for another four years. I'm a bit of an odd duck in that most people would be chomping at the bit to have done the things that I have done or to capitalize on them. I'm glad I got to do them but I didn't capitalize on them. I didn't see anybody going through it being really happy. I always thought that Roger had stepped into more than he wanted. He was probably having more fun getting there than after he arrived.

The one thing he used to say that I thought was a little weird was he thought that exposing himself to other things would taint his originality. In other words, he thought if he listened to a lot of other kinds of music that it would influence his craft. He wanted to be more of a true original. I don't know if I agree with that, but Roger always liked to convey that he was more mysterious and you couldn't quite get a handle on him. He always liked to convey the idea "You're never going to figure me out." He was a little bit elusive from that standpoint.

I think that he sized people up in two ways. If you were like a member of the audience, a member of the band and you laughed at his jokes, then he was warm and friendly because that made him the center of attention. But if it was someone like me who wanted or thought they wanted to be like him and were trying to be funny or write songs or tell jokes, he wasn't quite as open to it. He sort of liked people that he could play to, where he was the center of attention. That's typical with celebrities.

Roger was so enamored of Hank Williams I got the impression that he thought crashing and burning was a sign that he had arrived. In other words, to be self-destructive was a sign of being a star as well as being famous. Roger did act like he wanted to be thought of as a loose cannon. Who your heroes are can sometimes have unintended consequences.

Gary Mule Deer

Gary Mule Deer started his career in the entertainment business playing in The Back Porch Majority on Epic Records which evolved into the band Bandana. He is best known as a comedian/prop-comic performing on well over one hundred television shows and thousands of stages around the world. Gary is also an accomplished actor who has appeared in such movies as Annie Hall and Cheech and Chong's Up In Smoke.

Gary: Roger was a big part of my life. For about seven years, when I worked with him, it was some of the greatest times I've ever had on the road. What I can remember of it. I lived kinda like Roger did. I think that's why we got along so well. We were both kinda in that state all the time. I think that's why we felt a little too comfortable around each other a lot of the time. A lot of late nights and early mornings together… Roger was the type of guy who was up all night and I was too. Especially when he was working Las Vegas, because they would give him a house. Now that I look back on it, I wonder what the heck did we do all night? We kept each other amused is what we did.

We worked the Silverbird a lot. We would work there three times a year, three weeks at a time. We spent nine weeks a year there. He'd have the house and we would go over there afterward. I remember coming back to the hotel at five, six, seven a.m. every morning.

Roger and I had some great advertising. We were at the Silverbird Hotel on the final night of our three-week engagement. Just after our final show of that final week, the Silverbird went into bankruptcy, and they closed the casino that night at midnight. The next day everything was closed, but they left the marquee up for a year, so Roger Miller and Gary Mule Deer were on the marquee for a year in Las Vegas. The hotel wasn't open but it was great publicity. It was great to have your name up in Vegas for a year and not even have to be there.

One thing that is the most memorable for me is that the only show I have ever missed in my forty-two years in the business was with Roger Miller.

I had been up so many days and partying so hard… At least Roger would go to sleep after I would leave. Roger and I would stay up all night at the house in Las Vegas. I would come back to the hotel, Roger would go to bed. I would stay up and gamble all day until it was time to go to work that night, and I was doing this four and five nights in a row. I'd been up five days and I remember going up to my room an hour or two before the show. I sat down on the bed and the next thing I heard is security taking the door off the hinges to get into my room because they couldn't wake me up. I looked at my watch and it is 8:25, which means I should have been on twenty-five minutes ago. I jumped up off the bed fully clothed, ran down stairs, ran backstage, just as Roger was coming off. Roger had gone on with just him and his guitar. Then the band came on and played him back on doing his act. You know something, it was the best thing he'd ever done and he was so glad that he had done it. Normally he would never have been forced to do anything like that, just him and his guitar.

I'll never forget, I ran up the stage and said, "Oh God, Roger," like I was going to say "I'm sorry". And the people were still cheering because he was just walking back on with his band. He said, "You were great." And that's how I got out of it. If it wouldn't have been a great show and if he wouldn't have been in the mood to go on, it would have been a disaster. But I'll tell ya, it scared me to death.

Lyle: What years were you touring together?

Gary: '78 to '85 is when I worked with him the most, just before he started to work on *Big River*. I was with him when he was writing *Big River*. That was pretty incredible, to be on the road with Roger and go up to his room afterwards and he would say, "What do you think of this?" or "Listen to this." I got to hear all those songs at their very beginnings. I was the first one to hear little pieces, little bridges, little choruses. Sometimes he had the words but didn't have the music yet.

Roger was getting straight at that time and I wasn't. Roger was starting to straighten himself out. I remember the night we were at the Lone Star Café in New York City and I was opening for him. Some producers came in to talk to Roger Miller about doing a Broadway show and I remember Roger thought they were crazy. Everybody did. Nobody paid much attention to it. But they were pretty persistent. My God, did it pay off. It turned out to be one of the greatest things he ever did. It was really obvious to me that he was really straightening himself out to get this Broadway show done and he was doing it on his own. I could kinda tell, because he was still being nice to me but I could tell I was making him a little uncomfortable because I was still high and he wasn't. So I kinda backed off at that point, but I certainly admired him for what he was doing. He had to get himself straightened out because that was a big project, probably the biggest project he ever tackled. Also, at that time, he might have known he was getting sick too. I don't know if that was starting to come up or not, but right after that he was starting to go in for treatments, so that might have had something to do with it.

Lyle: I understand that early in the seventies Roger quit pills and even had parties to celebrate it and sent out press releases.

Gary: I think he was off pills and into other stuff, and that's kinda the way it was. In fact most people I knew who were on pills at that time were going to other things. I never saw him take any and I was never offered any. We did lots of other stuff, but it wasn't anything like that.

Lyle: I understand back then people thought cocaine was good for you.

Gary: Yeah, it was. That's when it was good for everybody and it wasn't addictive. People were saying there were temper tantrums and craziness. He could be crazy on stage. The band was amazing. They never knew what he was going to do next. And Roger was erratic that way. He would forget words a lot, but he would always get out of it. That was one of the funniest parts of Roger's show. He would be in the middle of something and forget the words. It actually became part of Roger. He would crack the band up, crack the audience up and he would always get out of it.

Lyle: Did you discuss the entertainment business with him much?

Gary: We discussed the entertainment business a lot. We were both kinda sour on different aspects of the entertainment business, because they didn't really want entertainers anymore so much as they wanted to put you in a niche. You couldn't be a comedian, a singer, and an instrumentalist. They didn't really like that kind of thing. I fought that all my life. I wasn't just a stand-up comic and I wasn't just a musician. It's taken me forever to get back on TV because of that. They always hated comics with guitars. A lot of times they didn't like singers with hit records who talked and were funny, although Roger did a great job hosting *The Tonight Show* and all kinds of things.

We did talk about the business a lot. I was having a hell of a time with it and he would boost me up all the time. They just used me all the time. I was the guy they called when somebody cancelled, because they didn't like Gary Mule Deer's guitar. They could always call me and rely on me to do a good job but it wasn't what they wanted for their image. I did *The Tonight Show* one night and got a standing ovation. When I walked off, Freddy the producer said to me, "Great show, Gary, but it's not *The Tonight Show*." That's what he said to me! Twenty years later I reminded him of it at a golf tournament, "Remember the night I got a standing ovation and you said 'Great show, Gary, but it's not *The Tonight Show*?' " He said, "Yeah, I remember it." There was a pause and he said, "I was right, wasn't I?" And he was! It was true because they did not accept the kind of entertainer that I was.

What he meant by the comment was, if I would have been out there in a suit just doing stand-up comedy, they would have had me back a lot. You walk out there with a cowboy hat and a guitar and props, and even though you do well, it's not their image. We'll let it get by tonight because we have a guest host, but you're never going to get on with Johnny. That's kinda what they were saying. I would be depressed about that a lot and Roger would always choke me out of it. One thing I remember about Roger was that he was always behind me.

Lyle: Was he frustrated as well? Because it seems like he wasn't taken seriously at times.

Gary: He was frustrated a lot about a lot of things, because he wrote so many real great serious songs. He had some of the greatest phrasing of anybody in the business. But at the same time we both realized that we did everything in our power to tank our careers at the same time. We would never take anything that seriously.

I remember a great incident. We were working in Atlantic City and Roger tells me one night, the night before Easter, "I'm going to be the Grand Marshall at the Easter Parade tomorrow, and if I have to get up at six a.m.you're getting up with me."

So I said, "Oh, okay."

We just stayed up, we didn't go to bed, of course. So at seven a.m. we go outside and there are five vintage cars. The first car was for the Grand Marshall, which was Roger and Mary, the second car was the mayor, the third car was the governor or something of New Jersey, the fourth was Miss Atlantic City, and the fifth car was the water commissioner. They would crawl at two or three miles an hour all the way up one end of the boardwalk and come back again. Well, the water commissioner didn't show up. Originally I couldn't go with them because there was no room, but they put me in the water commissioner's car and took the sign off the side. A lot of people didn't know who the hell I was. It was freezing cold in the morning with the wind coming off the ocean and we are coming back down the boardwalk, and I'll never forget this. Some little old lady yelled out, "Who are you?" and I yelled back, "Pia Zadora!" And without missing a beat she yelled back, "Your movies suck!" Roger and I will never forget that. That was one of the funniest things that ever happened. I tried to tell that on a TV show once but they wouldn't let me say "suck." That's how careful they were on TV in those days.

We had one airplane adventure that I'm kinda hesitant to talk about. I'll just say this: Roger and I were out of substance this one weekend. We knew we were going to be out for the weekend and we had like five or six shows to go, and we didn't know what we were going to do. We just had a small amount of a substance left. So one of us came up with the bright idea that if we did what we had left all at once, which was way too much for any two people to have, we would probably come up with a brilliant idea on how to get some more. So we did the whole thing at once and we came up with the idea to have a friend of his from Texas fly up in an airplane and bring us something. It was the paranoia thing that you don't want to ask anyone in town, you don't want anyone to think you're doing anything. However, you're being obvious as hell. So we had some guy fly up from Texas to bring us stuff. It cost me exactly what I made for the week. I don't know how much it cost Roger.

I was working with Roger and was gambling so much and got so out of control that I needed extra money. So one time when I was working at the Silverbird, what I would do was, I would get through working with Roger... We had two shows a night. In the morning I would get up at six a.m. in Las

Vegas and I would go to the airport and at seven-thirty I would fly to Anaheim, California. I would be picked up at about eight or eight-thirty by a representative from Disneyland. I would be taken to Disneyland, and at about ten in the morning I would do a show with the Kingston Trio. I would open for them and do another thirty minutes, then about one or two o'clock they would take me back to the airport and I would fly back to Las Vegas and work with Roger that night.

A guy came up to me in Vegas and said, "You know, there's a guitar player in town who has a brand new Gibson J200. He was playing with Engelbert [Humperdinck]. He only had a job with him for ten days, and he's never played this guitar other than those ten days. He wants to sell it. Would you be interested? He wants three hundred dollars for it, and it has two cases."

It was a beautiful J200 guitar. I said, "Sure, I'll try it out."

"Okay, try it out and see what you think." Later the guy calls me and says, "Well, I got to get the money. The guy wants the three hundred."

"Fact is, I don't have any money. I lost all my money."

"Well, I have to come and get the guitar. The guy wants the guitar back."

"Well, I'll be gone all day tomorrow to Disneyland."

He says "What time do you go?"

"Six-thirty."

"I'll be there at six-thirty in the morning to pick up the guitar."

So at six-thirty that morning I had seven dollars with me. I had borrowed five of it from a lobby porter. I had two dollars for cab fare, that's all the money I had. As I'm walking up to my room I put in a ticket for a dollar at the Keno counter. I walk up the stairs to get the guitar I had to return, walk downstairs, and I hit six out of six for a thousand dollars. So I walk right up to the Keno counter and get ten one hundred dollar bills. I see my friend walk in the door. I walk over to him give him three hundred dollars, take the guitar back upstairs, put it in my dressing room, come back downstairs and take a cab to Disneyland. And that's the guitar I'm playing with today!

Lyle: Did Roger gamble at all?

Gary: Roger didn't but Mary did. Mary played the dollar slot machines. Roger would kind of walk around and watch her till he got bored and then he would wander off. Mary gambled for both of them.

Lyle: Did he like playing Las Vegas?

Gary: He loved playing Las Vegas. We had great audiences. You have the best lighting and sound and stages, the advertising is good, and you get such great perks. You have great dressing rooms, you get lots of free food and drinks. There's not much not to like, especially in those days. We were really at the end of when it was really great. I mean, it got so corporate after that, that's why a lot of the places were going under. The Silverbird was originally the Thunderbird and after it went bankrupt it became the El Rancho. Then that went bankrupt. Now it's fully closed, it's not even there anymore. But those great places we used to play, it was wonderful during that time. I loved it up until the mid-eighties. After that it definitely changed.

We were together one night and wrote a great joke that both of us used after that. We were both talking about old marriages and alimony, and we came up with a line that everybody has stolen since then. I still do it in my show and Roger would still be doing it if he was around. This was the line: "Instead of getting married the next time I feel like it, I think I'm going to find some woman I hate and buy her a house." We came up with that at four o'clock in the morning at that house he was staying in when we worked at the Silverbird, back in probably 1981. That got out and it was one of those lines that spread fast. In fact, I did it one night and some guy walked up to me and said, "Hey, that's my line." I said, "You have no idea who you're talking to."

I've been in the business for forty-two years as a comedian and musician. I basically worked the comedy stores, I worked the Improv. I got to work with a lot of great stand-up comedians, everyone from Robin Williams to David Letterman to Jay Leno to Jerry Seinfeld. I went on tour with them for years, but my three favorite comedians were musicians. The three funniest people I've ever known in my life were Roger Miller, Michael Johnson, who had two hits, "Bluer Than Blue" and "Let's Spend the Night Together," and Vince Gill. They are the three funniest people I know in the business.

Lyle: Could you tell me anything about Roger that most people wouldn't know?

Gary: One thing that I do know is that he was a hands-on healer. Roger showed me a couple of times. One time I had a terrible pain in my lower back and he said, "I don't do this very often but I want to show you something." And he put his hands there and held them there for a while, and pretty soon they got so hot I could hardly stand it, which always made me wonder why when he got really sick he couldn't help himself. Maybe that didn't do any good. Every so often I would say, "Rog," and he would take my wrist or something, and I'm telling you, Lyle, it got so hot you could hardly stand it. He had that thing, he said it was in the family. I think he would use it for other people for headaches, backs, necks, whatever. But that's the one thing I knew that I don't think many people knew about. But he did it to me several times and it was amazing, the heat!

You know, one thing Roger did for me more than anything else—and I didn't live by it as much as I should have—was he told me, "Just be yourself." I was always up there trying to make sure I was making everybody happy, whereas I should have been a little looser like he was. I should have let myself just be what I wanted to be in the moment, experiment a little more, fool around. I think being with Roger loosened me up a lot. I wasn't as afraid to take chances up there, just more or less be myself.

Lee Rollag

L *ee Rollag was Roger's guitar player throughout the 1980s.*

Lee: I spent almost ten years traveling with Roger. I started in the summer of '81 and played my last job with him in 1990. The first job I did was *Theatre in the Round* in Fort Worth, at the Casa Manana Theatre. I really hadn't met Roger when we went to the first date. I hadn't met Danny Gatton or Shannon Ford, who was the drummer. They were both in New York and Roger was in Santa Fe. Once I actually got the job, they sent me a tape to learn the show from. They had a live cassette tape of a show they had done up in Canada, and that's what I rehearsed to.

I met up [with them] at the airport… I met Randy Hart and Ron Shumake in LAX [Los Angeles International Airport], then we flew to Dallas Fort Worth and I met Danny there. I didn't know anything about him. I didn't know who he was at the time. So we got there and met up with everybody and I still hadn't met Roger. We all just went to the bar of the hotel and I'm going, "Well, when are we going to rehearse? Come on, help me out, let's rehearse."

And they laughed and said, "We're going to go down and have some drinks."

I didn't meet Roger until soundcheck right before the show. He was real polite, "Glad you're here."

"We just play," is what he always used to say. It wasn't any kind of, "I want you to do this or do that." There wasn't an initiation or anything. Everyone was great.

I took Thumbs' place. When I went to check into the hotel his name was on my rooming list, on my invoice for my room, Ken Carllile. I was going, "My God, I'm taking Thumbs Carllile's place." I had seen Thumbs and I was a fan of his for years. I was in awe of him.

One time some drunk guy came up to the stage when we were playing. He was pissed off for some reason. He came up and said this saying that just kinda lived on. Roger would always say it. The guy said, "You can kiss my ass is all you are and I'm just the son of a bitch that'll do it!" One time we were playing at Ascuaga's Nugget in Reno when bass player Ron Shumake's alarm didn't go off. It came show time and he wasn't there. It was like the only time ever that somebody wasn't there for show time, so I played bass for the first five songs, then I saw Ron show up. He was at the side of the stage and had this panicked look on his face. In between songs he kinda slipped back behind the curtain and grabbed the bass and I got my guitar. After the show Roger said, "Ron, I want to talk to you. Don't worry it's not for a cup of coffee," because whenever he got rid of somebody he'd say, "Let's go have a cup of coffee." So Roger said, "Don't worry about it, man. I love you, you're a great guy." And he was really cool about it.

Lyle: At the time you were playing with him, Roger wasn't having the chart success he once did. Did that bother him?

Lee: Yes. I remember early in my time with him comments being made. I guess Willie and Waylon were doing really well at the time. I guess there were times when Roger was really happening and Willie wasn't. I do remember during that airline strike in '81 we were on a bus for about three weeks for a tour. Roger wrote a new funny song and Randy said something like, "Yeah, you know this one will get you back on top." And Roger kinda got real quiet and Randy kind of said, "Sorry." So I know it did kind of bother him. He didn't really have a record deal, but we would play all the same venues as whoever had the hit record at the time, because of who Roger was and what he had done.

Lyle: I ran into producer Harold Shedd and he said he recorded an album with Roger. That must have been in that same era you played with him. Do you recall if that was ever released?

Lee: I don't know. I know that occasionally he would do some recording in Nashville and I do remember a few of the new songs he had. He gave Danny Gatton a tape of three songs. That was part of what led to Danny's departure from the band… One night Roger on stage said, "I just recorded some new songs in Nashville." And we weren't sure which one he wanted to do first. He just sort of paused in anticipation of Danny kicking the song off, and he wasn't really sure which one because there were three new songs. So Roger just said, "Well, I write them, I guess I got to kick them off too."

For some reason that rubbed Danny the wrong way. Danny said something on stage and they argued about that after the show. Roger said, "You don't say that when I'm working. That was unprofessional."

And Danny said, "I can't read your mind."

Some things had built up between them over the years as time went by, and so after that it was like an "I quit," "You're fired" kind of thing. Danny was gone after that date. It was a mutual thing, like, "You can't fire me because I quit." They were both headstrong. It was a drag for all of us, we were like a family. We all thought he was going to come back. Of course he never did. I think once Roger knew that I could play the show, he could get by with one guitar player and save money. I felt a little weird about that.

Lyle: Did you still maintain a friendship with Danny?

Lee: Yes, all of us did. In fact, we played at Harrah's in Atlantic City a couple years later and Danny came and played with us. I thought Danny was just awesome. I used to put a tape recorder behind Danny's amp because I was always trying to learn his licks. He was great. He would show me whatever I wanted to know. He was a great guy. That's why it really shocked us to find out later what happened, because he would be one of the last people that I would expect that from.

Lyle: What happened to him?

Lee: What I had heard from conversations after the fact is that evidently he hadn't spoken to his wife in a few days. I don't know how much that had to do with it. Shannon seemed to think that him losing his record deal with Elektra didn't have much to do with it, because comments he made about that was, "They weren't letting me do what I wanted to do anyway." People had wondered how much that had to do with it. It still is a total mystery.

Lyle: Was it suicide?

Lee: Yes. The bass player that he was going to do a job with that weekend had talked to him earlier that day and Danny said, "See you at the gig." I guess Danny went out into his shed, had a 22 riffle, and hooked up some kind of way to push the trigger with a stick and shot himself in the head. He locked himself in there.

Roger was really an incredible performer… We played a gig in Santa Fe and we all went to his house to rehearse. I think we played about two songs for about five minutes and then went outside and started looking for arrowheads on his property. He was really into Indian artifacts and had found a lot of them on his property in Santa Fe. It was a ranch, but I don't know that it was a working ranch. I remember walking around the property and walking around back by the pool and seeing one of his Grammys sitting out there, and the emblem that said what it was for was missing. It was just sitting out there by the pool.

Lyle: I love Branson, Missouri but I find that a lot of the entertainers that have worked there don't. I was wondering what Roger's opinion of it was.

Lee: Other than making his jokes "There's more gravy here than I've ever seen in my life". Another thing he'd said is he went fishing with that oriental fiddle guy, Shoji "I went fishing with Shoji Tabuchi the other day and he ate my bait". But Roger liked Branson.

That last year that I worked for him, he cancelled some dates because he thought he had nodes on his throat. I guess that was the beginning of the cancer. Everybody thought it was throat cancer but it wasn't. He had a tumor that was pushing on his vocal cords. It was actually in his spine. It gave him the false sense that it was in his throat, that there was something wrong with his throat. Three or four months after I had done my last date with him, I heard through the drummer, Joe Doherty, "Did you heard about Roger?"

I said, "No, what are you talking about?"

He said, "He's got throat cancer and it's in remission."

That was the first I heard of it. They kept it really quiet. We didn't know what was going on. Finally Ken Stange, who was a keyboard player, a friend of mine that I got on the gig, actually talked to Roger. He was one of the last people I know of to actually talk to him. This was about six months or so before he died. At that time they couldn't find anything. He had radiation therapy or chemotherapy and they couldn't find any of the cancer, and when Ken talked to him he was going, "Yeah, you know they checked me out and it's gone and we're going to go back to work. We're going to start working again. Ken, I thought I was a goner!"

I talked to Ken about that and he said, "We're going to start doing some dates again."

Ron "Iceman" Shumake

Ron Shumake played bass and was the musical director for Roger from 1980 to 1992.

Ron: The highlight of my musical career was playing with Roger. At the time, in 1980, I was…kind of narrow-minded, so it was a heck of a thing when I got with Roger. He just opened my mind. The thing I got out of that was music is one of two things: it's either good or it's bad. If the music's good, the musicians are good, and the arrangements are great, I'm just as happy playing polka as be-bop or jazz or country, rock-and-roll, blues—it really doesn't matter. That's one of the things I learnt with Roger. His music had all those elements. He was the first crossover artist. He was the first country guy to go to Broadway. He showed me how to appreciate something for what it is and not to be such a bonehead about music.

I come to find out that one of the things that Roger really loved was jazz, Bob Wills in particular. He grew up listening to The Bob Wills Swing Band. He used to tell me he would sneak into wherever Bob Wills had played, underage, and listen to the music until tears came to his eyes. He was so emotionally moved by that. As a result, Roger always hired jazz-capable players. He didn't get stonewall country players to play in his band. He had all jazz players, which was right up my alley and fit with me perfectly. We could sit down and play be-bop tunes, any kind of stuff—hillbilly tunes, rock-a-billy, rock, blues, country—the whole gamut. We learned early on that he got the guys who were fast on their feet and had great ears and could follow him. I used to stand right behind him, right next to the drums, and I would cue off where he would put a bar chord from behind. I would look at his neck and that's how I knew what key he was going to play in. I could kinda guess what the song was. I got to be real good at that.

Lyle: So you guys didn't even know what song was coming up?

Ron: He would grab a bar chord on his guitar and I could see the position where his hand was. That was my only clue, because there was no telling what he would do. He never had a set list where he would do the same thing every night and tell the same jokes or anything like that. It was always by the seat of your pants. There was no telling what he would come up with.

He had one show that he would do for the audience and to keep the boys in the band laughing, he would add another show for us at the same time! He would turn around to the band and say something off to the side to crack the band up.

Roger was such a big personality with everyone, people would be thrilled just to sit there and listen to him talk. Sometimes they would say, "Screw the songs, we just want to hear Roger talk. Why don't you just let Roger talk?" Because he was a charmer.

I remember we played in Vegas one time when Thumbs and Danny Gatton were in the band. Between the two guitar players I would forget to play! I would sit there in awe, then I would remember I was playing the bass. Roger turned around, "Now Thumbs Carllile!" and Thumbs started playing a solo. Thumbs caught Roger's eye during this blistering solo, and all of a sudden Thumbs took his hands off—he played the guitar on his lap—lifted his hands off the neck, and put his elbow down and started playing with his elbow! Thumbs could play more with his elbow than most guys could play with two hands. Roger stood there in awe. Thumbs looked at him while he was playing his solo and he took a big yawn, and it killed Roger! Then it would be Danny Gatton's turn. There was a constant friendly rivalry. It was amazing.

Lyle: Was Danny Gatton famous before he started with Roger?

Ron: Danny Gatton had a reputation of being the most famous unknown guitar player. In Washington, D.C., where he grew up, he was real big. Everyone knew who he was. He would load the clubs up. He got fired from a lot of jobs in the D.C. area because too many people came! When too many people got in the room they couldn't serve drinks and they didn't make as much money. And then they would go up to Danny and complain, "Hey, man, this place is too crowded. We can't do any business." So Danny devised this little box, I don't know what it was. He would put it behind his amplifier and when the place got like that and they were complaining that they couldn't get around, he would flip the switch on this box and it would short out all the electricity in the place. They would call the electricians, the electricians would be running around and couldn't figure out what the heck was going on, and then people would start leaving. Danny would go outside and smoke a cigarette and have a few beers and wait for the place to clear out. When he thought most of the people had left, he would go back and the electricians would still be looking around, and he would flip the switch and go back on [stage] again. He was something else!

In Las Vegas especially, backstage was always a hang-out. Everybody in Las Vegas would come to see Roger and the band, so the backstage was a whole other show. There was no telling who would walk in there at any given time. I put a recorder in the room and would turn it on with ninety-minute tapes in it so I would get everything. I have tapes and tapes that I have stuffed away somewhere. All different people, lots of comedians of course. All the comedians would come in and that would start a chop fight right there, who's going to be the funniest. And then Thumbs would be sitting down playing the guitar, then Danny would be playing the guitar, so it was a whole other show backstage that was just as entertaining as the one outside, or maybe more so because everybody would let their hair down.

Thumbs told me one story… Roger went to England and bought himself a Bentley or something, a really nice car, and he was going to ship it over [to the U.S.]. He drove it around over there and he said, "The heck with it," and he just left it. He just abandoned it.

Roger used to fret away hours in the hotel rooms with a soldering iron and a bunch of coat hangers, just to amuse himself. He would make these little characters, little horses and stuff like that.

I got married in Reno, and Roger and Mary were my best man and best woman. We were playing in Reno and I said to my girlfriend at the time, "Let's go get married." So Roger and Mary stood up for me.

Lyle: Do you have any photos from that?

Ron: I think my ex-wife has those.

Lyle: Did he ever talk to you about the movie *Songwriter*? [This is a movie with Kris Kristofferson and Willie Nelson in which Roger was supposed to have played a music publisher but for some reason didn't appear in it.]

Ron: I don't know what happened about that, because him and Willie were best buddies. We would never know when Willie would show up. He would come in and play with us all the time. In fact, we did the *Austin City Limits* show and there was a rumor that Willie would show up but we weren't sure. We were used to being surprised all the time, we would just be ready for anything. While we were doing the show, at one point Roger looked over and said, "I'm going to ask a friend of mine to come up. Willie Nelson!" And I go to myself, 'There it is.' Roger gave Willie the guitar and picked up his fiddle. We didn't know what song we were going to do, what key we were going to do it in, what was going to happen. All we did was just lock onto Roger and go. He picked up the fiddle and he goes with the bow, "Domp, Domp," and then we're into "Milk Cow Blues." If you listen to it and look at it, it looks like we had rehearsed it, but we didn't know anything!

Lyle: How was it being around Roger when he first started having problems with his voice?

Ron: He was mad at the time that he wasn't feeling good, and he got bitter. He was mad that he was sick and he couldn't put his finger on it and nobody really knew. I don't think he knew exactly, I'm not sure that the doctors knew until pretty late that it was spinal cancer. We had played in Colorado—it was probably the last gig I played with him—and he was trying to walk up the steps at this outdoor festival and his back was killing him. He barely made it up the stairs to do the show, he was just suffering. At the end of the show he walked off and they took him off in an ambulance. He didn't know what it was. Later on a lot of my friends said that they'd been in to see Roger and it's spinal cancer and it had gone to his brain and confused him. He didn't know he was going to die. They were thinking there wasn't much they could do for him at that point. They were going, "I feel so sorry, he doesn't know that he's going." Shannon Ford went to see him with the Gatlin Brothers, and Roger looked at him and said, "Do I know you?" He didn't remember, he was deteriorating. I couldn't go, it would just hurt me too much to see him like that. I just prayed for him.

Roger [died October 25, 1992], Thumbs [died July 31, 1987] , Danny [died October 20, 1994]...a couple of years back in the nineties there I went through some real emotional trauma losing all those guys. They were the greatest guys I've ever known in my life. When I sit around and think about it, it's just really sad, especially the way Danny went, because I had just talked to him.

You know, out of all the country guys Roger stands alone. All the country people were there at one time or another. They would walk on stage and we'd play with them, so I've played with all of them, just about...the most important ones. And of all of them, Roger was the most interesting and had the most personality.

Larry Graham

arry Graham is Ferlin Husky's drummer and manager. He was the drummer on Jim Reeves' last tour and luckily refused a ride on the flight that ended Jim's life. I met him at the Grand Ole Opry, where he said to me, "I could pretty much tell you anything you want to know about Roger. I was his roommate."

Larry: We had an apartment on West End for a while. It was in the sixties. He was playing drums with Faron Young. He was like the rest of us—we were all musicians, dirty apartment. We were just everywhere in Printer's Alley, and Tootsie's was our home base. He was like the rest of us, living day by day.

Lyle: Who else was living with you?

Larry: I think Jimmy Day. He was a steel guitar player with Ray Price. You may wake up one morning and there would be six or eight musicians in your apartment, on the floor, in the bathtub, anywhere.

Lyle: It must have been something else being around in those days.

Larry: You had a lot of good times, but you didn't remember them.

When Roger first met you it was like he knew you your whole life. He was a big practical joker, a meddler. He would find out something on you, he would set you up.

He would disappear for a couple of days at a time. That was just Roger. He mellowed out in his later years…nothing like he was when we were all just musicians. I remember the first CMA Awards when he was Entertainer of the Year. I never will forget, he had a solid black tailored suit with a high collar. I said, "Well, Roger, you have some great clothes." And he said, "Yeah, I've got good clothes, but I'm still the same."

Roger was a joyful person to be around. If Roger liked you he would give you his last nickel. If he didn't like you, he would tell you and wouldn't have anything to do with you. Even after he really made it big he was always sentimental to musicians, the sidemen.

It was an honor just to know him. Roger came to Nashville with nothing and he left with a lot—that's friends, not money.

Ken Stange

Ken Stange took Randy Hart's place as Roger's keyboard player in the eighties.

Ken: Roger was pretty into blow and cocaine in the 'eighties. He never drank that much. That was weird. He was doing that stuff but he wouldn't drink. That usually went hand in hand. I survived the eighties and as a musician I was into that shit. It was just too bad after he cleaned up and adopted the kids, because the damage had been done. It really affected me because…I've played with a lot of artists—I'm playing with Dennis Quaid right now, and I might do the Rod Stewart tour—but Roger is the only guy that I have met in my whole life that I would truly call a genius on a musical level. He was like the Mark Twain of music and he was a comic genius on the level of Robin Williams. When you play with a guy that does a comedy music thing, they do the same thing over and over. After a while the band is like, "Ho-hum." Not with Roger. His improvisational skills on a comedy level were so amazing that the only guy I could compare it to would be Robin Williams. There wasn't a show that we would do that he wouldn't crack us up!

When we were playing he would complain about his voice. He was clearing his voice but he couldn't sing and he didn't know what was wrong. That's how they found out about the cancer. There was cancer somewhere in his spinal cord that affected his vocal cords. I remember him always going, "Man, there's something wrong with my voice." We'd go, "Well, Roger, you haven't sang in awhile." We would have never thought it could be something like that.

One of my favorite memories is when we were playing at John Ascuaga's Nugget in Sparks. My daughter was just a little over a year old. She's eighteen now, in college. She was real musical, just a brilliant kid, so I taught her "King of the Road." She learnt to sing it and she could barely talk. Backstage I was holding her and Roger was hanging around, it was after the show, and I said, "Audrey, sing." And she sang "King of the Road" to Roger Miller. He just flipped! He was banging the walls, he couldn't believe it. I was so proud.

During that same time we were backstage after a show, we had just played, and Roger really liked what he heard. He looked at me—and this means more to me than any other artist I have ever played with who has ever given me any compliment—he said, "Stange, you're a find." I just swelled up because he hardly ever gave out compliments, or at least not to me or the other guys in the band. But he always liked me because I played harmonica and keyboards, because I could play the *Big River* stuff on harp.

After he cleaned up and sobered up, he started remembering tunes and we started doing all different kinds of tunes. I was with him during that transition. All of a sudden he would start playing these songs that he wrote when he was a kid for different artists when he was just a staff writer. In the show he would do a little chronological musical history of his work.

Roger didn't want us to wear hats. He wasn't into the country stigma—you know, boots and hats. We didn't do that. We were like jazz guys from L.A., we weren't country artists. We could play that stuff, we did it, we'd play everything. You got to to make a living. When I first got the gig Roger himself taught me how to play country piano. I didn't really know and he sat down at the piano and said, "Here's how you do this." Every show when he introduced us, he would tell something about the guys in the band. He would say, "Ken teaches jazz at Pepperdine University." That's the kind of stuff that impressed him. He didn't want any pedal steel. We'd play Branson and the local guys playing music would go, "Where's your steel player?"

"Well, we don't have one."

"Well, where's your banjo? Where's your fiddler?"

"Well, Roger plays fiddle."

They couldn't believe it. We would call ourselves "Assholes from L.A.". This was a Ron Shumake thing, "We're assholes from L.A. and we don't jam." We were just kidding, of course. That was impressive to Roger, that we weren't country guys, because he wasn't a country artist. He wrote stuff that went in that direction, but I wouldn't really call it country and western or "country and restroom" like Roger would say.

Marshall Grant

"He's been with me from the first," Johnny Cash would say as he introduced Marshall Grant, one of the original Tennessee Two. Besides playing bass, Marshall was also Johnny's road manager. He was a friend of Roger's right from the beginning of their careers._

Marshall: One time Roger was at my house with Luther Perkins. I was an original member of the Tennessee Two, Luther Perkins was the other member. Roger got up from the table and opened the refrigerator door and the light hit him in the face, and he started doing his little routine there and sang. Then he stepped back and said, "I thought I was on stage when the spotlight hit me in the face." He spent quite a bit of time in my house in Memphis. He was just Roger everywhere he was at, whether he was on stage, backstage, in your house. He was a lovable guy.

Lyle: I understand that Roger toured with you and The Johnny Cash Show.

Marshall: Yes, he did. He was on tour with us, but he was playing fiddle for Ray Price. I'll tell you what he did do though. John was having some pretty bad times then with his drug problems, and a lot of places John wouldn't show up. I would always call Roger to see if I could get him to come fill in. He probably filled in over the period of a couple of years probably fifteen or twenty dates where John just didn't show up. If we were on a three or five day tour and John didn't show up for the first day, I would keep him there to fill in for John for the entire time. That happened an awful lot.

Lyle: How did the crowd react to that?

Marshall: They loved him. John wasn't the biggest thing in the world at the time. He was still in his growth period and Roger was the same thing. In years to come, '68, '69, '70, nobody could have filled in for John, but at that time he could because we weren't playing to monstrous crowds.

Lyle: I guess at that time Roger was struggling with his own addictions too.

Marshall: Yes, he was, he had a pretty bad run with it. But Roger was a little bit different. Where John turned everything in his life 180 degrees, Roger just got more lovable and funny. So with Roger's addiction, it wasn't as bad as other people I've known. He did no harm to nobody.

Harry Anderson

hen I was a kid, one of my favorite shows was Night Court. I've always enjoyed the magic and sarcastic humor of Harry Anderson, so it was great to find out that he was friends with Roger.

Harry: I was his opening act at the Silverbird [in Vegas], back in the eighties before *Night Court*. I was a popular opening act for country and western shows. I had just done Freddy Fender the week before when he fell over backwards on stage, he just passed out. I was there opening for Kenny Rogers at the Riviera quite a bit, and Dottie West, The Gatlin Brothers. So I was kind of a known as that kind of conman character, city slicker. It went well with the country western things. I was asked to do Roger's shows. At that time he was just trying to swear off junk, and everybody took shifts staying with Roger just making sure he was not tempted. I was the new kid so I got the late shift, so we hung around late at night.

One of my favorite memories is something he told me once when we were staying up late, putting nickels into slot machines, just anything but doing junk. He could drink, he could do anything but junk. So we're standing there putting nickels in slot machines, we're both pretty hammered, and Roger says, "You know, Harry, I've written hundreds and hundreds of songs, and some of them were pretty good. But some guy comes along and writes one fucking song, *one song*, and that's all he writes and that's all anyone can talk about is this guy and his one song." Then he paused and he said, "Fuck Francis Scott Key."

[Author's Note] If you're not from the USA and didn't get the last one (like me), Francis Scott Key wrote "The Star-Spangled Banner."

David Allan Coe

Richard D. Moore

Not many artists stick to their guns and say and do what they want, but singer/songwriter/actor/magician/author/ex-con David Allan Coe does. He is as 'outlaw' as it gets in country music.

David: I met Roger when he owned the King of the Road Hotel in Nashville. He used to have these songwriter pulls in his hotel room, where he would invite songwriters and we would sit around in a circle and play our songs. Roger introduced me to Willie Nelson at one of those things. I was there, Jackson Browne, Mickey Newbury, Charlie Rich, Billy Joe Shaver, Roger and Shel Silverstein, and somebody knocked on the door. Roger told me to go answer the door. I opened the door and there wasn't nobody there. I couldn't see nobody. Then I felt something against my legs and I looked down and it was Willie Nelson. He was on this hands and knees crawling in the room with a handful of joints. That's how I met Willie.

I used to hang out with Roger all the time. One of my favorite memories with Roger was at one of these guitar pullin's. All these great songwriters passed this guitar around and played and sang their songs, and we handed the guitar to Roger and he started tuning the guitar like we had all been playing it out of tune!

Lyle: Did Roger spend much time at the hotel?

David: At that time period he did. I don't know if he really owned that place or if they were just using his name but he sure acted like he owned it. I didn't realize until I went to Branson. Everyone has their name on those theatres but some businessman owns them, he's just paying them to use their name. At the time we just assumed Roger owned the place.

Roger said many times that he thought I was the most unusual and outspoken songwriter that he had ever met. I did a couple of x-rated albums years ago and when Roger heard them he said, "That's the funniest shit I have ever heard in my life. I have written a thousand songs like that but I would never have the nerve to play them for anybody, let alone record them."

I asked him, "What's one of them that you wrote?"

And he said, "If I Can't Be Your Number One, Then Number Two on You."

Lyle: I had heard that Roger liked to write some x-rated songs.

David: A lot of them guys did, they just never had the nerve to record them. Shel was the one who talked me into that. I was living in Key West at the time. We were over at Shel's house, sitting around. He was playing me "Freakers at the Freaker's Ball," and I said, "You think that's the shit, listen to this shit." And I started playing him some of those songs and he just fell over laughing. He said, "David, you have to record them songs, people need to hear that." Some people said it was the biggest mistake I ever made in my life, but at one time I made my living off of that stuff. I can't complain.

Lyle: You definitely stick out from the rest. It must have been tough losing friends like Roger and Shel.

David: I do tributes to them every night in my show. I talk about Roger, Mickey, Shel, Waylon, John Hartford, all the people I was lucky enough to be friends with. I was lucky enough to play with Bill Monroe and played with him three days before he died. I was with John Hartford at his house the day before he died. I read about Mickey dying in *Rolling Stone* magazine. Nobody even called me and told me, I had no clue.

The thing that really pisses me off about shit like that is that they're doing a tribute album to Waylon and they're putting people on it like Sheryl Crow. Waylon didn't even fucking know who Sheryl Crow is! Nobody's asking me to be on a Waylon tribute album. That's the kind of shit that makes me mad. I mean, even Jimmy Buffet, as much as he doesn't like me still mentions me in his books. And I really like Jimmy Buffet, I always have liked him. When I wrote the song, "Jimmy Buffet Doesn't Live in Key West Anymore," I wasn't criticizing him. I was criticizing the press that was comparing me to him. I was trying to say that we are two different people living in the same environment, and Jimmy doesn't live here no more and I do and I have every right to write the same kind of songs he was writing about the ocean. I live on the ocean! I have every right to write these songs without being compared to his songs.

Dennis Linde

I think the first song I ever learned to play on guitar was Elvis' "Burning Love," written by Dennis Linde. Dennis' songs "Crystal Day," "Tom Green County Fair," "TJ's Last Ride" and more are on Roger's 1970 album. It's those three songs that made me into the Roger Miller fan that I am. Garth Brooks had a hit with Linde's song "Callin' Baton Rouge" and The Dixie Chicks had a number one record with his "Goodbye Earl."

Dennis: The first time I met Roger, he was playing the Fairmont Hotel in Dallas. Billy Swan, Kris Kristofferson and I all had cuts by him on that *1970* album. I'm not sure if Billy did or not, but Billy was with us. Roger flew us out to the Fairmont to listen to him play. I met him before the show—nice guy, and crazy. We went to the Fairmont and we were dressed like our normal selves, jeans and everything, and they wouldn't let us in. So Kris talked to someone and it ended up that they loaned us sport jackets that we had to wear. Billy and I had these gigantic ones. We were like one hundred and sixty pound guys and they gave us these two-hundred-pound guy jackets. Kris got one from someone in the band and it was this checkered car-salesman type jacket. But it fit and they got us in and we got to watch the show. At one point Roger introduced us and we got to stand up. We looked ridiculous.

His band live was such a knockout. That's when he had Thumbs Carllile playing guitar, that crazy flat guitar. I'd never seen anything like that. The band was great, Roger was great. He did his big hits and some of his new stuff. He did one of my songs, one of Kris'. It might have been "Bobby McGee." I'm really not clear on it. I was sort of in a daze. I think we all were.

Lyle: How did it come about that he was recording your songs?

Dennis: I think he had been going on the road like crazy during all of '69 and he just didn't have any time to write any new material, so he put the word out that he was looking for material. Naturally he was looking for stuff that was off the wall, because of the way he writes. I think that I just lucked out. Jerry Kennedy heard my songs and he really liked them. I only had one cut before that. Roger was one of my heroes. It's nice just to know he listened to them. It turned out he cut four or five of them! It was like a dream. When I heard "Where Have All the Average People Gone?", it just floored me! It was just the fact that it was Roger Miller and it was on the radio. I remember I was in my Volkswagen and it was like time was standing still for three minutes. It was just an awesome experience.

Lyle: I think my favorite song of all time is "Crystal Day."

Dennis: Wow! That was a song I thought would never get cut by anyone. To see Roger do it was just a miracle, and to do such a nice production and everything.

Lyle: Was that close to what you had in mind?

Dennis: That's what I had in mind, but I sure didn't have it on my demo. I couldn't have asked for a neater cut than that. It all flowed. He had that sort of light, dreamy feel to it that I hadn't heard him do before. But he did it so great, he made it sound so natural.

Lyle: I find that song has a "Sergeant Pepper" feel to it.

Dennis: Yes, an abstract kind of thing. Somehow Roger himself was so abstract that he picked up on it. He could get things into songs that worked that I don't think other people could. And it worked for outside material too. I was so proud of the cuts he did of mine, and still am.

Lyle: Can you share a little as to what inspired that song?

Dennis: It was just a feeling, one of those things. I was living up in St. Louis with a nice family and there was a little basement studio they fixed up for me. I was walking around the clay mines out around that area and there was this day that just struck me, this wintry day. It was bright and clear and I thought, 'What a crystal day.' The whole thing just went from there—imagery and whatever fell out of my pencil, it just came together. I have very few quick songs and that was one of the fast ones.

Lyle: I know Roger didn't cut it, but I was wondering if there is a story behind "Burning Love"?

Dennis: That was really easy because Pam and I had just gotten married. The love part was no problem whatsoever. It was going to be rock-and-roll, because I bought a set of drums that day. I never really played drums, but I had to do something. I had this one rhythm down and I had to write something to play it on quick. I guess in thirty minutes I wrote "Burning Love." I was thinking if anyone cut it, it would be Sam and Dave. I was a big fan of theirs. Elvis was so far out of reach. Well, even Sam and Dave were really out of reach at the time.

I did an album at the time, I think it was on Intrepid Records, and I think at some point Arthur Alexander, the R&B soul singer, cut it. Somewhere or another my father-in-law, publisher Bob Beckem, played it for Elvis' producer, Felton Jarvis. Felton loved it. I don't think Elvis was knocked out with the idea, but I thought he did a great job with it. Some people say he didn't really like the song that much, but you wouldn't know from hearing it.

Lyle: Did you ever get to meet Elvis?

Dennis: No, I never did. But I played on "Burning Love." I got to overdub the guitar. They said Elvis wouldn't be there in the studio. Some people said it was recorded in Memphis, but I know it was done in Studio A in Nashville. My overdub anyway. I played the sliding whiny guitar and a couple of little background electric parts. I was afraid Elvis was going to show up. That was the most nervous I've ever been playing. He didn't. It was just me, Felton Jarvis and the engineer. I'm actually glad he didn't because I wouldn't have been able to play at all. He's so big in my mind he couldn't have possibly lived up to that…the King. It did scare me pretty bad thinking he might be there.

Lyle: Do you have any advice that you could give on songwriting?

Dennis: If you got an idea, just let it fly. Don't try to edit yourself. And if you do, wait until late in the game when the song's pretty well along its way. That's pretty lousy advice, really. I guess it's sort of a kamikaze school, an instinctive thing. I let the idea itself sit there for a long time before I even start the song, usually, except in the case of "Burning Love," which is really exceptional for me. Once you get into it, don't be afraid to go into stupid places if it wants to lead you there, and hope for the best!

Harold and Don Reid,
The Statler Brothers

The Statler Brothers are a huge talent in the country music scene. They had their own television series, The Statler Brothers Show on TNN from 1991-1997; they were regulars on the ABC series The Johnny Cash Show; they were Johnny's backup singers on the road and in the studio for decades, and have dozens of great songs of their own. Don Reid wrote an amazing song that Elvis Presley recorded in 1975, "Susan When She Tried."

Harold: We did a Christmas special [in 1985] and Roger was one of our guests. He came one morning to tape and we got to playing around as you always do with Roger, telling stories and laughing. That day we had every guest sing a song and then tell a Christmas memory. Roger's memory, of course, was one that just completely set us all on edge. It was about how he would wet the bed when he was a kid and his sister would tell him that Santa Claus wasn't going to come and see him. That was his Christmas memory.

We probably wasted more time with Roger on the set then we did with anybody else, because you couldn't work with him there. You were having too much fun and that's the truth! We had music going in and out of each interview. Somebody was taping, some other guest, and we were standing backstage with Roger giggling. They were playing "Deck the Halls" and we're standing there talking and he just starts singing "Check the balls on that big collie, fa-la-la-la-la-la-la-la-la."

Lyle: When did you guys first meet Roger Miller?

Don: We used to perform in The Johnny Cash Show and Roger took his place a couple of times, so we probably worked with Roger the same time that we met Johnny. We're talking about the late sixties some time.

Lyle: When Roger was taking his place, did it upset the crowd?

Harold: I don't remember anybody being upset. I know what you mean though. If people don't get what they paid for, they'll sit back, enjoy the show, then ask for their money back. Roger was a great entertainer. He would pretty much make you forget anyone you came to see. Roger had such a classic mind that he would say things off the top of this head that would almost wind up as Americana or folklore. For example, I've heard this from many comedians but I believe Roger came up with it: He went to Las Vegas and somebody said, "You went to Vegas. Did you win?" He said, "I guess I did. I went there in a ten-thousand-dollar Cadillac and I came back in a two-hundred-thousand dollar Greyhound."

Don: He was such a warm-hearted person. I loved his writing even when you cut through the humor. I think "Husbands and Wives" was the best thing he ever wrote. He was the same way with his personality. You could just laugh all day, but then when he got serious and wanted to say something serious, it was meaningful.

We recorded a song from *Big River*, "You Oughta Be Here With Me." Roger came to the session when we recorded it, and it was nice to have him in the studio while we were doing one of his songs.

Harold: He was pleased that we had done it and what we had done with it. That's always nice to have approval from the parent, especially someone you respect like Roger.

Don: I remember the last time I saw him, I remember the last thing he said to me. We were backstage at the Opry at the Minnie Pearl salute, and he was saying, "I've got this throat cancer but I'm going to beat it." Of course the sad thing about it is that he didn't.

Lyle: I think it hit most entertainers pretty hard. He was real loved among his peers.

Don: Absolutely. I don't know anybody in the business that didn't like him. I can't name anybody else that we could say that about. Nobody ever said anything bad about him, and I could think of something bad to say about most of them.

Harold: You want some of that, Lyle? That could be another book.

Lyle: Did Roger Miller have an effect on your lives or your careers?

Don: He had an effect on my writing, for sure...in the way that he wrote. Here's how I always saw him as a writer; he never had a throwaway line. One of his lines, most songwriters would take and make a song out of, but Roger would just take it and use it as a line.

Where most people would write around their best line, with Roger every line mattered, every rhythm was good. He was just a perfect writer. I learned from him: don't use any throwaways, make every verse count, make every line count. In the early days he was the last person I remember really waiting to see what that next release was going to be. You remember that from your youth when you're thinking, "I wonder what so-and-so's new record is going to be." Roger was the last one I remember really anticipating what it was going to be, was it going to top the other ones. He would always top himself!

Lyle: My favorite Johnny Cash album is *Ballads of the True West*. I couldn't find a credit but that is you singing on there, right?

Don: Yes. That was quite a project. That was a big project at the time. We enjoyed doing that.

Harold: I think the most interesting thing about that album was the album cover. Don't hold it close to you. Keep it as far away from your face as you can—it's pretty scary.

Don: That was a strange one. Every Johnny Cash session was different from any other session in the world. He didn't run the show like anybody else. Sometimes he didn't run it at all!

Harold: Sometimes he would go to lunch.

Don: When we cut "Flowers on the Wall," he went out for lunch. He just stopped in the middle of a song and said he was going out to get some biscuits and gravy, and he left the studio! He left us and all the pickers inside, just sitting there. The producer came back to us and said, "While we were waiting for John to eat lunch, is there anything you want to record?" And that's how it happened. That was pretty typical. He would just stop and start whenever he wanted to. He would go take a nap whenever he wanted to.

Harold: To this day, as far as we know—and I'm serious—there's no official session when we recorded "Flowers on the Wall." It was on the tail end of his session, we were just sitting there waiting on him and they said, "Let's record something." People have asked us before, "Why did you use a banjo? Why'd you use this on that song?" Well, we used it because that's the people that were sitting in the studio.

Don: If there had been an accordion there it would have been on there too!

Bill Mack

Bill Mack is one of country music's most famous DJs. He's also an accomplished songwriter with songs recorded by over sixty artists. In 1997 he won a Grammy for the Best Country Song of the Year; "Blue," recorded by LeAnn Rimes.

Bill: It all started out in Shamrock, Texas. He was raised in a little town Delhi, Oklahoma, not Erick like everybody thinks. Delhi is just right outside of Erick. He married a Shamrock girl. His first wife was from Shamrock, my hometown, and that's where I met him. He used to hang out with an old boy named Cleland Bircham, who had a big old garage out in Shamrock, population about thirty-five hundred people. Shamrock was dry, they didn't allow booze. But Cleland would get him a tub filled up with beer, and after he closed his shop he would get out his guitar. Roger connected up with him someway, and that is how Roger first got started out—in Cleland's garage, sit in there and pick. At that time he was still in high school out in Oklahoma. There was a place in Shamrock called Jay's Hamburgers, the best hamburgers in the world, located just outside the pool hall. To us they tasted like the best hamburgers in the world, plain old greasy, hotplate hamburgers. Roger and I were seated together at some big function in Nashville back in the seventies—it was one of those award shows—and they brought us one of those tough steaks. Roger nudged me and said, "Hey, Bill, what would you give for a good old Jay's hamburger right now?"

You know, I hired Roger. He played fiddle for me one time when I formed my band in Wichita Falls.

Lyle: Yeah, I heard that he played the same song on the fiddle all night.

Bill: "Bile Dem Cabbage," that was the tune he knew. I first met Roger when I did a show out in Oklahoma. He had won the fiddling contest that they had before my show went on in the auditorium and he said, "If you ever need a fiddle man, let me know." I hired him to do a Christmas party 'cause my fiddle man was sick. The party was in Childress, Texas, and I thought, "I know this kid in Oklahoma." I just happened to have Roger's number and I called and said, "Are you going to be busy…?" whatever the night the Christmas party was taking place.

He said, "No… I'm free," acting like he was booked every night.

He met me in Childress. We were doing Christmas songs and I asked him, "Are you sure you know all these songs? My songs?"

He said, "Yeah, I know them. You just do them and I will do my bit."

And the only thing he played all night was "Bile Dem Cabbage."

Lyle: Did Roger only play fiddle with you the one time?

Bill: That's it. He was a big fan of Hank Williams. When he was in Erick, Oklahoma, he would call me when I was on the air in Wichita Falls asking if I would play a Hank Williams song. This was after I fired him! It wasn't like a "You're fired" kind of thing—I just never hired him again. There was a difference. I would always say, "I didn't fire you, I just didn't hire you again." He liked to go around telling everybody that I was the first one to fire him.

I moved to Lubbock, Texas, and he was living in Fort Worth at the time. The guy that was in charge of the radio station in Fort Worth was also a songwriter and he was jealous of Roger. He got the word out, "Don't give Roger Miller any jobs." He wanted Roger out of Fort Worth. Roger called me and I got him a job working at a radio station in Amarillo. I tried to get him a position in Lubbock but there was no openings. But the guy who owned the radio station had another one in Amarillo and Roger worked there as a disc jockey, wrote songs, wrote jingles. After they fired him his jingles were still played. He wasn't that good of a disc jockey, but they kept him on because he could write jingles and they could get some advertisers because of his talent to write jingles.

Roger told me one time, he said, "Man, they fired me from the radio station. After I hit, I was playing a show in Amarillo and they were still playing my old jingles!" This was four years after they had fired him. "They interviewed me on that radio station and treated me like a star when I went back the second time. It seems so strange. I was sitting in the hotel room listening to the radio station, and they were playing those same jingles that I had written. They didn't pay me for them. They made a lot of money off of them and then they fired me."

Lyle: Was he singing them as well?

Bill: Yes. I was doing the same thing in Lubbock with the radio station.

Lyle: Do you know why he left Nashville for California?

Bill: When he was with RCA he wasn't happy. He told me they were not letting him do what he wanted to do, they weren't capturing him. Chet was an important person, but Roger told me that he confronted Chet and told him that he wanted his contract back, and Chet let him have it. Roger wasn't really a strong person on the Nashville scene. I think that Roger was ahead of his time, he was one jump ahead of most of the people. He never had the dream or desire to be on the Grand Ole Opry. He said that wasn't a big dream of his. He appeared there and everything, but I think he wanted to get more into movies. He had a lot of friends in Nashville, but he wasn't that crazy about living there. He loved the people but he wasn't doing the Nashville Sound, he wasn't jiving with the Nashville atmosphere. It wasn't that he was so terribly uncomfortable, but he wanted to go to a different atmosphere. He wanted the West and West Coast.

Roger liked to entertain and he liked to pick the guitar and he liked to sing, but primarily his great love in those years when I first got to know him well was his songwriting. One of the greatest thrills was... He called me one time and said, "Ernest Tubb has recorded 'Half a Mind.'" I will never forget that. He would call me and tell me when somebody had recorded one of his songs. One of the happiest moments for him was when he told me that Jim Reeves had recorded "Home" and Little Jimmy Dickens recorded "When Your House Is Not a Home." These were monumental moments for Rog. That's when I would really see the excited Roger. He would call me and say, "Go get that record now. I want you to hear it."

Lyle: With you being a popular DJ, was he trying to get you to play his music?

Bill: Yes. He expected us to and I did. I was proud he was my friend. His music was so good that if I had not known him [I'd still play his music]. His work was so strong lyrically. He was and still is one of the greatest that I think ever lived. He had that soul and it showed in all of his work.

He was on my radio show in San Antonio one time. Minnie Pearl had a bar downstairs in her home and her husband had his foot stuck in the bar stool and broke his foot. Roger was on my show and I brought it up. I said, "I just heard that Minnie Pearl's husband broke his foot on a bar stool." And Roger said, "A bar stool? That's something you stumble over in the woods." A bar stool! Back then you couldn't say stuff like that on the air. That's how innocent radio was in 1960, '61.

Another funny thing... While living in San Antonio in 1961, I purchased a new Martin guitar. I was so proud of it. I was hosting a country music show at the San Antonio Municipal Auditorium. It consisted of a bunch of big names, including Roger. Backstage, I pulled my new Martin out of the case, handed it to Roger and said, "I want you to be the first to sign my new Martin, Rog." I handed him my Marks-A-Lot pen and watched as he scribbled on my new guitar. When he handed the guitar to me, I noticed he had signed 'Bill Mack' instead of his name. I shouted, "Roger, you signed my name! What are you doing?" He gave me that Miller sneer and yawned, "It's your guitar, not mine."

BJ Thomas

BJ Thomas has sold more than seventy million albums! He does excellent versions of "I'm So Lonesome I Could Cry," "I Just Can't Help Believing" and Roger's "Husbands and Wives." BJ has lived the rock-and-roll lifestyle, seen the world, and has been through life's ups and downs. He now focuses his energies on religious music and spending time with his wife, Gloria.

BJ: I met Roger when I was playing the Palomino nightclub in California. Roger came to see the show and we got acquainted and spent a lot of time together over a few years in the early seventies. Roger and I had a lot in common, because neither one of us thought we could have a good time unless we were *using* something. We both lived in California, so we attended a lot of parties out there together and spent most of the time in the bathroom. As far as abusing drugs together, that was a real negative, but the time we spent together was really great. Roger was a genius in spite of the drugs. He had a way of looking at things and speaking about things that was beyond clever. It was so unique and insightful, and he had that timbre in his voice that automatically made people want to listen to what he was saying. He had a real relaxing and calming affect.

We spent some time together at his house. I think it was Katharine Hepburn's old house. One time I was over there when I was temporarily separated from my wife, Gloria, and he was divorced for a few years, and we were both unhappy with the way things turned out. I had my guitar in the car so I said, "Let's write a love song together." And Roger said, "Well, I don't write love songs anymore." That always stuck with me, that his divorce had such a profound effect on him that he didn't write love songs anymore. There was a real sadness over the failure of that relationship.

We never did write anything together. If we would have started writing that song, I don't think we'd even been able to write it anyway because we were both real confused. I am basically a positive, up person and he was too, but I think he felt things in a very deep way. Where a lot of people would be in denial and not see something for what it really was, I think he really connected with the sadness and had a lot of remorse and regrets he was feeling from the end of that relationship.

A while later, somebody in my family was in drug rehab in Escondido and I would call them up to see how they were doing. Roger happened to be there at the same time, so whenever I'd call to talk to them I would talk to Roger also. Roger realized he was going to have to get sober and he was trying to. I think he was in there for about a month. It was kind of funny because when you go into rehab it's all about staying sober. You can't do *anything*. But Roger had his own room with a color TV and they went to McDonald's for him every day to get him a double cheeseburger. So he had a way of even working rehab to suit him. I don't think they were going to McDonald's for anybody else in rehab.

I was aware of Roger before I had my first hits, and I was, like most of the world, affected by the string of hits he had: "Dang Me," 'King of the Road." I always thought his records had an extremely high quality to them. He had a purity of sound in his throat that was unbelievable. There was no copying or matching his sound with anybody else's. A lot of people in the music industry are influenced by somebody and try to sound like them, and in the process they end up losing their own sound. He had an effect on me to always stick to your sound and sound like yourself. I tell you, the music business could sure use somebody like him right now. When you talk to a lot of the older guys like myself, it's kind of hard not to have a kind of resentment toward the music industry now because we don't have a place in it. There's such a sameness and imitative thing going on today. But back in Roger's time, everybody had a different sound and stayed true to themselves. We're missing that now.

Lyle: Did you hang out at the King of the Road Hotel at all?

BJ: Yes, we had some good times there. It was a great place. My wife and I used to go to the club on the roof and we'd rent out the suite on the top floor with the swinging double bed. We would swing that thing so high that we'd almost kill ourselves.

One of my favorite things that Roger used to say when he was talking about somebody "You know he's got more talent in his whole body than I have in my little finger." You know, a lot of times when people are like that they are irritating and overbearing but not Roger. He wasn't trying to be humorous or intelligent at somebody's expense. I think he made a real effort not to ever hurt anyone. I had a great deal of respect for Roger and I'll never forget the times I spent with him.

Steve Wariner

At the age of seventeen Steve Wariner joined Dottie West's band. He had a close relationship with Chet Atkins who signed him to RCA in 1977. Steve is a talented singer/songwriter who has had eight number-one singles and has been a member of the Grand Ole Opry since 1996.

Steve: Roger was the first guy I know of that crossed so many genres. I remember as a kid he was showing up on tons of television shows that you'd never see country artists on. He took country into places it had never gone. I always thought that was so impressive and so cool. I first met him through Dottie West when I was playing bass in her band when I was seventeen. I was in awe of Dottie. I played with her for three years. Dottie admired Roger so much, she talked about him a lot. Any time songwriting came up, she raved about Roger Miller. When I first started working for Dottie, they all went to see Roger in concert one time in Reno. I was so disappointed because I was underage and couldn't get in. I eventually got to meet him. I got to know him over the years. When I started making records and having hits, our paths would cross. I admired him so much that any time I was around anywhere near that he was performing, I'd stop in and say hello to him if I could.

The last time I saw him was very special. Chet called me one afternoon and said, "I'm getting ready to have lunch with Roger Miller. Why don't you meet us down at Maude's?" That was a place down on Music Row. I was just thrilled because I hadn't seen Roger in quite a while. I knew Roger was going through treatments for his cancer. I was so excited and proud that Chet included me. Roger couldn't speak that well, he was sort of whispering, and I remember vividly him making jokes about it. Chet asked Roger if he was feeling okay and he responded, "Let me put it this way, Chet: I've taken 'Cattle Call' out of my show."

Chet and Roger did a lot of catching up and reminiscing. Roger looked well and was in good spirits. It wasn't long after that he passed away. Looking back, I think those guys knew it was an important lunch. In some way it might have been their goodbye.

Chet asked me to play at Roger's service at the Ryman Auditorium. That was the most graceful and beautiful ceremony that I've seen in my life, and I've been to a bunch. That was the most tasteful and classy memorial. The place was packed with people that loved Roger. People would get up and sing, and then later they got up sharing stories about Roger, and then they showed old clips of television appearances and things that he had done. One minute you were laughing your head off and the next you were crying. I got up with Chet and he played "Amazing Grace" and I sang part of it. Waylon Jennings was in the front row just weeping like crazy, he loved Roger so much.

You know, I just love hearing Roger Miller stories. There are hundreds of them. One of my favorites is from back in Roger's early roarin' days. There was a bunch of guys out one night at a club and Roger kept looking over at a table saying, "That SOB is staring at me."

The other guys said, "Don't worry about it, Roger."

But Roger noticed that the guy kept on staring. So after a few minutes of it, he got real mad and went up to that guy and said, "Listen, buddy, I've got a list of everybody's name in this place whose ass I can kick and your name is at the top of it."

And the guy got up and just kept getting up! He was well over six feet tall and he said, "I don't think you can kick my ass."

And real quick Roger said, "Well, I'll just take your name off the list then!"

Marc Durham

Bruce Sexton

Marc Durham is a songwriter/ musician who has been entertaining crowds for over forty years. He played in Roger's band in the 1970s.

Marc: Roger and I grew up in the same small town in Oklahoma—Erick. We were a generation apart, around ten years or so. I was just starting to play about the same time he started having hits in the early sixties. I started playing with Micheal Smotherman, another guy who ended up playing with Roger down the road.

You know, it's funny how things change. Before Roger started having those hits he was 'that damn Miller boy.' Roger was mischievous and ornery in his younger days. He wasn't a bad kid, he was just different. Then when he hit they named a street after him and had Roger Miller Day.

Lyle: A lot of talented people came out from that way.

Marc: Yeah. We were talking about that one day and someone said, "Must be something in the water."

And Roger said, "More likely, the lack of water. Hell, I never saw a river with water in it until I was fourteen."

It was real dry out there. The north fork of the Red River ran out north of town but there was never any water in it.

I was playing in a band with Micheal Smotherman and we knew Roger was coming to our small town. We set up our band in an abandoned feed store, where we would practice, and we wanted to get Roger to come and hear us. So he drove up and we just swarmed his car before he could get out of it, "Mr. Miller! Mr. Miller! We got a band and we want you to come and hear us." And he did. He came down later that day. We were pretty bad. We played just a couple of songs and he stopped us and pointed at me and Micheal and said, "You and you, y'all keep practicing." And he pointed at the other guys and said, "And you and you, I think you might want to go to college and get a job. I don't think you guys have it, but I can see the passion in these two other boys."

So Micheal and I kept playing over the years, through high school and college. I got a job with IBM, then I decided to go to L.A. with Micheal and we played in a band called Buckwheat and got a record deal on London Records. We did four albums and we had some success, mostly in Canada. Then the band broke up and I hooked up with Billy Burnette. I was in his band and we also played some shows with his dad, Dorsey. We were playing at the Palomino one night and Roger came in to see Dorsey. After the show, Dorsey introduced me to him and said, "Roger, you may remember this boy, he's from Erick."

I said, "Twenty years ago you told me to keep practicing."

And Roger said, "Well I think you did, didn't you?"

After that we all went to my house, ate, picked and grinned. Then a few days later, I got a call from him saying, "You know, I've been thinking about changing bass players. You want to come and work for me?" That was in '74 and I was with him until '77. I told Roger about Micheal and he said, "Well, bring him on up to the house."

We all sat around playing and Micheal joined the band. Then next thing we knew Billy Burnette was in the band and Steve Turner, who also played with Billy. We all became very close. Micheal and I did a lot of songwriting together and we started playing our songs for Roger and he signed us to his publishing company in Nashville.

Lyle: Did you guys discuss the art of songwriting?

Marc: We talked about songwriting quite a bit. I don't think he considered it artistic. To him it was just making up stuff. He said, "I guess I got good with words because that's all I had to play with when I was a kid." His advice on songwriting was: "Always write from the heart, don't write for the radio, or for the pocketbook. Write songs that mean something to you."

He'd help us if he had an idea to make the song better. He'd say things like, "It's your song, but have you thought about this…" And if a change was made, he wouldn't take a writer's credit.

Roger loved a good song and respected anybody with a good song. After the show we always hung out and would play each other music. It wouldn't be just us, it would be all kinds of people and huge stars like Willie and Waylon or Merle Haggard. We would take the turns passing the guitar around. It was quite an experience for a kid from Oklahoma. He was always very gracious with his stage with us. He'd let us do a song on our own.

We were in Atlanta playing in some dinner theatre in a hotel and the CMA Awards were coming up the next day. We were all sitting up and it was three a.m. and Roger said, "Have you guys ever been to those awards?"

We said, "No."

He said, "Well, hell, let's go. Get the phonebook and see if you could find us a jet somewhere."

I got the phonebook and I started calling around and I found somebody that said, yeah, they'd meet us out at the airport at six or seven a.m. We went ahead and stayed up and partied. We called for a couple of limos and went out to the airport, got on a Lear jet and went up to Nashville. The next thing I know we're at some swanky hotel and Willie, Waylon and Jessie Colter were there. I can't even begin to name all the people that came through that hotel suite... We never made it to the awards. We just partied through the whole thing. He was known to grab a Lear jet at just the drop of a hat.

Roger always said that he was born about twenty minutes behind his time because he was always late. We were playing the Golden Nugget in downtown Las Vegas and they wanted the show to start promptly at whatever it was, 8:05 or 8:17. It was some really weird number like that. They held the show a few times and they told him if he wasn't there on time [again, he'd be fired]. He might come walking up one minute before the curtain was drawn back. He wasn't real happy about playing there anyway because we were in the lounge. This was kind of a starting of a bounce back thing. Roger was the kind of guy that'd say, "We'll just see about that." It came time for the show and Roger wasn't there and they just opened the curtain to an empty stage. I think we might have been on stage. He came strolling up after that. He was fired at that point.

Roger was just a very eccentric, crazy guy. He was not very political. It kind of surprised me, but we played the White House when Gerald Ford was in office. Roger was kind of apolitical. We all were. I was still coming out of the hippie thing. We weren't really into particular candidates, we didn't really talk about what a great job the President was doing or what a crappy job he was doing. We'd joke about it and he'd find jokes about them.

Lyle: Do any memories come up from that White House performance?

Marc: It was just quite amazing. Henry Kissinger was in the audience and all these heads of state and dignitaries from foreign countries. Elizabeth Taylor was there, I danced with Betty Ford. It was quite a deal. It was us, Ella Fitzgerald and Tammy Wynette…kind of an odd combination of performers. It was out on the lawn…just awesome.

We socialized a lot the time that I was with him. Our split was somewhat strained because of something that happened with the band as a whole, a situation that happened. I can't really go into it. He was having a problem with his accountant at this time. His accountant ran off with his ex-wife. I don't know if they ran off together, but they were kind of in cahoots. From what I understand during that time, that would have been in the seventies, he wasn't sending the taxes in and they were siphoning money off. That's kind of the way I understand that it went down.

Another funny thing was when he got his divorce he bought a new 450 SL Mercedes and he went up there to see his ex-wife, to do whatever… He was just going up there to show the car off, a convertible. Unbeknownst to him some bird had crapped down the driver's side door, just run all down the door. Then she walked around the car and said, "Oh, I see you had the family emblem put on the door." I guess that was Leah.

Lyle: I heard that Glen Campbell ended up dating Roger's ex-wife….

Marc: I think so at one point. But I think that was before Sarah, Glen's wife, who was Mac Davis' wife. When that happened Roger and her were already over, and I don't think it lasted very long between Glen and her. I don't think Roger ever really held that against him.

It was just a wild time. We hung a lot and sang a lot, partied with Campbell and with just whoever. You'd hang out with Roger and Glen and you'd go to Glen Campbell's show the next night and hear a couple of Rogerisms. Roger didn't mind. He said, "Hell, that stuff's not mine anyway. It just come out of my mouth and I don't know where the hell it comes from."

Steve Turner

Steve Turner has been a premier drummer and percussionist for more than 25 years. He has appeared with many artists on numerous gold and platinum hit sessions and television appearances. His friendship with Micheal Smotherman (Roger's pianist) helped land him a place in Roger Miller's band. He took Marty Allred's place as the drummer in Roger's band in 1975.

Steve: I sort of rode the gig down. I was working for him for about a year and a half. He was going pretty good when I first started with him but towards the end he started sabotaging [*his career*], he was doing a lot of drugs. Cocaine, that's the first time I ever saw anybody playing with that.

Some of it was that, and staying awake, and all those guys were doing that, Glen Campbell, that's the first time I met him. Glen worshiped Roger, he would quote him, "I may be schizophrenic but we'll always have each other", which is a Roger Miller line. And Glen would always end the quotes by saying "Roger Miller". Another one he'd say was "I'd give my right arm to be ambidextrous."

His humor was funny, but a lot of it you'd crack up on the way home thinking about it. A lot of his humor you had to think about, it wasn't an immediate face value response. Towards the end of working with him, maybe it was paranoia but if the crowd wasn't laughing, Roger would walk off and leave. I mean he left a number of shows half way through. He'd say "Now that was funny! Fuck y'all!" and he'd walk off the stage. And we'd finish the set out, Micheal Smotherman would sing a song, Billy Burnette, Marc Durham. We'd all play something just to appease the crowd.

This one time at the Fairmont Hotel, this is when his career was going down, from a lot of that kind of stuff. This manager guy who ran the room was a prick, he came in during a show. It wasn't full, it was spotted around in tables. Roger was talking and telling some jokes and this manager comes to the front of the stage and turns his back to Roger and he started talking to somebody while Roger's trying to do his show. Roger said "Excuse me" but the guy just kept on talking, so Roger said "Hey! You know what? Fuck you and fuck this rat hole!" and he walked off and split. The next night he wouldn't come down to do the show so they cancelled the rest of the shows there. But Roger was going through some tough times, his accountant was embezzling from him. I went a month working for Roger without getting paid but eventually things got straightened out.

Lyle: Would he come back on stage after getting mad at a crowd?

Steve: Sometimes he would but sometimes he'd get in a car and speed off.

Lyle: Do you have any favorite one-liners of his?

Steve: One of my favorite quotes of his was when he'd go up to people and say "Am I who you think I am?"

Roger used to tell me stories about him and Johnny Cash painting their way out of a room. They got pissed at a guy and painted a room black, everything, the windows, curtains, the bed, the floor. Then they set the paint can down and left.

You know, I always listened to rock-and-roll. I was playing jazz and reggae when I started working with Roger, but he turned me on to country music. I started seeing the soul that was in it. I got my Bachelor of Music from Florida State but I got my Master's from the Roger Miller School of Music.

John Byner

*J*ohn Byner is an actor/comedian/impressionist who starred in his own television series Bizarre and as a regular on many series, including my personal favorite, Soap. He's appeared in many movies and television shows, and on stages worldwide.

John: Roger blew up the train when his show was ending. He had this train that he'd sing on and sing songs about. When he was cancelled, the last show, the last minute, he took one of those plungers that they have when they blow up mines and things and blew up the train.

Lyle: For real?

John: For real. He blew up the train because it was the last scene in the last show that he was going to do. I admired him for doing that. I thought it was the funniest thing. It wasn't a violent thing, it was just a toy train. We sort of clicked when I saw him do that because it was a very bizarre thing to do back in those days. I think it was black and white television, that's how long ago it was. He said the show was a struggle for him. He had not had as good a time as he wished he had.

Lyle: Do you know why the show was cancelled?

John: I don't remember what it was. I can remember Glen Campbell's show being cancelled because so-and-so's wife didn't like country music. I'm not going to name names but…those things happen.

Roger would grit his teeth once in a while if he didn't like something. I was showing [my friend] Dennis some pictures of Roger and he had these sandals on. Roger was kind of peeking around the back of this motor home that they had gotten for their honeymoon and he's wearing sandals with socks on. Dennis said, "Is that as down as Roger gets? Sandals with socks on?" Not thinking it would upset him, when I saw Roger the next time I told him what Dennis had said and it really ticked him off. He gritted his teeth and mumbled, "Son of a bi…" Really angry, he'd do that. He'd grit his teeth and talk through them.

We'd talk about friends in the business and I'd say something and he'd say, "That was in the seventies, wasn't it?"

And I'd say, "Yeah."

Roger would say, "I don't remember the seventies."

Lyle: Did you ever talk to him about songwriting?

John: Oh yeah, he'd kick around tunes he was working on. In fact, the one about old friends… There was a line in there [about] linking arms, and he'd say, "What do you think?" You'd say, "Well, I think it's a great tune but maybe it should be like arm-in-arm or something like that," and he would just fluff it off. He'd never make any changes. If he said the grass was purple and you'd say, "But wait a minute, Roger, the grass is green," it stayed purple. He'd run his new tunes by me and he'd run into his stonewalls. He'd have something leading up, it was really cooking, and then 'Wa, ba, ba bap pa pah…'—that's as far as he got. He'd rattle off about six or eight of those songs that he got to a certain place at and would have to quit because he couldn't get any further without having it sound like something else or somebody else's thing. He had a slew of those.

Lyle: Do you know any behind-the-scenes stories on any of those songs that he wrote?

John: Well, I know for sure he wrote "King of the Road" on an envelope riding on a plane. In fact, the envelope still exists. It used to be in a case in his living room. It was written on the back of a business envelope.

Lyle: Do you have any favorite one-liners of his that come to mind?

John: You know how somebody will say "How's that?" when you're talking to them and they don't understand? Especially country folk. Well, he would say it so fast that people, especially strangers, wouldn't understand that he'd said "Cow's ass?"

One afternoon I was hanging with Mary and Roger at their place and Roger said, "Hey, Byner, guess where I'm going tonight?"

"Where?"

"I'm going to James Cagney's house."

I said, "What I wouldn't give to go to James Cagney's house."

I go home—I'm raising my kids by myself on the beach there in Malibu—and the phone's ringing, the dog's barking and the kids are having a fight about something. One of them answered the phone upstairs and leans over the balcony and says, "Dad! James Cagney is on the phone."

Evidently, Roger called him and told him and so Cagney called me at my house. [*Imitating his voice,*] "John-o! It's me, Jimmy! Jimmy Cagney! Why don't you come over tonight? We're having a smoker. Just you, me and the boys."

That's exactly how he said it. I went over there and I sat to his right and heard some great stories and told some great stories. Donald O'Connor was there. At the end of the night, James Cagney and Pat O'Brien walked me to the door. I had to pinch myself, 'My God, James Cagney and Pat O'Brien seeing me to the door!'

I was asked back a second time and it was all because of Roger. Cagney liked me. First thing he said when I met him [*imitating his voice perfectly,*] "I just saw you do something straight. It was marvelous, marvelous!"

It was fun. Donald O'Connor and I got up and did "Yankee Doodle Dandy" for him. It was a hell of a night.

Larry Richstein

L arry Richstein was Roger's road manager from 1986 to 1992.

Larry: I hooked up with Roger in late '84. I was his soundman for a week with him at the Golden Nugget in Las Vegas. Then I didn't see him for about a year and a half because *Big River* was about to open. *Big River* opened up in the spring of '85 on Broadway and of course it was a big hit. But he didn't work much for a while because of having done that. As I recall, back in the spring of '86 he decided he was going to start working some again. Well, Randy Hart had been his road manager, but Roger had been off so long that Randy went with Steve Wariner. It all came back together on short notice. There wasn't a lot of warning. Roger had some dates booked, they called me, and I said I'd road manage him if he wanted me to. So, I became his road manager and did sound and stuff...took care of the dates. That's when I started to get to know him.

As far as the Vegas days and a lot of the crazy stuff... When I went with him there was a little bit of crazy stuff, but I'll tell you something; Roger was getting a little older and he and Mary, and a few years down the line there they had the kids. First they got Taylor and then a while down the line the same people got pregnant again, which I thought was interesting, so they got the brother also. Roger and Mary were so happy with these children. Adopting those kids at his age…changed things for him. He changed his ways somewhat. He told me an interesting story when he adopted Taylor. He had had other marriages and had children from those marriages that he raised—his son Dean and a daughter. Roger said to me that he thought he was doing it for Mary, because he had raised kids and was a little bit older. He said to me, "The minute I put that little girl in my arms the other day, I was a goner." They just were so happy raising those kids.

He told me a story one time. He worked with the band, and then after they had the kids he wanted to work a little bit more. I think he wanted to make a little more money now that he had the kids and stuff. They were comfortable, he did fine, he worked a certain amount every year. I don't think he wanted to work a tremendous amount, didn't want to kill himself.

So his manger, Stan Moress, mentioned the possibility of doing some solo shows. At first he kind of balked at the idea. He wasn't too keen on it. He mentioned it to me and I said, "I think you oughta try it, because your persona, once you get out there you kind of make people feel like they're in your living room anyway."

So we booked a small fair date in California. Just he and I went. We'd meet at an airport. I kept his gear, I kept his guitars, his amp and stuff like that. He'd carry his fiddle, but of course on the solo dates he didn't use the fiddle, because it's pretty hard to do a fiddle thing just by yourself. So we'd meet at an airport, get a Lincoln, get in the car and go do the job, just him and me. He'd be a little nervous. Roger could be nervous going into a situation, but once he'd get out there he'd relax. Sometimes he'd balk at wanting to do autographs or talk with people and stuff like that. He'd say, "Aww heck, I don't want to do that." I'd say, "Well, you gotta do some of this. It's best." I'd talk him into it and as soon as he'd get out there he'd meet some people and he'd just get chatting away.

But he went out there and it would be just great. He used an acoustic guitar, sat on a stool, did the songs, talked with the crowd, did his usual banter, and it went just fine. It was interesting that a guy that's been at it that long he was a little nervous about it.

We were playing Branson there for a couple of years—'89, '90, '91—and we were playing Roy Clark's theatre once a month during the season. We had been there once in '86 and he didn't like it, but now it was starting to grow and we started playing it. One time we're driving into Branson and Roger's looking at all these buses and at the people getting off the buses and going into the buffets and all of that. He said, "Boy, I've never seen so many unhealthy-looking people in one place in all my life."

Well by this time I'd been with him for a while and I'm going, 'Aw shit, when is this going to show up on stage?'

Sure enough we were doing a matinee one day and he said it on stage right there in Branson! [At another show] he said, "You know, folks, you know how you stay in a hotel and at night they come in and turn down your bed and they leave you a nice chocolate or a mint by your pillow? Not here in Branson... Chicken-fried steak!"

When Waylon had some heart problems there was a time when Waylon was going to play this fair date up in the middle of Idaho and he got sick about three or four days before and couldn't do it. So they asked Roger if he would do it and he said he would. We got the band together and we met in Boise. It was right up in the middle of Idaho, which was some of the most beautiful country I'd ever seen. The band was in one car and Roger and I were in another. We get there just in time to get on stage and do the show. I had the band get the stage ready, because the sound company was there and they were waiting for us. We were just gonna go and plug in, we didn't sound check or anything. I took a look around and I said to Roger, "Let me go get the dough before we go on. Let me get this taken care of." We were gonna get in the car right afterwards, because there was no place to stay up there. We were going to drive back down to Boise and just fly home.

This whole thing looked suspicious to me, something wasn't right, so I wanted to get our money. I get with the guy handling it and he said, "Well, we got a little problem. We don't have all your money."

I said, "What do you mean you don't have all our money? Waylon got sick and we're covering so you can still have your show and now we show up and you guys don't have the money?"

I was pissed off. I wasn't real nice about it to these old cowboys. I said, "Well what do you got?"

They had some of it. I had this guy's kid going to get the popcorn money.

I said, "I want every dime you got in this place. I want every dime!" I had them running left and right.

Meanwhile I go talk to Roger, "Roger, these guys don't have the money."

He said, "Shit! I haven't had to deal with that in twenty years."

I said, "What do you want to do? Do you want to leave?"

Roger said, "No, we'll play. The audience is here to see a show. They haven't done anything wrong. We're here, they're here to see me. We'll go on."

That tells you an awful lot about him in my opinion. That showed me the stuff he was made of, that he went out and did it.

Gail Davies

Jim McGuire

*G*ail Davies is a singer/songwriter best known for her hits "Jagged Edge of a Broken Heart" and "You Turn Me On, I'm a Radio." She is also known as being one of the first women in the music industry to produce her own albums.*

Gail: Roger and I met at the Troubadour in Los Angeles. I was singing with a group called The Midnight Band. We played at the end of each evening to close out. Roger came in one night and heard me sing. I also met Frank Zappa during that same time and both of them asked me to tour with them. Roger had actually asked me out on a date when we first met, then called a few days later saying one of his background singers had left the group and he needed to replace her immediately. I told him I wasn't interested in being a background singer because I was trying to become a quality songwriter and artist myself, but he said it would only be for a few weeks, until he found someone, so I agreed. That's how I ended up on the road with him.

This was back in the mid-seventies, before I had anything going on in my career. I was just singing background on his songs, wearing long evening gowns in posh, high class show rooms and being the cute little girl singer. He always called me his "pretty lady" and sometimes, if he was irritated with me, "the little bohemian."

Roger featured me quite often during his shows and I made my television debut on the *Merv Griffin Show* singing a duet with him of the Johnny & Jack classic, "Ashes of Love."

Lyle: Did Roger give you any advice on songwriting?

Gail: Roger gave me tons of advice, all the time. I sat up with him many nights after the shows and he would try to write songs and talk about songwriting. He told me it was hard to have kittens with somebody watching.

He did tell me his life story one evening, about how his father died when he was a little boy and his mother, who thought it was in his best interest, gave him to his aunt and uncle who lived on a farm in Oklahoma. He loved them very much but always missed not having his mother around. It was a very sad story and quite interesting so I went back to my room that night and wrote a song called "I'm Hungry I'm Tired." When I played the song for Roger he got tears in his eyes. That was, to me, the moment I became a real songwriter.

Roger was one of the sharpest and funniest human beings I ever met but he was also very frustrated that he was always "expected" to be funny. He felt that people never took his love songs seriously. "Husbands and Wives" is one of the greatest lyrics and melodies ever written but that's not what people wanted to hear. He felt they just wanted the funny Roger, not the serious Roger. I remember one time he told me someone had sent him a letter or telegram that said, "sorry to hear your clown died." That hurt him tremendously. I thought it was cruel that people didn't want to let him grow or expand as an artist. This was long before he wrote the score for *Big River*.

I do remember that we were walking through a hotel lobby when some young kids walked by and started singing "King of the Road." He was feeling a little paranoid that evening and thought they were making fun of him. He was pissed off but when we got into the elevator I told him that they didn't mean any harm. They were just trying to identify with him and didn't know what to say because he was a big star and people sometimes say and do silly things when they're at a loss for words around someone who's famous. He thanked me for helping him see things in a more positive light. He said I gave him a sense of balance.

Besides the music part of our relationship, Roger was also a friend and concerned about me and my life. I was talking to him one night about the fact that I hadn't seen my real father, who was a country singer back in the fifties, since he and my mother divorced, when I was five years old. He got angry with me and said I needed to look him up immediately and go see him. I took that advice seriously and located my dad in San Antonio, Texas. At Roger's insistence, I finally met my dad again and then he died a few months later. I have always been grateful to Roger for making me do that.

Lyle: Did you keep in touch with Roger throughout his life?

Gail: Not too much. I didn't know that Roger was madly in love with, and also dating, Mary from the Kenny Rogers band. I was madly in love with Roger at that time but after I found out, I left the band and we didn't see much of each other again until my career was taking off. We did play a couple of shows together in California. Both he and Mary were very kind and gracious to me but we were never close after that.

Roger and I were very close but only for a short time. He was a great man and as I mentioned in the song I wrote about him, I will love him till the day that I breathe no more.

Dwight Yoakam

Richard D. Moore

Dwight Yoakam has truly earned his title of "Country Music Artist" with his distinct style. Along with his talents in songwriting and singing, he is an excellent actor, and screenwriter and has some of the coolest stage moves since Elvis. He's also one of the few people that co-wrote with Roger Miller.

Dwight: It was an honor to have known Roger. I actually met him first at Willie Nelson's Farm Aid in 1986, and he had heard of me and heard "Honky Tonk Man" on the radio. He came up and introduced himself and I was just ecstatic to meet somebody of that legendary proportion. He was talking about his son having been a fan and introduced him to my music. We then met again at a tribute to Willie Nelson a couple of years later in Hollywood, at the Pantages Theatre. Roger and I were both singing a Willie song separately, we were both on that part of the show. He and I were chatting and I was telling him what a huge fan I was of him as a writer. I told him I had an idea that I had in my hip pocket for a song. I just basically had a title and I thought it might be a cool shuffle; the title is "It Only Hurts When I Cry." His eyes lit up and he said, "Now I like that."

I said, "Well, would you even consider writing with me?"

"Yeah I'd love to write that with you. You know, I've never co-written with anybody." I was shocked and he said, "Well, there's been some people's names on some of my songs but I never actually co-wrote."

The title itself was kind of a hook, tongue-in-cheek. "It Only Hurts When I Cry", I think, appealed to him. We got together about a month later at my house in Hollywood… We sat down together and just started swapping lines. My old Weimaraner [dog] Jack befriended Roger. He'd always ask about Jack when he'd call. We sat there, the three of us—Roger, myself and Jack, although we kicked Jack out of the room so we didn't have to give him a writer's credit. It was a phenomenal experience.

Somebody asked me one time what it was like to write with Roger and I said, "Staying up with his wit and how his mind worked and the speed of his mind would be like trying to ride a bicycle alongside a taxiing Lear jet and keeping up." It felt like that at times. Interestingly enough, we were literally trading line for line. He'd say, [quotes the first line from the song]. He started that melodic approach on that first line and I'd answer him. That set the pattern for the rhyme scheme of the song and how we were going to play off each other...kind of posing comments, the juxtaposition... The irony being that the only time is all the time, right?

So once we kind of caught the sparkle in each other's eyes, the reaction, the response to each of those lines, it just pushed us through writing it fairly quickly. We got it done that day, pretty much. We talked on the phone one other time and just kind of batted back and forth. Then he came back out and sang some harmony with me on it. When he was singing harmony on the track...he came back into the room and they were asking him... Because of the INS [musician's union], you had to get a driver's license from everybody. This was in 1990-1991. Some new legislation had been passed where they required everybody to put up their social security number or show some sort of ID to be confirmed by whomever the session leader was on that day. Roger came back into the room and they had forgotten to ask him for that earlier. He had just sung a take, and he walked back into the room and they said, "Roger, we need to have your drivers license." And he said, "Well, how fast was I singing, Officer?"

Lyle: Was there any reworking of the song before it was recorded?

Dwight: Not really. We put it down in a shuffle pattern and the melody and everything was there, pretty much. I might have massaged how we did the bridge, just in terms of my vocal approach to that—how I was going to do it. No, there was not much real reworking.

We did discuss writing some other songs together. He called when we had the number one with that together. He called and was very excited about it and I was equally excited, just elated that we had done it together. We talked at that time about writing another song and getting together and doing it. Unfortunately, as illness would have it and life would have it, we were never able to realize that opportunity.

He was a really phenomenal thinker and truly worthy of the term "genius" being applied to his musical prowess. It's not over-used when it comes to Roger Miller. You go back and listen to the rhyme scheme and the way he approached writing "Engine Engine #9," and it's as good as anything by the Tin Pan Alley guys, the twenties, thirties. It's shoulder-to-shoulder with

Johnny Mercer or Cole Porter. In my opinion I just think he's a true songwriting genius, a lyrical genius. I'll always owe him a debt of gratitude for writing that with me. It'll be one of the truly cherished moments in my career, him sitting in the front room of my house that day writing that song.

Lyle: What was it like sitting across one of your heroes and writing a song with him?

Dwight: Well, Roger was a person who wiped that from the room the minute he came in. He just acted like another human being, interacted that way. It was really only the coming and the going of it that were moments where I was able to think to myself, "I'm here with the King of the Road, the man who, when I was a kid, had the biggest hit in all the world for that two month period."

Lyle: Did you talk to him about the art of songwriting?

Dwight: Yeah, he said to me…and it's the simply the best way I've heard anyone put it, "I always figured songwriting was kind of like a cat having her kittens; something you went off under the porch and did yourself." I don't think I've ever heard a more apt description of the process given. I concur wholeheartedly with his reference to the solitary nature of writing.

We chatted a lot about a lot of different things: his love of the West, the insanity of touring, and about playing with Ray Price's band. He told me about leaving Nashville. He was going to California to become an actor…not to be involved in music anymore. He made the *Dang Me* album as a fulfillment of a commitment to his label, and gathered enough money together by making it to go out to California in 1963. It was originally titled *Roger and Out*, in reference to him leaving the music business. He found himself about three months into it, having a hit single with "Dang Me." They re-titled the album *Dang Me*, and the rest is history, as they say.

Lyle: Did knowing Roger have an effect on your life?

Dwight: Yes it did. It has continued to serve as a point of inspiration and a moment that I'll cherish always and it continues to be a point on the horizon that I aspire to as an artist—Roger Miller's work.

It Happened Just
That Way...

By singer/songwriter/record producer **Norro Wilson**:

Many years ago when I first came to Nashville, I joined up with a gospel quartet and tried to make a living singing gospel music. Well, I needed to make more money than I was singing, so I went to work for a company selling bibles. That's where I first met Roger Miller. We ended up becoming good friends. We met at a meeting the guy who owned the company put on about how to go on the road and sell bibles to people on the street and to little old ladies and stuff. So Roger and I went out on this great adventure of selling bibles. We only lasted three days. Later, somebody asked Roger how come we got out of selling bibles and he said, "The Lord called us out of it."

Roger used to rent Lear jets all the time and he'd do crazy things like fly from LA to Nashville to pick up Krystal Burgers for his friends. Anyway, Minnie Pearl was putting on a Heart Telethon in Chattanooga. I was in Printer's Alley and Roger came by and we had a couple of drinks and next thing I know we get in his car and we're at the airport in a Lear jet and I had never been in one before. He didn't tell me he was even taking me. We were rocking it pretty good hightailing to Chattanooga and about half way there Miller yelled up to the pilot "Do a loop!" And they just did a complete rollover before you knew it—it warped my mind!

● ● ● ● ● ● ● ● ● ● ● ● ● ●

By singer/songwriter, **Tommy Cash**, *brother of Johnny Cash:*

Back in the sixties and seventies, Roger was well known for going into places where people were working and getting up on stage with them to do a song. I was in Los Angeles working at the Palomino Club—this was '74 or so—and I had a full house that night. I had a few hit records in a row about that time, "Six White Horses," and a couple of others. Roger came in with Hoyt Axton and they were partying. And right in the middle of my second show I asked Roger if he'd like to get up and do a song. "Hey Roger Miller's out here. You want to get up and do one?" Well, he come up and took my guitar and he just went into his act, and Hoyt Axton came up and joined him and they finished off the night. I never did get back on stage! The club owner said, "Hey, you've done your part, just let 'em go on, let 'em rave on, let 'em do whatever they wanna do. Here's your pay. Don't worry about trying to get back on stage and finish your show." They just took over.

• • • • • • • • • • • • • •

By Cajun-country singer/songwriter **Jimmy C. Newman**:

I knew Roger Miller before he was a star. I knew him when he was playing fiddle for Minnie Pearl. And then I used him on the road as a sideman too. I remember one specific date, it was South Carolina and he was playing drums for Faron. There was a guy who would book these shows so he could be on it and sing too. We were outside between shows and this guy who booked us so he could be on the show strolled over to where Roger and I were visiting and says "Roger, have you heard my last record?" and Roger said "I certainly hope so".

Another time we [went] to a BMI party, Broadcasting Music Incorporated. My wife and I walked through the country club and there was a big reception in a tent and we walked out of the building and into the tent where everybody was milling around, band playing, people drinking. He's standing right next to the tent and we visited. We both turned around at the same time and on the wall of the tent was [a label] "Nashville Tent and Awning Company". At the same time when he saw that and I was looking he did this [*looking inside his suit jacket at the label*] to see if it was the same brand that made his coat that made the tent. He was a great, great guy and a great friend and we'll always miss him here in Nashville.

• • • • • • • • • • • • • •

By "The Gentle Giant" singer/songwriter **Don Williams**:

He was in my estimation just one fine fella, incredibly talented. I did a show out in L.A. years ago and Roger came to it and after the show was over he invited me to go home with him for just a bit because I think I had two shows that night. So I did, so when we went behind the venue and got into his Rolls Royce, he tried to start it and it wouldn't start so he got out and lifted the hood and did a little tinkering, he closed the hood and he got back in the car and it started and we drove out to his house. After I was there for an hour, hour and a half, he went out to start it and the same thing happened again, and he said "Don, that's proof positive that it doesn't make any difference if you're a country boy, I had the same problems when I had an old Chevy pickup and now I have a Rolls Royce and I still have to lift the hood up to get the thing to start." Roger was just a good ol' boy.

• • • • • • • • • • • • • •

By singer/songwriter **Helen Cornelius**:

My son was killed in an accident and I hadn't seen Roger for quite some time. It had been probably, oh—I guess, two years after that. I ran into Roger and his wife at the CMA Awards and of course, it was all gala going over the big red carpet from the Grand Ole Opry to the hotel where the big reception was being held after the awards. Roger took time to get out of line from where he was and came over to me and he said, "I have worried about you so much with what you've gone through", and he said "Are you okay"? And he just showed that real tender, gentle side. And I thought that was very sweet and I appreciated that. He was a sweetheart.

• • • • • • • • • • • • •

By singer/songwriter/comedian **Jim Stafford**:

All the guys used to go to Tootsie's Orchid Lounge. You'd give her your picture, she'd write your phone number down on a piece of paper or put it on the picture—whatever. And if somebody came in looking for a sideman she would give them your number and help you get a job. I remember seeing a picture of Roger on her wall along with all the others and underneath it, it said "To Tootsie—I love you like a cat loves cream."

I do remember one thing that was pretty sad; I actually watched the sign go down across the street about Roger Miller coming [this was at the Roy Clark Theater in Branson in 1992]. Obviously Roger Miller's people were calling saying he ain't gonna be working anymore. He's too sick to work. He died shortly after that.

• • • • • • • • • • • • •

By Grand Ole Opry Member **Little Jimmy Dickens**:

Roger used to live about three doors from me in East Nashville. And he used to come by my house a lot on his way home. He'd pass by and stop in if he seen me in the yard and visit for awhile. One day I was working on a swing set for my little girl and I was trying to set it up. And he came by and said, "What are you doing?" And I said, "I'm trying to get these darn bolts in the right place and I find out I don't know much about it." And he said, "You're standing too close to it and you're getting feedback." Crazy guy!

• • • • • • • • • • • • • •

By **Hargus "Pig" Robbins**, *piano player on many of Roger's recording sessions, including "King of the Road" and "Dang Me":*

I'm blind, and it was around Christmas time, and he's talking about how he's gonna get this for so-and-so and that for so-and-so. He said, "And, Pig, I'm gonna get you a seeing eye hog." We were all swinging from the rafters!

• • • • • • • • • • • • • •

By songwriter/producer, **Billy Arr**:

One time Roger gave me a birthday present. He was the only one to get me anything and I was real grateful to him for it. It was all packaged nicely. He had me open it in front of everyone, and I took it out and it was a real nice expensive ball pen. Roger then said, "Can I have your autograph?" and handed me a napkin to sign. So I started to sign it and I said, "There's no ink in this pen!" Roger said, "Just a hint—get out of town! Don't need the competition. Every time you try to write a song, use that pen."

• • • • • • • • • • • • • •

Canadian singer, songwriter, impressionist **Ronnie Prophet**:

I walked in Roger's dressing room and he had one ear up against the wall. I said, "What are you doing Roger?"

He said, "Come here listen to this."

So I put my ear against the wall and I said, "I don't hear a thing."

He said, "I know, and it's been like that all day."

He would say things like, "What's the difference between a duck? One leg is both the same." I think that's just hilarious but most people with a right mind would say that doesn't make any sense. Right! It doesn't make any sense, but listening to Roger tell it you're falling on the floor.

• • • • • • • • • • • • • •

By songwriter **Sonny Throckmorton**:

If somebody were to ask me, "Who was the greatest songwriter?" I would have to say Roger Miller. I just believe he's one of the greatest minds of our time. Roger once said to a guy who asked him if he'd catch dinner—he looks to Roger and said "Can you buy dinner? I didn't bring any money with me." And Roger said "Yeah, and I bet you didn't leave any at home either."

• • • • • • • • • • • • • •

By manager **Rick Marcelli:**

Roger used to say, "When you're at a table it's funny how people get shellout falter when the bill comes." We had fallout shelters because of the air raid and we'd call it "shellout falter", meaning that people would look the other way when the bill came to the table. They wouldn't pick up the tab. They had shellout falter.

He also talked about how he loved to go fishing for a cab in New York. He related getting a cab in New York as going fishing.

• • • • • • • • • • • • • •

By **Ken Stange,** *one of Roger's keyboard players in the eighties:*

One time we were in an airport just hanging out waiting for a flight. A couple of rows over Roger was sitting reading the paper and this little midget who worked at the airport comes over to him and he was talking to him. And we were looking over there, because we would always run interference for him to make sure nobody bugged him. We realized it was no big deal. The guy leaves, Roger gets up and walks over to us and we said, "What did that guy want?" He said, "He wanted to go up on me!"

• • • • • • • • • • • • • •

By songwriter/musician **Donnie Fritts:**

I met Roger before I had started [playing] with Kris Kristofferson and I was just starting out writing. It was about '64, I had just signed with Shelby Singleton's publishing company in Nashville. And I saw Roger as he was coming in the back door of the publishing company and he said to me "Hello, I'm Roger Miller and I'm a Coke sucker"—he was drinking a Coke!

• • • • • • • • • • • • • •

By Singer/songwriter/producer **Billy Swan:**

When I was playing with Kris Kristofferson in 1970, Roger came to see us at the Troubadour, and Kris wasn't there yet, it was a night that he was late, anyway Roger came up on stage to sing a few songs, and I just started playing bass and I wasn't all that familiar with it. So Roger got up on stage with us and it was Dennis Linde, myself and him and he turned and said "'King of the Road', B natural"—My God! I immediately whipped that bass off and gave it to Dennis Linde, I didn't know what the hell B natural meant, G okay, F okay, B natural—I guess he might have been joking.

• • • • • • • • • • • • • •

By **Reggie Young**, *arguably the most famous session guitar player in the country music industry:*

Roger once said to me, "I don't believe in astrological signs. I never really got into all that stuff, but me being a Capricorn, that's one of my traits." Roger got stopped by the cops and said, "I don't know why you stopped me. I've been passing people all day long going faster than me."

• • • • • • • • • • • • • •

By **Bill Anderson,** *reprinted by permission from his book,* I Hope You're Living As High On the Hog As the Pig You Turned Out To Be:

A newspaper reporter asked Roger in an interview, "Do you have any plans for the movies?" To which Roger replied, "I sure do. I'm going to see *Driving Miss Daisy* next week."

• • • • • • • • • • • • • •

By *singer/songwriter,* **Marty Stuart**:

Glen Campbell said he'd been born again, and Roger said, "It must have been rough on your mother."

• • • • • • • • • • • • • •

Favorite Roger Miller one-liner of producer/singer/songwriter **Cowboy Jack Clement**:

"Here's a song I wrote while I was singing that one."

• • • • • • • • • • • • • •

By *singer/songwriter/manager* **Merle Kilgore**:

At the airport a guy stopped Roger and said, "Oh, Mr. Miller, I play all your music and I want to make it big time in Nashville. Can you give me a show biz tip?" Roger said, "Okay, keep your pills and your change in separate pockets. I just took thirty-five cents!"

• • • • • • • • • • • • • •

By *singer/songwriter* **Thom Bresh**:

We were in a plane and it was bumpy, and Roger said, "Man, they must be working on this part of the sky."

People used to say "No sweat" but Roger said "Negative perspiration."

. . . .

*By actor **George Lindsay**:*

He looked at a wall thermostat and said, "You know, I'm gaining weight."

. . . .

*Favorite Roger one-liners of recording artist, **Bobby Bare**:*

"My mom and dad were first cousins. That's why I look so much alike."

"We were so poor at our house, we had to jack off the dog to feed the cat."

. . . .

*By **Randy Hart**, Roger's keyboard player and band leader from '78 to '84:*

I remember we were in Vegas one time and there was a lady near the front of the stage that kept having to get up and apparently go back to the ladies room. About the third time she got up, Roger said off-mic, "You oughta eat some cheese."

We were in Reno one time riding in a cab somewhere and they were building or tearing down a church. Roger looked over and there was a bulldozer sitting there, and he said, "Look, they tore down that church and look what was inside!"

. . . .

*By Roger's long-time friend, **Chuck Blore**:*

One time we were on an airplane and Roger asked the stewardess, "Hey, Ma'am, how high is this airplane?" She said, "Oh, I would guess maybe 30,000 feet." He said, "Holy shit! How wide is it?"

"Cupid shot an arrow in the air, it fell to earth and hit me in the leg. So now my leg loves you."

. . . .

*By legendary session player/and president of the Nashville Musician's Union **Harold Bradley**:*

Buford Pusser, the *Walking Tall Sheriff* walked up to Roger and said, "Roger, you know, I got seventeen holes in me." And Roger said, "Well, lay down and open your mouth and we'll play a round of golf." He was just clever beyond imagination.

• • • • • • • • • • • • • •

*By **Lee Rollag**, Roger's guitar player from 1981-1990:*

We crossed the country on a bus tour and passed the arch in St. Louis. Roger looked out and said, "There's the tomb of the unknown hamburger."

• • • • • • • • • • • • • •

*By session guitar player **Steve Chapman**:*

They asked him one time in an interview about the new Civil Rights Bill. He said, "I think they ought to pay the damned thing."

Thumbs was telling me that there was a cop that stopped him in L.A. and said, "Can I see your license, sir?" And he said, "Can I shoot your gun?"

• • • • • • • • • • • • • •

*By singer/songwriter **Johnny Bush**:*

The thing that really knocked me out besides his songs that I could quote would be he said "The Tennessee State flower was Martha White".

• • • • • • • • • • • • • •

*By **Don Reid**, of The Statler Brothers:*

Roger said on our TV show, "The strongest man in the world should be able to grab himself in the ass and lift his feet off the floor."

• • • • • • • • • • • • • •

*By American television legend **Dick Clark**:*

Of the thousands and thousands of people I have met over the years professionally, I have never socialized with more than probably half a dozen of them, of which Roger Miller was one. I treasure that, because, well, he must have had thousands of friends, but I was one of them and that was outstanding for me.

One peculiar thing he'd do every now and again… He'd catch me in the middle of a workday, all hell would be breaking loose and they'd say, "Roger Miller is on the phone." I'd obviously pick it up thinking it was something important and nine times out of ten it had nothing to do with anything other than he'd heard something funny. He'd call me up and say, "Dick? Roger. Did you hear the one about the one-legged crow that flew over the moon?" He'd tell me a joke and then hang up.

• • • • • • • • • • • • • •

Conclusion

When asked how he wanted to be remembered, Roger replied. "I just don't want to be forgotten."* Roger Miller is unlike anyone in the entertainment industry I've ever heard of; he left behind an unbelievable catalog of songs and a mark on his peers like no other, but perhaps was lost by the mass public because of his uncategorizability or his own eccentricities. This book is really only a few drops in the bucket of the memories, one-liners and stories Roger left behind.

Roger Miller in his legacy serves as the ultimate teacher in originality, artistic integrity, music, life's ups and downs, what to do and what not to do. If this adventure has taught me anything, it's that I was born twenty-five years too late. As a music fan and a singer/songwriter I feel like I missed it: the days of open doors in Nashville, of listening to great songs in the top ten, and when it was possible to catch Roger Miller, Bobby Darin and Elvis Presley all in the same weekend in Vegas. I do have an amazing consolation prize though; I met all my living heroes and had questions answered, stories shared and even advice right from their mouths. Writing this book was a surreal learning experience.

I must say that it's disappointing to sit back decades after Roger's peak and turn on a radio. You'd think with evolution, technology, and history to learn from that the music industry would be releasing some of the most amazing material ever, but it isn't. It is truly sad that stars that shine 1/1000th as brilliant as Roger Miller have received a thousand times more media attention.

The loss of not having Roger creating down here anymore has had an effect on me, and I never even met him or was lucky enough to see him in concert. I imagine losing Roger must have been devastating to his family and friends. Luckily Roger left all of us his music to spark old memories, create new ones and bring happiness to us through what he did best. Thanks for the music, Roger, and for providing the better part of the soundtrack to my life. Roger and my other musical heroes have been there to enhance those amazing times life has to offer, serve as comfort in the rough times, fill in the mundane and inspire me to contribute to the industry that I've taken so much enjoyment out of.

*Quote from www.rogermiller.com

The original title of this book was "Old Friends: Fuzzy Memories of Roger Miller"; perfectly fitting, but didn't quite have the same effect as "Ain't Got No Cigarettes" did. Those words spark something with people, a smile, perhaps a snapshot of times past or a memory of singing along with Roger on the radio.

I think the underlying goal of any songwriter, or any creator of anything, is to leave their mark, and Roger Miller left his, in fact he left many. The wit, the music, the memories and the impact of his genius will never be forgotten.

– Lyle E Style

Special Thanks

I 'd like to thank all the interviewees, their management, publicists and staff who helped me arrange the interviews along with my family and friends who supported me. There are so many people who helped me on this journey and here are just a few by name: Gregg Shilliday and the staff at Great Plains Publications, my wife Angela, my folks Mildred and Eugene Baraniuk, Jenna Young, my sister Lori (Gaybee) Caldwell, Ron Sawchuk, Bill and Nancy Dees, Judy Hardin, Toby Keith, Robert Oermann, Joe & Kim Canino, Franco DiGioia, Curtis Beyak, Gordy Collins, Cindy Cruise, Kyra Williams, Tegan Feilberg, Arthur Buenahora, Nikki Mitchell, Jerry Bridges, Barbara Hodson, Richard Moore, Dale Cummings, The Country Music Hall of Fame, Dawn Oberg, Jay Orr, Denny Adcock, Cindy Westmoreland, Mason Williams, Cort Cassidy, Gary Mule Deer, Bobby Goldsboro, Clark Thomas, Jackson DeParis, Mel Tillis, Mike Clark, Michelle Peters, Kevin Dunn, Larry Schwartz, Lee Rollag, Onalee Ames, Randy Hart, the Relish Design Team, Greg Humphrey and all the folks on this and the other side that helped pull strings for me.

My apologies to all the interviewees that didn't make the cut due to space issues: Harry Dean Stanton (the coolest of actors), Jerry "Jigger" Bridges, Johnny Counterfit, Billy Sanford, Jessi Colter, Charles Cochran, Buddy Harmon, Charlie Lamb, Shannon Ford, Billy Walker, Billy Ray Reynolds, Ray Edenton, Kenny Malone, Bill Dees, Leona Williams, Dave Kirby, Billy Graham, David Briggs, Larry Gatlin, Don Markham, Vernon White, Lou Robin, Melba Montgomery, Ronnie Hawkins, Ferlin Huskey, Jim Ed Brown, TG Sheppard, Jody Payne, Kay Bradley, Chip Young and all the others whom I met that shared a story or a warm memory of times they spent with Roger.

Harlan Howard and Johnny Cash—sorry the timing didn't work out.

I believe that time is the most valuable thing a person could spend. Thank you for your time!

For questions and comments, or if you have any Roger stories or rarities you'd like share, don't be a stranger—I'm at www.doitwithstyle.com

Index (select)

Page numbers set in *italic type* refer to photographs